FINDING A VOICE

FINDING A VOICE
Family Therapy for Young People with Anorexia

Greg Dring

KARNAC

First published in 2015 by
Karnac Books Ltd
118 Finchley Road
London NW3 5HT

British Library Cataloguing in Publication Data

A C.I.P. for this book is available from the British Library

ISBN-13: 978-1-78220-186-1

Typeset by V Publishing Solutions Pvt Ltd., Chennai, India

Printed in Great Britain by TJ International Ltd, Padstow, Cornwall

www.karnacbooks.com

CONTENTS

ACKNOWLEDGEMENTS

I wish to express my thanks to friends and colleagues who have provided helpful comments and feedback on parts of the text. In particular thanks are due to: Lindy Clark, Sam Clark-Stone, Jacqui Sayers, and Jane Thomason.

My thanks are also due to the late Dr. Karen Boucher for her comments and support in the writing of this book.

The chapter entitled "Anorexia is not an inherited disorder" incorporates material from Dring (2014) "Anorexia runs in families: Is this due to genes or family relationships?" in the *Journal of Family Therapy*, Chichester: Wiley. Published online at http://onlinelibrary.wiley.com/journal/10.1111/(ISSN)1467–6427/earlyview

ABOUT THE AUTHOR

Greg Dring is a Clinical Psychologist and Family Therapist. He trained as a Clinical Psychologist in the National Health Service. He subsequently took a Master's Degree in Psychotherapy at the University of Warwick which focused both on practice and research in psychotherapy. He trained in Family Therapy at the Institute of Family Therapy in London. He has worked in both adult and children's mental health services in the UK. From 1995 to 2010 he was Consultant Clinical Psychologist at the Young Peoples' Service in Bath, a specialist out-patient treatment service for young people with serious mental disorders. There he gained intensive experience of family therapy for young people with anorexia, and also of multi-family groups for the same client group. He now works in independent practice and provides supervision for therapists working with young people with eating disorders and their families.

CHAPTER ONE

The challenge of finding a voice

This book is written for family therapists who treat young people with anorexia. In the United Kingdom these therapists work predominantly in the National Health Service (NHS) in Child and Adolescent Mental Health Services (CAMHS). The book aims to empower family therapists to provide effective treatment. The intention is to support family therapists both as therapists and as members of multi-disciplinary teams. In addition the book addresses the question of how best to organise effective treatment services for these young people. The evidence is that family therapy is an effective treatment for the young patient with anorexia, at least within three years of onset. Despite that, it seems clear that effective treatment is not always being provided in the United Kingdom, judging from the data provided by Gowers et al (2007). If we do not achieve this with young patients with anorexia the consequences are very serious for them. Steinhausen (2002), in a meta-analysis of anorexia outcomes studies made during the twentieth century, found no evidence for improvement in outcomes for adults with anorexia. The implication is that despite the development of creative new treatments for eating disorders, patients with anorexia still have a poor prognosis. As yet, there is no very effective treatment for adults. It is therefore crucially important to provide effective treatment for young patients in the early phase of anorexia.

Today, Maudsley Model Family Therapy is being implemented in several regional areas of the NHS as a treatment to be delivered by clinicians who are not trained as family therapists. Family therapists in CAMHS will be expected to supervise and support these clinicians and need to be well informed about the issues involved.

The argument

The argument presented in this book questions the prevailing orthodoxy about family therapy for anorexia. Even to write the words "family therapy for anorexia" is to contradict the orthodoxy, since it maintains that this is not "family therapy", but "family work". This means that the goal should not be to change the family relationships, but only to overcome the anorexic behaviour, and its effects on the family, and only then normal development will re-assert itself. That is the proposition of the current treatment manual, Lock et al (2001) and Lock and Le Grange (2013). For this reason some people argue that family therapy skills are not required.

The Academy for Eating Disorders position paper by Le Grange et al (2010), on the family and anorexia, sets up unhelpful dichotomy. They reject "any etiologic model of eating disorders in which family influences are seen as the primary cause of anorexia nervosa or bulimia nervosa Le Grange et al (2010, p. 1)". The old Psychosomatic Family Model of Minuchin et al (1978) is criticised by Le Grange et al (2010) both for its inaccuracy and for making families feel blamed. This position reflects that taken by Dare and Eisler (1997) in the paper that introduced the current Maudsley Model. It is also the position taken by the authors of the treatment manual, Lock et al (2001) and Lock and Le Grange (2013). Despite this the Academy takes the position that the family may make some contribution to the aetiology, probably in conjunction with other influences such as genetic factors.

Curiously enough, students of individual therapy may now have a better grasp of family issues in anorexia than family therapists, who are expected to accept the new orthodoxy. It is time to move on from a preoccupation with the Psychosomatic Family Model and to reconsider the existing research. A model derived from clinical observation and systematic research in the 1970s is unlikely to be either right or wrong in all respects. Family therapy thinking itself has moved on considerably since the 1970s. Knowledge of child development and the interface between family relationships and child and adolescent development has also advanced providing some new perspectives, and a much larger evidence base. There is sufficient evidence that the families of anorexic patients are not a random selection of families. There can be little serious doubt that family experiences contribute to the development of anorexia. Some of these influences were recognised by Minuchin et al (1978), while others were not.

The development of family therapy models for anorexia

It will be argued in the next three chapters that it is useful to distinguish at least three distinct *evidence based* models of family therapy for young people with anorexia. The first is the Structural Family Therapy model of Minuchin et al (1978), the Philadelphia group of therapists. This was the approach that first demonstrated that family therapy was an effective treatment for anorexia. It is the approach that subsequently became most controversial. Like other early approaches to family therapy for anorexia it saw the patient's experience in the family as the cause of her anorexia. The second approach is that of Dare and Eisler (1997). They proposed a new model, but retained important ideas from family therapy. However, they specifically stated that family pathology was not a major component of the aetiology of anorexia. The declaration of this position to the family was part of the treatment. The third approach is to be found in the Family-Based Treatment (FBT) manual by Lock et al (2001) and Lock and Le Grange (2013). They presented an approach that owed a great deal to Dare and Eisler, but with a different emphasis in which the contribution from family therapy is virtually absent.

It has been claimed that the series of changes that have transformed the family therapy approach to anorexia are based on evidence. This evidence is reviewed and it is argued that although all the approaches that have been tested are likely to be more effective than traditional treatments, such as in-patient refeeding, or individual therapy, the empirical arguments for the change of approach are hard to sustain. The overall conclusion drawn from these chapters is that all three approaches demonstrate impressive effectiveness in reducing the core symptoms of anorexia: low weight, dietary restraint and amenorrhea. On the other hand it cannot be demonstrated that the successive changes to the treatment approach initiated by Dare and Eisler, and continued by Lock and Le Grange, have improved outcomes, reduced drop-out rates, or improved the *quality* of outcomes when judged in terms of broader indices of the patients' mental health. In fact the evidence demonstrates very significant levels of continuing neurotic difficulties in a patient population treated with FBT. It is suggested that the current model sacrifices much that family therapy might offer to these families, and that this may account for the substantial continuing psychopathology demonstrated to exist in patients treated with this model, as demonstrated by Lock et al (2006a). This in turn reflects the assumption that family relationships are not a significant factor in aetiology. Probably family therapists who understand the way that anorexia arises in a family context would have more to offer the patient and her family, and would expect to produce a more complete recovery.

The aetiology of anorexia

There has always been a tension between hereditary and environmental explanations of anorexia. In the past, leading authorities on anorexia, drawing on family aggregation and twin studies, argued that genetic factors probably account for more than half the risk of anorexia. Advances in genetic research have altered the position completely. Recent studies such as those by Pinheiro et al (2010) and Wang et al (2011) demonstrate that there are at most only very slight associations between genetic variations and anorexia or anorexia sub-types. These recent failures to confirm genetic hypotheses shift the balance of the argument back to an emphasis on environmental factors.

To understand the aetiology we need to understand anorexia as a psychological phenomenon. Anorexia occurs most commonly in a young person who has low self-esteem, usually in a girl who has been made vulnerable as a result of the development of an anxious approach to life, accompanied by ideals of perfectionism and obsessionality. It develops in girls and young women who have great deal of difficulty in expressing their own needs, a pattern of behaviour known as "self-silencing". In this situation anorexia develops at a time of stress. It can be seen as performing a function for the patient, in reducing distress that she is not able to manage in other ways, such as turning to her parents for support. Outside the field of family therapy this is the dominant view of the development of anorexia. There is a long history to this line of thinking. It can be traced back at least as far as the work of Bruch (1974, 1981). Bruch thought that the development of anorexia could be explained by problems in the very early relationship between the infant and her mother. She thought that it was the mother's inability to respond sensitively to the infant's needs that set the scene for the development of anorexia in adolescence. It is impossible to know how much weight to give to difficulties in this early relationship, except insofar as they have been validated by studies of the impact of obstetric losses and high concern parenting in the early years on the development of anorexia, Shoebridge and Gowers (2000). However, a great deal of evidence indicates that a variety of family experiences shape the patient's vulnerability to anorexia.

An overview of research on family interaction and parenting, and their relationship to anorexia, provides abundant evidence of the link between family relationships and anorexia. The old Psychosomatic Family Model is not confirmed by research. On the other hand it is far from true that the evidence indicates that family relationships are not a major factor in aetiology. However, there may be limited value in attempting to link anorexia to family variables such as "conflict avoidance" since it is most likely that it is the specific way in which each child experiences their relationship with their parents, siblings, and other family members, that affects the outcome in terms of mental health. Despite this, three factors stand out. The first concerns the emotional life of the family. Typically the patient does not feel well supported in her family. A lack of effective parental care and closeness can be seen to undermine the development of self-esteem. Insecure attachment is the crucial issue here. In addition, parental vulnerabilities lead the child to put her own needs and feelings second and attend to those of her parents. The second factor is parental psychological control. Despite their consciously benevolent intentions, the parents' own needs are prioritised over those of the child. The expression of the parents' needs and attitudes, in the form of parental psychological control, contribute to the development of perfectionism, leading to the development of internalising disorders, including anorexia. Third, parental attitudes to eating, weight, appearance and, more generally, to acceptable self-presentation, prompt attention to the control of eating. In the difficult years following puberty, girls who are vulnerable because of these factors encounter circumstances in which they need to turn to parents for support. Instead of doing so, some turn away and find a temporary solution to the difficulties they face by achieving success in their control of eating and weight. This transition, this turning away from parental support, embracing self-silencing, is the point of entry to anorexia itself.

A family model of anorexia

A number of conclusions can be drawn from the research. Many factors contribute to the development of low self-esteem, internalising disorders, eating disorders and anorexia. Insecure attachment, and resulting deficits in the ability to regulate emotion, affects the patient and often her parents too. This probably accounts for the patient's difficulties with self-esteem, in managing emotion, and in asserting her own needs. Parental psychological control is a factor in the development of internalising disorders, including eating disorders such as anorexia. It may be the factor that contributes most strongly to the development of the pathological self-control and the perfectionistic and obsessive attitudes that underlie anorexia. Parental attitudes to eating and weight, and related attitudes to appearance and achievement, are also important. It is probably often this kind of family influence that causes the underlying psychopathology to be expressed as an eating disorder rather than as, say, an anxiety disorder or depression. Each of these factors could be seen as overlapping with and having implications for at least one of the others. Each can be seen as reflecting the parents' own vulnerabilities, psychological problems and insecurities. Other family factors, such as the impact of the behaviour of siblings, have received little attention from researchers. Nevertheless family therapists will often see them as having an important impact.

Influences outside the family have to be acknowledged. Many patients suffer very acutely from their experience of cultural influences, peer group influences and extraneous events, such as sexual assaults. Nevertheless, resilience in the face of adverse factors reflects young people's experience with their carers throughout childhood and adolescence. The effect of current disturbance arising from such factors is mediated through relationships with parents. Therefore, these influences do not act on the individual young person independently of family factors. Some influences outside the family may be helpful. For example, some schools and peer groups may help girls manage feelings about competition, or problems about bullying, better than others.

A crucial issue is that we should not be looking for a general model that describes all cases as the same, like the Psychosomatic Family

Model. Instead we need a model rich enough to identify different influences which give rise to vulnerability to anorexia, and the family influences which prevent the patient finding a more functional way of dealing with distress at the point in time when anorexia begins.

Alternative approaches

In recent years, a number of authors have published accounts and case studies of family therapy for anorexia. These accounts present anorexia in a family relationship context. In these approaches, family relationship issues are the focus of the work at an early stage. They present a set of perspectives on treatment that are quite different from the current Maudsley Model and FBT approaches. These approaches cannot yet be described as evidence based.

Micucci (2009) gives an account that is closest to the structural/systemic family therapy tradition. He sees improving family relationships and communication as essential to removing the anorexic symptom. He presented the case of "Tina", a teenage girl who developed anorexia in the context of triangulation in the parental relationship. In this case study a relational reframe is presented at an early stage. The message to the family includes the observation that "She is wasting away not only from lack of food but also because of the absence of nurturing and sustaining relationships in her life … I will work with you all, as a family, to give you the chance to begin building more sustaining relationships, so that Tina may begin to grow again", Micucci (2009, p. 123). In this case the parents were separated and the father had grown distant from the family while each parent believed the other was responsible for the problem. Micucci presents a way of uniting the parents in managing refeeding with Tina despite these difficult circumstances. He draws on older family therapy ideas, but also on ideas about attachment, in his account of the development of the anorexia. His approach is different from the Maudsley Model and Family-Based Treatment approaches in addressing relationship issues between the patient and each parent at an early stage.

Zubery et al (2005) present a very different model. In this approach, separate treatment for patient and parents takes place at the first stage. The expectation is that parents will prepare food, present it and be present at meal times, but that it is the patient's responsibility to eat. A parents' group and multi-family groups are very significant components. Direct communication between parents and patient is expected to improve only at a late stage of treatment. The emotional entanglement between parents and adolescent child are seen as very important in this approach. They describe a case in which this approach successfully engaged a family despite the parents' initial reluctance to join in the work.

Dallos (2004, 2006) describes an Attachment-Narrative approach to family therapy for anorexia. He developed this idea partly because of his subjective experience as a therapist and partly because of his knowledge of research and theory about attachment, and how it relates to people's styles of relating to one another and the sense they make of relationships. Dallos (2004) commented that "For years I have wondered whether there was something wrong with myself … since I had great difficulty in helping families where anorexia was the presenting problem, in engaging in conversations about their difficulties, their feelings, the impact of their problems on the relationship and vice versa", Dallos (2004, pp. 41–42). But, he says, he discovered that this was a common problem for therapists working with these families. He came to see the issue within a frame of reference about attachment and its impact on the ability to express and think about relationships. He thought that attachment insecurities reflected the family relationships of the patient, and those that her parents had experienced in the course of their own development. Dallos (2006) and Dallos and Vetere (2009) describe cases of family therapy for anorexia. The management of the patient's eating is not the focus of the therapy. The approach integrates approaches from the narrative tradition in family therapy with attachment theory approaches. Again the emphasis is very much on relationships, concentrating on closeness and on comforting in the patient's relationship with her parents, and on similar issues in the parent's family of origin. The approach is one that is very relevant to the understanding and management of the parents' own vulnerabilities and the way that the patient herself is caught up in responding to these vulnerabilities. The approach is not presented as sufficient in itself for the management of an acute anorexic crisis. As it is presented it would seem to be appropriate to a case in which weight had at least been stabilised or one in which the management of weight and eating was in the hands of another clinician. However, ideas taken from this and other attachment-based approaches to family therapy for anorexia could be integrated into an approach that engages the family in the acute stage.

Beyond Maudsley Model Family Therapy

This book proposes to change the therapy model by integrating aspects of attachment approaches with more traditional structural/systemic approaches. This is not a treatment manual as such, and should be read alongside Minuchin et al (1978) "Psychosomatic Families" and the FBT treatment manual by, Lock et al (2001) and Lock and Le Grange (2013). The FBT manual contains much that is useful, but omits much that has the potential to maximise outcomes. A number of technical issues are tackled with a view to helping family therapists make the most of their skills in helping these patients and their families. The proposals draw on ideas taken from older family therapy traditions as well as from attachment therapists such as Dallos (2006), Dallos and Vetere (2009), Diamond and Stern (2003), and Hughes (2007).

Managing guilt and blame

In the present state of our knowledge it is hard to justify the statement to the family that families do not "cause" anorexia. It now seems very likely that anorexia is in fact largely the result of the child's experience of upbringing. Family relationships are likely to be the largest influence on the development of the vulnerabilities that give rise to anorexia. It would be hard to justify the statement even if the strategy was consciously intended to manage the sensitivities of a particularly vulnerable group of parents, which may have been the original intention. Hughes (2007) has addressed the management of feelings of guilt and shame, especially in parents, and sees the management of these feelings as a central issue in setting up and maintaining a secure base in family therapy. To achieve this, the therapist needs to be constantly monitoring the state of their relationships with the family members. To Hughes this is a technical issue about therapeutic relationships, not a scientific issue about the cause of the problem. That is how we should see it.

The context of treatment

Family therapists recognise the importance of context. It is important to address the question of what they need in order to provide effective intervention. In addition, the model has implications for the way that mental health professionals work together. Issues to do with co-working and supervision are important. Another important issue is the integration of the work across levels of service; across out-patient, community outreach and in-patient services. Their approaches need to be coordinated in order to provide a coherent service, a service which provides containment for the families' anxiety, while fostering the patient's capacity for self-expression.

A note on language

Probably one in ten young patients with anorexia is male, but for the sake of brevity and simply to avoid the constant repetition of the formula "he or she", the patient will always be referred to as female.

CHAPTER TWO

The roots of family therapy for young people with anorexia

The influence of the Philadelphia group

Minuchin continues to be seen as in some sense the founding father of the approach. There are probably three reasons for that. First, Minuchin et al (1978) were the first to document a series of cases in which the recovery rates achieved far exceeded the rates achieved by traditional approaches to treatment such as in-patient treatment and individual therapy. Second, Minuchin and his colleagues were the first to present the idea that parents could be put in charge of their daughter's eating, illustrating this with impressive examples of cases in which the use of this strategy initiated rapid therapeutic improvement. Third, Minuchin was an effective exponent of his approach and was willing to subject his work to observation. Even today there are probably more published transcripts of therapy sessions conducted by Minuchin and his colleagues in the Philadelphia group than of all the other approaches to family therapy treatment of anorexia put together.

The structural family therapists' understanding of anorexia—the "psychosomatic family"

Minuchin et al (1975) at the Children's Hospital of Philadelphia provided a concise description of a theoretical position subsequently outlined at greater length in the well-known book "Psychosomatic Families", Minuchin et al (1978). They argued that there were close similarities between the families of young people with anorexia and those of families with children who presented with repeated crises with asthma or diabetes. They referred to these as "brittle" diabetes and "psychosomatic" asthma, to distinguish these cases from others in which families worked together successfully to manage their children's conditions. Physiological vulnerability was seen as a component of the problem in these cases, but *not* necessarily in the anorexic cases. The families of the patients with anorexia were seen as tending towards a preoccupation with somatic concerns, and often specifically with preoccupations about food and diet, table manners and food fads, hence the patient's "choice" of anorexia as a symptom. But it was the family structure, and the role the problem came to play in that, which necessitated that the "choice" be made.

The "psychosomatogenic family" was later called simply the "psychosomatic family". It was characterised by four transactional patterns: enmeshment, over-protectiveness, rigidity and lack of conflict resolution. However, this was not enough on its own to account for the symptom. It was also necessary that the child played a role in the regulation of conflict between her parents. According to Minuchin et al (1978), this was universally the case for the anorexic girls treated in the long treatment series, as in the fifty-three cases they reported.

Enmeshment was described as a relationship pattern which was highly responsive and over-involved. Signs of this would be members of the family speaking for each other and, for example, finishing off one another's sentences. Discussions between two family members would be diffused by the involvement of other family members. Life spaces might be intruded on so that, for example, family members might not, literally or metaphorically, close the bedroom door. Another sign of this kind of family pattern was that family members would have difficulty speaking about individual qualities of family members, tending instead to generalise about the family as a whole. Sub-system boundaries would be weak in this kind of family since children could take inappropriate parenting roles, and could enter into inappropriate alliances with one parent against the other, in these ways making the parental couple less effective as the parents in the family.

Over-protectiveness was indicated by over-concern about slight signs of illness or distress. Any sign of tension or possible conflict would activate anxiety arousing behaviour in children in order to distract parents, in particular, from demonstrations of conflict or distress. The family tended to think in terms of protective concerns in ways that served to undermine the child's development of autonomy and competence. The children, especially the symptomatic child, would feel excessive responsibility for the welfare of other family members. The sick child might protect the family by distracting them with her symptoms, and this could be "a major reinforcement for the illness".

Rigidity was seen as a family need to maintain the status quo. Minuchin et al (1975) described this in terms of the family sticking to its habitual pattern of interaction, even when this was no longer appropriate. Parents would have difficulty adjusting to the developing needs of adolescent children.

Minuchin et al (1975) described various different behaviour patterns in relation to conflict in these families. He argued that these families had three very different ways of dealing with conflict. Sometimes one spouse was a conflict avoider. This spouse responded to conflicts raised by their partner by detouring or in more extreme cases by simply leaving the house. Other families disagreed openly but constant interruptions and subject changes concealed any issues of conflict before it could be resolved. Some families saw "no need" to disagree and openly rejected any conflict. Hence the model said that all the families were uncomfortable with and alert to conflict. But the issue was not conflict avoidance *per se* but rather it predicted that the families, although displaying a wide range of overt behaviours, would be alike in failing to achieve conflict resolution.

The families were seen as very uncomfortable with conflict, and this discomfort was seen as the immediate reason for the last of the conditions required for anorexia, with "the use of the sick child" in parental conflict regulation. This did not always take the same form. In fact, three different mechanisms were proposed for this important function in the model: "triangulation", "parent–child coalition" and "detouring". In triangulation the parental conflict was acknowledged and the triangulated child found herself constantly asked to take sides (as if she were the adult in the relationship perhaps) and was typically silenced by this. In parent–child coalition the anorexic patient was simply aligned with one parent against the other. This could be a covert alliance, and the child might verbalise the criticism of one parent while the other parent (the ally) remained surprisingly silent, or argued ineffectually against his or her allied child. Further variety was introduced here by the possibility that the excluded (allied against) parent might or might not challenge or try to break up this alliance against them. In a detouring pattern, concern about the child with the problem became a distraction from acknowledging and confronting parental relationship difficulties. The description maintained that families might show quite a variety of behaviour in relation to their style of managing conflict, and in relation to the way the symptomatic child played a role in the parental marital relationship. At the same time all this was seen as indicative of the pattern of underlying transactional difficulties in the families.

* * *

The Psychosomatic Family Model was focused on contemporaneous transaction patterns in the family rather than on their impact on child development. Nevertheless, these could be inferred to be of long standing, and hence to have contributed to those difficulties in the child's development which ultimately gave rise to anorexia. Sargent et al (1985) explicitly acknowledge this, saying that the psychosomatic family characteristics produced a context in which the psychological features of anorexia nervosa that had been identified by Bruch (1974) were adaptive. Sargent et al argued that the patient's difficulty in perceiving her own feelings could be attributed to her over-sensitivity to family members, and to her over-focus on others feelings and needs, both qualities resulting from the family transactional pattern. Sargent et al argued that the family context in which everyone seems to be vulnerable and in need of protection prevents the development of interpersonal trust. Failure to resolve conflict prevented the child developing a sense of competence in interpersonal relationships, and confidence in her own problem solving ability in relationships. The family context was therefore one that encouraged developmental delay. Following from this, the child became even more over-involved with her parents and family just at the point of development when she should be becoming more intensely involved in peer relationships. They argued that as parents had difficulty in working out effective roles with each other they were unable to provide effective leadership in the family. The lack of effective boundaries between individuals and sub-systems in the family, as well as an overly-restrictive boundary in relation to the outside world, interfered with the family's effective achievement of its tasks. It failed to support the adolescent development of a move into greater involvement with the outside world, and it could not provide a mutually satisfactory relationship for the parental couple that would be left behind when the younger generation left home. As the symptomatic problem developed, the family responded by becoming even more protective, so that the problem exacerbated the difficulties that had caused it.

* * *

The use of the terms "psychosomatic family" was unfortunate, as it naturally suggested that the theory was intended to explain all psychosomatic illness. Yet it is clear from the texts that Minuchin et al (1975) saw the theory as applying to "brittle diabetes" and "psychosomatic asthma" and that these were differentiated from ordinary cases of diabetes and asthma by the failure of the family to succeed in controlling the illness using treatments that, from the medical point of view, should have been effective. Minuchin argued that the presence of physiological vulnerability was debatable in anorexic cases and, in this respect, drew a clear distinction between them and the diabetic and asthmatic cases. As he says, "The psychosomatic element lies in the emotional exacerbation of the already available symptom. In the 'secondary' psychosomatic disorder, no such predisposing physical disorder can be demonstrated. The psychosomatic element is apparent in the transformation of emotional conflicts into somatic symptoms", Minuchin et al (1975, p. 1033). Of course, one could accept the whole of Minuchin's description of the anorexic person and her family and not see in it any "psychosomatic" element at all, and family therapists have rarely followed Minuchin's lead in referring to anorexia as a psychosomatic disorder.

The model of treatment for young people with anorexia

The "Psychosomatic Family Model" generated a treatment for anorexia. Aponte and Hoffman (1973), Minuchin et al (1975), Minuchin et al (1978) and Sargent et al (1985) provide accounts of this approach. Structural family therapy was used to remove the patient from her central role in the parental relationship. To achieve this, the parents might be asked to manage the patient's symptomatic behaviour (her eating and any abnormal weight control strategies) in the early stages. In some instances the therapist took on this role instead. Either way, the intention was to remove the patient from her central role in the parental relationship at mealtimes, as a precursor to removing her from that position at all times. Family relationship problems were targeted in order to achieve this. In this way, the patient would be released to develop into a young adult. All the problematic transactional patterns would be the target of this therapy, and all the techniques of structural family therapy described in, for example, Minuchin and Fishman (1981) could be used. Sargent et al (1985) who were members of the group at the Philadelphia Children's Hospital provided a useful and concise account.

Beginning treatment

Sargent et al (1985) described a process of engaging the family, usually by asking that all members of the family living at home come to the first appointment. In the event that this was difficult, the therapist's role in convening was to arrange for effective leadership in the family to make treatment possible. In some circumstances, after the first session, the therapist might arrange to see one parent separately, both parents separately, or another combination of family members, bearing in mind the essential issue of leadership in the family. They described a process in which the therapist created a therapeutic system made up of the family and therapist. They did this by expressing professional concern and appreciation of the family members' concern for the patient, as well as by conveying their own familiarity with the problem of anorexia. They argued that the therapist should first get to know about the family members as individuals, learning about their interests and their competencies, seeking to make them comfortable in the situation, and ensuring that contact had been made with each member of the family. The therapist then enquired about the problem. They proposed that the therapist should start with the parents, and be insistent on getting the views of each parent, and what each had tried to do to resolve the problem, as well as getting a description of the impact of the problem on each of them. After this, the therapist obtained the same information from the patient and her siblings. At this stage the therapist might empathise with any distress the patient expressed about herself, but was not to counter this with reassurance. During all this the therapist initiated the therapeutic task of boundary making by gently discouraging interruptions. At the end of this initial meeting a treatment contract was made that was "concrete, specific and problem centered." It included a contract for a specific level of regular weight recovery. It focused on the problems of the anorexic patient. Other problems, such as discord in the parental marriage, were to be addressed at a later stage. They argue that the therapist should draw attention to the patient's emotional and social difficulties and frame those in developmental terms. This, they argued, was less threatening for the family than framing the problem in terms of serious family conflicts.

Family lunch sessions

Today, family lunch sessions are seen as an opportunity to put parents in charge of the patient eating but that was not their purpose in the early stages of the development of the treatment model. Instead, they were seen as an opportunity to assess the family dynamic and to intervene in a way that started the process of restructuring the family relationships. This was not always done in the same way. Rosman et al (1975) presented different approaches to such sessions. They derived their information by observing a series of family lunch sessions which were conducted at the Philadelphia Child Guidance Clinic. They described three quite different strategies which therapists had employed, all of which, they said, had proved equally effective. In the first, the goal was to put parents in charge in order to highlight the interpersonal difficulty. The therapist would instruct one parent, then the other, to take charge of the meal. As each failed to get the patient to eat, the therapist supported them but observed the other parent undermining these efforts. Finally, the therapist united the parents' efforts, and, with the support of the therapist, the parents got their child to eat, or she started to eat spontaneously. The second strategy was almost the opposite of the first. In this strategy, the therapist first prompted each parent to take charge in turn. When the patient's capacity to defeat her parents was demonstrated, the therapist used himself as a boundary between parents and child, saying that he would in future make this a private issue between himself and the patient, thus prohibiting further conflict. The third strategy was one of distraction. The therapist again used himself to make a boundary, this time by engaging the family in discussion of issues about anything but food. He was able to open up discussion about issues that had to do with the parents or siblings, and as he did so the patient began to eat. Rosman et al (1975) argued that the first strategy might be more suitable for younger adolescents, the second with older adolescents who would naturally be moving towards greater autonomy within the family, the third where the family structure was already more flexible or where the child was already eating a little. They thought it was the first two of these strategies which were more appropriate to the situation in which the child's refusal to eat was provoking a crisis. Rosman et al quoted Minuchin (1974) "… when a *family* crisis is organised around the symptom it is not the symptom itself but the interpersonal negotiation of parents and children around eating that gains salience", Minuchin (1974, pp. 243–244).

Rosman et al (1975) argued that there were a number of underlying aims in these sessions. The first was to challenge the idea that the problem resided in the patient and to reframe it as located in the family relationships. To do so the therapist would reframe in a way to normalise the behaviour, describing it as rebellious or defiant rather than as a symptom of mental illness. The problem of the symptomatic child was seen as being the way that she was caught up in this pattern of family relationships. The second aim was to highlight the current transactional significance of the patient's refusal to eat. The refusal to eat was to be seen in terms of such issues as parent–child problems in communication, struggles over autonomy and control, or adolescent rebellion against parental authority. The final aim was to block the parents' use of the child's refusal to eat as a conflict detouring device. The parents would then need to be helped to achieve more direct and effective conflict resolution. Although the three strategies seem very different they shared the same aim. As they put it, the intention was that "*the* usual *pattern of parental interaction around the symptom be inhibited or changed in such a way as to bring about a separation, an increase in distance, between parents and child*" (my italics), Rosman et al (1975, p. 851). The aim was *not* simply to re-establish parental authority.

At the risk of labouring the point, the central issue in getting the patient to eat again was to remove the daughter from her role in triangulation, coalition or detouring in her parents' relationship at meal times. This could be achieved either by getting parents to co-operate wholeheartedly in managing the meals, or by taking them out of that role and allowing the parents difficulties to be managed another way.

It was not about re-establishing parental authority at meal times. Having achieved the goal of getting the patient eating again, therapy could proceed towards separating her from her over-involvement in the parents' relationship in general, enabling her to pursue age appropriate developmental tasks. Rosman et al (1975) presented data drawn from the records of eight patients that demonstrated that the family lunch session resulted in a change from weight loss to gain, or accelerated weight gain, when the days before and after the session were compared.

Sargent et al (1985) did not regard family lunch sessions as necessary in every case. They suggested they should be used in those cases where the patient was unable to eat without undue distress, or when weight loss continued despite the treatment contract for weight recovery. They argued that the session presented an opportunity for the therapist to work with the parents on what the patient should eat. The goals were that the patients should eat in a context in which they could see their parents co-operating with one another, without other aspects of family relationships intruding into the situation, and increasing mutual support and collaboration between the parents. If they were in conflict the therapist would help them to co-ordinate their efforts.

Middle phase

Sargent et al (1985) argued that once the patient was regaining weight, even if the rate of weight recovery was slow, the focus should move on. It would now be on the psychosocial difficulties of the patient and/or the unresolved conflicts in the family. Parents could be helped to think about the stresses that may have contributed to the development of the problem. The parents and patient could then be encouraged to find other ways of coping with these stresses. The therapist had parallel goals. For the parents these would be to foster mutual support and improved conflict resolution, that is, in the parent's marital relationship. For the patient, it was the development of increasing autonomy and self-respect. Central to this second goal was that the therapist helped the patient to speak for herself, to assert herself with her parents, and to express in her own words the difficulties she was experiencing. They commented that the patient in this phase might become depressed and even suicidal, and that the family should be prepared for this possibility, and told that signs of troubling emotions are also signs of progress. Also at this stage the therapist helped the family recognise that disagreements between parents and adolescent children are part of family life, and that separation can be a difficult and painful process. As this stage continued, a range of difficulties might emerge affecting parents individually or affecting their relationship. These might become the focus of further therapeutic work, since to leave the difficulties unaddressed invited relapse in the patient, or the engagement of another sibling in difficulties. Individual sessions for the patient and marital therapy for the parental couple were indicated at this stage, as well as sessions to strengthen the ability of siblings to support one another.

Final phase of treatment and ending

In the final phase of treatment, Sargent et al (1985) recommended that the therapist carry on both individual therapy for the patient and marital therapy for the parents while also keeping the whole family as a group in mind. Nevertheless, they suggested that family sessions should continue, on a monthly basis, to ensure that changes achieved in other sessions were "meshing" in the family context. Marital work with the parents was intended to help them to improve their ability to negotiate, and to compromise with each other, and to improve the partners' capacity for mutual support. There might even be a need to achieve forgiveness for past resentments. At the end of treatment they suggested follow up meetings for two to four months and telephone contact after that.

Controversial issues in the Philadelphia group's approach

The therapist's style

The style of the therapist in Structural Family Therapy was one that was warm, immediate and direct. This is the style of the work described by Sargent et al (1985) and illustrated in the publications of Minuchin et al (1978) and Aponte and Hoffman (1973). In describing this style Sargent comments that the therapist should use warmth and sensitivity in order to make a therapeutic relationship with members of the family. They say that the therapist must also be comfortable with creating and maintaining conflict to the point of resolution, even when family members are uncomfortable with this. They also emphasised the importance of the therapist's colleagues in providing support and supervision to allow therapy to succeed in working with a very challenging situation. The style is well illustrated in the paper by Aponte and Hoffman (1973), in the first session in the case of "Laura R.". This very early paper (which can now be downloaded without charge from the Wiley Online Library) illustrates the approach. It is a transcript of the whole of a consultation session in which Aponte and Hoffman observed Minuchin meet the family with the therapist who was to carry out the work, except that there were gaps in the session where the cine film had to be changed. It includes the comments of Hoffman, and another observer, as they discuss the therapeutic interaction. The session was set up as a family lunch session, but lunch did not arrive in time and putting the parents in charge of their daughters eating did not become the focus of the work. It is interesting that in this very early example it is clear that Minuchin was willing to target changes in the family structure at an early stage, and saw that as a precondition for success with the refeeding task. He joined the family warmly, and focused on what he saw as age inappropriate closeness between the father and daughter, and the need to modify this by strengthening the parental marital relationship. The frame of reference was developmental. He thought the patient, aged fourteen, needed to have privacy and space to develop peer relationships without her father interfering. The parents needed to be enjoying one another's company in preparation for the time when the children would leave home. The patient is presented to the family as using her fasting to express needs that she could not express otherwise. Minuchin ensured that during the session the patient said something about her need for privacy, something the father was perhaps not yet ready to hear. This illustrates what Sargent et al (1985) meant when he talked about framing the patient's needs in developmental terms. It also illustrates the structural technique of under-focusing, since Minuchin did not directly allude to marital problems, yet was able to imply them in a less threatening way by talking about how the marital partners would change to allow the daughter her privacy.

Joining, intensification and relational reframing in family lunch sessions

Some of the family lunch sessions will be described in detail, as events in them may illustrate aspects of the structural approach that were subsequently felt to be unacceptable. There are six published transcripts of structural family therapy for anorexia, and in each case the description of the work is dominated by a description of first or early sessions in which the family lunch was to be included in the assessment. Joining with the family before the lunch, and the management of the family situation during the lunch, dominates these descriptions, which set the scene for all the subsequent work. That subsequent work is described briefly, and only in outline, so that what we have is mostly the transcript of the initial session, with the therapist's or observer's comments. Four such transcripts, the cases of "Deborah Kaplan", "Judy Gilbert", "Miriam Priestman", and "Loretta Menotti" make up more than half of the book "Psychosomatic Families", Minuchin et al (1978). In addition we have the case of "Laura R." already described in the paper by Aponte and Hoffman (1973), and the case described as "Judy Brown" in Minuchin (1974). It is interesting that in only three of the six cases does the therapist pursue the strategy of putting the parents in charge of their daughter's eating during the session. Therapists who are concerned to know more about how this work was done should read these transcripts. For the purpose of this discussion a brief summary of some of this material is provided here.

* * *

In the case of Deborah Kaplan, right at the beginning, Minuchin et al (1978, pp. 142–201) used an incident in which her parents helped her to take off her scarf to highlight enmeshment, in a gentle, under-focused way, and continued to use this through the session. At one point he used the metaphor provided by the patient's brother "Simon said that mother sometimes takes his voice" (Minuchin et al, 1978, p. 150)—here Minuchin seems to imply that the mother stole her son's voice by speaking for him. The issues of conflict management in the family, and boundary issues, were the focus of this part of the session. After some time food arrived and Minuchin left the room while her parents were left in charge of seeing to it that Deborah ate. Minuchin observed the interaction through a one-way screen and described it like this: "Each of the family members was controlling the others. In response to my demand, the father took a stern attitude: 'You will eat.' The daughter responded with an oblique complaint about over-control. This triggered her mother to say to her father, 'Don't be so harsh'. The mother took over, pleading, and the daughter responded by rejecting the request. This activated her father to take another stern position … ." (Minuchin et al, 1978, p. 162) and so the interaction continued round and round.

Minuchin then put her father in charge. Her father attempted to insist that Deborah eat, starting by being reasonable, but her mother continued to intervene, and when her father continued to insist that Deborah ate, her mother tried to over-rule him by saying to Deborah "You don't have to eat that much ...". Minuchin returned to the room, saying "The problem here is you two! You (to father) say, 'You should eat' and mother says, 'You shouldn't eat!'" (Minuchin et al, 1978, p. 165). This led to an interaction in which Deborah's mother first rejected what Minuchin had said, but then explained her comment, saying "Because he is just upsetting her, and that she is going to rebel all the more." This led to a further exchange in which Minuchin told Deborah's mother to express her disagreements directly to her husband, but not through undermining him about food.

Minuchin then put Deborah's mother in charge of the meal, and removed her father and brother to the observation room. Her mother tried reasoning and begging, without success. Minuchin then put her father back in charge and he tried reasoning and became angry with his daughter's continued refusal, and Deborah ended this sequence by crushing the food in her hands. At this point her father was angry and said he would like to hit Deborah. Minuchin told the parents they had each tried their best and Deborah had defeated them, and that "She is really involved in a battle with both of you, in which she wins. And that is all that is important for her." (Minuchin et al, 1978, p. 178). He congratulated Deborah on her victory and described the crushed hot dog in her hands as the symbol of her victory. He asked her, "Why do you want to defeat them? You feel that you have been so controlled that this is one of the ways in which you will express your autonomy?" (Minuchin et al, 1978, p. 179). Minuchin ended the session saying to the parents "We will help you." The response to this was that after the session Deborah began to eat, and self-starvation never again became the issue. In the next session the focus of therapy switched to the question whether the parents could let Deborah grow up, and Deborah asserted herself about her right to go out and socialise. In addition, her mother was given the task of helping her father not to over-burden himself. In subsequent sessions the parent's marital relationship, in which Deborah's mother was seen as defining her husband as the authority, but covertly resenting him for that, became the new theme. Both partners were encouraged to communicate more directly with each other while Deborah was encouraged to stand up for herself. Work continued with the family for six months, and included marital and sex therapy for the parents, and individual sessions for Deborah. The patient returned for some individual sessions with the therapist four years later after she had left home, and these focused on her relationship difficulties and use of bingeing to manage distress. Reading this account it is clear that the meal session achieved a very high level of intensity, and may have been very uncomfortable for both Deborah and her parents. A relational reframe was offered at the end. Clearly, in view of subsequent events, a therapeutic alliance was maintained with both the parents and the daughter.

Much the same was true in the second case. "Judy Gilbert" was fourteen at referral and had already been hospitalised three times and was being fed through a surgically implanted tube at the time of the assessment. In an initial joining phase Minuchin again focused on parental protectiveness, and framed Judy as stubborn rather than ill. When lunch arrived Minuchin put the parents in charge. Judy was "nasty" in her interactions with parents about food, and her parents alternated between efforts to be authoritative, and placating, and reasoning with Judy about eating, as well as appeals to family loyalty "You don't love us? Is that it?" Minuchin et al (1978, pp. 205–238). After a while Minuchin interrupted this sequence, saying that Judy felt herself to be stronger than both her father and mother. He then put her father in charge. Her father tried again and his wife joined in much as before. The intensity of the situation built up with Judy behaving in a defiant, childlike way, and both parents became obviously angry. Now Minuchin put her mother in charge of getting Judy to eat. She attempted to do so, and this time the father joined in. Minuchin framed Judy as rude to her father, and challenging her mother, who Minuchin saw as inappropriately comforting Judy at this point, and insisted that the parents were treating Judy with a respect she did not deserve, especially in view of the way she was treating her father. Minuchin escalated the situation further when Judy's parents, working together, had got Judy to eat a tiny amount. During the next sequence her parents worked together to make Judy eat and put the food into her mouth and the conflict escalated to the point where both parents slapped Judy. After a while Minuchin intervened again, and this time set the parents the task of negotiating with Judy what she would eat. The conflict between Judy and her parents continued, with her parents putting food in Judy's mouth. Sometimes this was eaten, and sometimes spat out again. The session ended with Minuchin congratulating the parents on the progress they had made, and setting up daily sessions to continue with this every day, which the parents accepted.

After this session, Judy began to eat and recovered weight sufficiently to go home from hospital. Family therapy continued with a focus on helping Judy to detach herself from a "little girl" position stuck between her parents, and helping her develop appropriate involvement outside the family. At the same time the father was encouraged to become more assertive with his wife, and some work focused on reinstating him in a relationship from which he had been both emotionally and physically absent. This therapy supported the family through some further difficulties about Judy's eating, and she achieved an appropriate degree of independence. At three-year follow-up she was functioning well from a psychosocial point of view, and was regarded as having recovered from anorexia. It is clear from the descriptions of these sessions that a very high level of intensity was achieved. This was seen by Minuchin as necessary to make the structural changes required for the patient to eat.

* * *

High intensity was also achieved in such sessions when the parents were *not* put in charge, as in the case of "Loretta Menotti". In this session intensity had been achieved even before the food arrived for the family lunch. Minuchin had challenged the mothers' over-control of all her daughters, framing this as a cross-cultural issue. He thought her mother had brought more restrictive rules from the parent's home culture of Italy, while the girls held American values implying more freedom for them. Loretta's mother resisted this view while Loretta accepted and argued for it, with a little support from her father. Minuchin maintained this focus throughout the session. Having experienced Loretta's difficulty in establishing her individuality in the face of her mother's control he decided not to put her parents in charge of her lunch, and instead permitted her not to eat during the session. The family was set the task of allowing Loretta to eat alone, her parents were not to know what she ate, and the therapist took responsibility for the task of monitoring her weight to ensure she was safe. Loretta was given the task of getting to know her father better, and both were to spend half an hour together twice a week. Weight recovery was achieved over the following three months. Family therapy lasted for four months, focusing on supporting individuation and age appropriate autonomy. In this case, intensity was already achieved in the first session in the conflict between Minuchin and Loretta's mother, and between Loretta and her mother, with Loretta standing up for herself, and these factors may have indicated to Minuchin that it was not necessary to create intensity by enacting the conflict over eating.

* * *

In another case described by Minuchin et al (1978), "Miriam Priestman", intensity was achieved in another way, this time through a deepening of affect. She was another very regressed anorexic girl admitted to hospital. This time the therapist, Liebman, used himself to make a boundary in the session, keeping Miriam out of the triangulated position, and supporting her in eating. Miriam ate, almost unnoticed, while Liebman focused the conversation on family communication instead of food. Liebman understood the anorexia as reflecting her parent's inability to achieve conflict resolution in their own relationship. Instead, all marital attention and energy had centred on Miriam. The focus of this lunch session became the discontent between the parents, with the therapist responding by reframing what each parent had seen as negative aspects of themselves, or the other, as positive. Eventually this led the father to talk about the bitterness he felt about his family of origin, and about the death of his first wife, Miriam's mother. At the same time, Liebman worked towards strengthening the relationship between Miriam and her step-mother, framing her step-mother as someone who could help Miriam with problems in expressing herself. Like Deborah and Judy, Miriam responded to this session by beginning to eat and regaining weight. After discharge her parents were put in charge of her eating through a behaviour modification programme. Weight recovery was achieved in the following two months. Family therapy continued with the aim of strengthening the parental relationship, and using the older sister to help Miriam engage in more age appropriate activities outside the home. Miriam, too, was reported to have achieved a complete recovery at the follow up five years after the end of treatment.

As can be seen, the Philadelphia group of therapists had considerable flexibility in their approach to family therapy in general, and specifically to the family lunch sessions. What was common to the approach at the beginning of treatment was the goal of removing the patient from her problematic role in her parents' marital relationship. The therapists' approach to family lunch sessions could be calibrated on the family's degree of resistance to the patient's expressions of autonomy, and the degree of family resistance to discussion of difficulties in relationships. In the cases of Laura R., Loretta Menotti and Miriam Priestman this did not involve putting parents in charge of their daughters eating during a family lunch session. The therapists were willing to tackle parental marital relationship issues early on, when they saw this as necessary to success with refeeding. On the other hand they often presented the issues in terms of the patient's developmental needs, with less focus on the marital issues, as in the case of Laura R. The approach was one that allowed the therapist a great deal of flexibility about the strategy to pursue. The therapists drew on their experience of the interaction within the family to decide upon the best strategy.

In these sessions the patient sometimes ate without her parents taking charge of her. The structural therapists understood this as reflecting their success, *at that moment in time*, in removing the patient from her detouring position in the family relationships. When the real issues could be directly discussed, as they could at that moment in the cases of Loretta and Miriam, the patient did not need to refuse to eat.

Outcomes from the structural approach

Minuchin et al (1978) reported a series of fifty-three cases. Three refused family treatment, and fifty families were treated. The average duration of family therapy was seven months, ranging from three to sixteen months. A research follow-up was made with the patients on average two years eight months after their treatment. They were rated as "recovered", "fair", or "unimproved" on a measure of anorexic symptoms. Patients were considered "recovered" if their weight was restored and their eating behaviour was normalised. Their condition was rated as "fair" if their weight was restored, but they still had eating disorder symptoms. Eighty-one per cent of the patients were considered to be "recovered". A second rating was made, this time of psychosocial adjustment in three areas; family relationships, school or work relationships, and peer relationships. In these ratings "good" meant good across all three domains, "fair" indicated good across two domains and "unimproved" meant that there were continuing problems in two or more areas. Eighty-one per cent were rated "good". Seventy-nine per cent were rated as *both* "recovered" in symptomatic terms, and as having a "good" psychosocial adjustment.

Other early approaches

A number of other approaches have offered perspectives on anorexia. In the 1970s Palazzoli (1974, Palazzoli et al, 1978) were influential. They shared Minuchin's idea that anorexia played a role in the family, stabilising the parental marriage and thus providing security for all family members. This may have contributed to the continuing concern, even in the current treatment manual, to strengthen the boundary around the parental marriage in later stages of treatment. However, Palazzoli did not put parents in charge of their daughters eating.

Palazzoli (1974) described families with anorexic daughters. They thought that in these families it was usual for each member to reject other family members' self-definitions. It was usual to blame his or her decisions on others. Decisions were always seen as being made for the sake of another person, not for oneself. In addition, a system of alliances and coalitions across generational boundaries was seen as a central feature. In this the symptomatic child had a special place that distanced her from her siblings. She would take on the role of expressing the views of one parent about the other, only to be disconfirmed by the behaviour of the parent she seemed to support. No direct communication could develop between the parental couple. Each person implied that they always took a self-sacrificing position. The underlying dynamic was one of blame shifting.

Palazzoli (1974, Palazzoli et al, 1978) described a therapy approach in which therapists always worked together in pairs, one man and one woman. Dealing with these families the therapists always found family members disqualifying the therapists' views. They concluded that it was essential that families should never feel blamed by the therapists, and so developed the practice of "positive connotation"; everything done by family members was seen as done for the most altruistic reasons. In 1974 they reported a range of therapeutic interventions. These could include some interventions aimed at breaking down the family behaviour which disqualified the emotional content of the communication, for example by refusing to go along with the idea that cruel behaviour could be a source of humour. Sometimes therapeutic tasks were prescribed in order to intensify a relationship in which a hidden cross-generational coalition prevented parents from forming an effective alliance. The intensification could make the alliance too uncomfortable to maintain. Another therapeutic strategy involved the prescription of a family ritual, which was devised in such a way as to make it extremely difficult for family members to disqualify each other's communications. For example, this might be done by requiring family members to give each member the floor for fifteen minutes and listening to them without commenting or intervening. Finally, they developed the approach that came to be seen as most typical of their work. This was the counter-paradoxical intervention in which family members were told to continue in their current pattern of relationship, and the patient was told to continue to restrict her food intake, since this served to protect all members of the family from the dangers that would arise if the family broke up. Later, in the book Paradox and Counterparadox by Palazzoli et al (1978), this last technique was presented as the main means of intervening.

Outcomes from treatment using Palazzoli's approach

Palazzoli (1974) reported that in a series of twelve families with an anorexic daughter, nine recovered in less than twenty sessions, and three broke off treatment "because of our therapeutic mistakes". No details of the treatment series were given and there was no information about follow-up. Stierlin and Weber (1989) reported a follow-up study of patients treated with this approach. It did not provide convincing evidence that the treatment was effective.

Behavioural Family Systems Therapy

An approach that drew heavily on Minuchin's work was the Behavioural Family Systems Therapy described by Robin (1994). In this method the first phase involved a more directive, coaching approach to help parents with refeeding; family structure and relationships became the focus of the second phase, while fading out parental control over eating; supporting the patient in engaging more with peers, and decreasing her involvement with parents, were aims of the final phase. Robin took a directive approach to the first phase of treatment. Parents were given a clear eating plan and expected to implement that with their daughter. Robin used a coaching approach to helping parents achieve this. He saw family dynamics in much the same way as Minuchin had, particularly in terms of the effect of a weak parental coalition. This became the focus of his second phase of treatment. He was less emphatic than Minuchin about the causes of anorexia, regarding family relationships as one of a number of factors that predisposed a person to developing it. Robin et al (1999) provide a useful description of this approach. It is clear from their account that they saw the refeeding situation as one that the therapists would use to help them to understand and intervene in unhelpful family processes. Robin's therapists would seem to have had more freedom to intervene early in family relationship issues than either Maudsley Model or Family-Based Treatment approaches would encourage today. Robin et al (1995) reported that this treatment was effective in a small study. Six of eleven patients had recovered at the end of a treatment lasting on average sixteen months; nine had done so at one-year follow-up.

White's Narrative Therapy model

Another approach that may have influenced later developments was the Narrative Therapy model developed by White (1983). White saw anorexia as reflecting a rigid family belief system especially in relation to a daughter's role in the family. White was influenced by the problem solving approach to family therapy. His stance was one of agnosticism about the source of the problem. A central concern for White was to counteract the family's burden of guilt about the illness, by specifically denying that the family had a role in the development of anorexia. The incorporation of this belief into Maudsley Model Family Therapy represented a significant shift in approach. Each of these approaches made some contribution to the development of the Maudsley Model, to which we will shortly turn.

Contrasting positions about direct communication

There are two contrasting positions in these approaches. Minuchin et al (1978) used relational reframes in their work. This did not take the relatively guilt inducing form that would be conveyed by any message that said "Your daughter has anorexia because you are using her in your relationship to avoid having to face up to negotiating conflict, intimacy and distance between you" although that is, crudely, a summary of what they thought. Instead they usually used a developmental framework, seeing the issue in terms of the patient's need for autonomy. The comments that these therapists made that other therapists may have been most uncomfortable with are perhaps those that directly addressed interactions around food. For example Minuchin's "The problem here is you two ..." addressed to the parents of Deborah Kaplan, is about the way that the parents were unable to co-operate in the refeeding task. His comments to Judy Brown and her parents, framing Judy as "rude" to her father and so on goes exactly in the opposite direction that we go when we see anorexia as an "illness", and "make allowances" for the resulting behaviour. Minuchin spoke in that way because he wanted to intensify the message that the parents must unite against the anorexic behaviour.

By contrast Palazzoli et al (1978) provided a frame of reference that warned therapists against any kind of direct communication with family members because of their perception that the families' strategy was always to defeat the therapist. Both groups of therapists were working strategically of course, but Minuchin seems to have assumed that the families had a much greater latent capacity for direct honest communication, and on the face of it his results proved his point. Minuchin's perspective was far more respectful of the family's capacity to process honest communication than Palazzoli's. However, there has always been a twenty to forty per cent minority of families who did not respond positively to any of these treatments, so it is not possible to assume that the same approach would be the most successful in every case.

CHAPTER THREE

The development of Maudsley Model Family Therapy

Dare and Eisler (1997) rejected an approach that was built on the view that family dynamics are the cause of anorexia. Instead, they took the view that family relationship problems might arise as a result of the anorexia. Such problems might then become maintaining factors. They were concerned that family models of anorexia created a context in which parents would feel blamed. They thought that blame would lead to feelings of guilt and this in turn would cause the parents to be critical of their daughter. Such difficulties could be seen to follow naturally from the therapist's relationship restructuring goals. They would prevent therapeutic progress or lead to withdrawal from treatment.

Instead of seeing the family as the source of the problem, Dare and Eisler preferred to focus on influences outside the family, primarily socio-cultural influences, and to emphasise the impact that the anorexia had on the family rather than the impact that the family had on it. They regarded the changes they proposed as being empirically based. They maintained there were three reasons for the changes. First, research did not consistently support the psychosomatic family model. Hence, they were no longer confident that family relationships accounted for the onset of anorexia. Second, they had become convinced that "confrontational" techniques derived from the structural model could exacerbate family difficulties, reducing therapeutic progress. Third, they felt that these techniques could also lead to families dropping out of therapy. Central to this new approach was the idea that families do not cause anorexia. Nevertheless they presented an approach to family therapy that drew on aspects of the Systemic Family Therapy approach.

Subsequently, Eisler (2005) proposed that the apparent difficulties of families with daughters with anorexia should be understood as the result of the illness. These difficulties could then be seen as having much in common with the difficulties experienced by families in which a family member had any long-term illness.

Maudsley Model Family Therapy used a particular strategy at the outset. It was that parents were put in charge of their daughters eating in order to achieve weight restoration. As we have seen the strategy is derived from the family meal enactment described in Minuchin et al (1978), although Minuchin used this as an assessment device and did not always pursue this as the basis of the early stages of therapy. The strategy of putting parents in charge remains, but family lunch sessions in the consulting room were dropped from the Maudsley Model after the second family therapy outcome study, Le Grange et al (1992a, 1992b) and Squire-Dehouk (1993).

The First Maudsley Model

Dare et al (1990) described the approach used in the First Maudsley Study. This is the approach that pre-dated the current Maudsley Model. It was an eclectic approach drawing on the work of Minuchin et al (1978) and Palazzoli et al (1974). Dare and his colleagues said that, in contrast to the Philadelphia group, they would maintain the focus on food and starvation for a longer period in the early stages of treatment. In the first phase of treatment they described arousing anxiety in parents in order to motivate them to take firm control of their daughter's eating. Praise and positive feedback to the family served to protect the therapeutic alliance from tensions that might arise in this approach. In the second phase the therapist worked to achieve steady weight gain in the patient, with a minimum of conflict. If the family raised other issues these would only be discussed in terms of their impact on the task of refeeding. In the third phase, when the patient's eating was no longer a problem, control over food was handed back to the patient, and family discussions were focused on the adolescents increasing autonomy, and the establishment of healthy relationships between young adults and their parents. In the same paper they indicated their aim to work along the lines of the Milan school in the second or third phases of treatment. They stated, "We use an intergenerational understanding to make systemic interventions in the style of the Milan school ..." and that "These are propounded as expressing the family's need for the symptom ..." Dare et al (1990, p. 43). They saw this as reducing resistance to treatment. Other aspects of treatment, such as offering to continue individual work for the patient, and marital therapy for the parental couple, were dropped from the approach.

The current Maudsley Model emerges

Subsequently Dare and Eisler (1997), in developing Maudsley Model Family Therapy, rejected the earlier model but maintained that as far as treatment was concerned "The model of therapy utilised with adolescent patients with anorexia most closely resembles the Structural Model ... Like the Philadelphia group, we commonly support the parents in taking control of their daughter's eating ... . However, in engaging the family around this task, we make no assumption that the observed pattern of family functioning is dysfunctional or that the aim of therapy is to reverse this dysfunction", Dare and Eisler (1997, p. 319). Dare and Eisler (1997) presented what was essentially a reflective, systemic therapy stance. They expressed concern that some structural interventions are experienced as "covertly blaming the family, and perhaps in particular the mother", Dare and Eisler (1997, p. 319). In so far as they observed the family functioning in some respects much as Minuchin had seen it, they were inclined to comment on the interaction rather than assertively seeking to change it along the lines of structural family therapy. For example, they said that if they see that parents are "pulled in opposite directions" when it comes to managing the symptoms, then they would seek to explore the impact of the anorexia on the system "in which one parent speaks for caring closeness and the other for respectful distance", Dare and Eisler (1997, p. 319). This suggests an attitude of therapeutic neutrality consistent with the later developments of the systemic approach that was popular at the time. They took issue particularly with the use of structural techniques designed to "break a habitual pattern of conflict avoidance", Dare and Eisler (1997, p. 319), which they thought might be unnecessary or even harmful, especially in the early stages of treatment. When research indicated that insofar as parental (or at any rate maternal) criticism predicted a poorer outcome from treatment, they thought that the structural therapists assumptions about the cause of the illness, and direct approach to therapy, would make matters worse.

At what stage did the shift to the Maudsley Model happen?

In another discussion of their treatment approach, Dare et al (1995), say that their original approach to treatment in the First Maudsley Study was influenced by the approaches of Palazzoli and Minuchin. They say that at that time the Maudsley group shared the view that the families of patients with anorexia were dysfunctional, and that the therapeutic goal was to change family relationships. The change of approach preceded the next two studies, which I will refer to as the Pilot Study and the Third Maudsley Study. It seems to follow that the choice was made in the light of research results and clinical experience arising from the First Maudsley Study. Dare et al (1990) said, again referring to the First Maudsley Study, "Our 'neutral' stance as to the origins of the 'disorder' is a position that is the least likely to induce disabling guilt in the family members and also accords with our scientific viewpoint", Dare et al (1990, p. 42). This neutral stance was that of Milan-Systemic Therapy, a stance that concealed the therapist's real belief that the anorexia existed and was maintained because it served a function in the family system. Subsequently, drawing conclusions from the First Maudsley Study, they became more concerned about the possibility that parents would feel blamed. This led them to develop the stance specifically denying that parents played a role in the aetiology of anorexia. From that point they declared to families that "families don't cause anorexia" or that parents are not the "root cause" of the disorder. The position was reinforced by the failure to confirm the accuracy of the Psychosomatic Family Model in a study by Dare et al (1994). On balance, it seems likely that the work of Minuchin was very much more in the minds of the therapists during the First Maudsley Study than it was subsequently. In these respects the shift in approach reflected the ongoing changes in British family therapy at the time. No doubt there was a process of mutual influence between this group of therapists and the professional culture.

It is not really clear what attitude Dare and Eisler (1997) had to relational reframing. On the face of it their way of thinking does not need to prevent the therapist from seeing ways that family relationships may be unhelpful, impairing the daughter's development of autonomy for example. Many of the "confrontational" techniques used by the structural therapist were framed in this way. Their discussion does seem to indicate a reluctance to raise such issues. The model requires therapists to think of them as secondary to the "illness".

Empirical evidence for the change of approach

Dare and Eisler regarded the changes they had made to the treatment model as evidence based. They were involved in three substantial studies of the outcome of family therapy for anorexia in adolescent patients. Of these, the First Maudsley study (Szmuckler et al, 1985; Russell et al, 1987; Dare et al, 1990; Eisler et al, 1997) confirmed that family therapy was an effective intervention for young people with acute anorexia. This is the only one of the three studies to pre-date the change of approach. It was the first of the studies in which ratings of Expressed Emotion (EE) by parents were obtained, prior to the start of out-patient treatment. Expressed emotion was measured by rating families on warmth and emotional over-involvement, warmth and hostility, and by counting the number of critical comments and positive remarks in a clinical interview. This research on expressed emotion provided the objective evidence behind the change of approach.

Parental criticism and withdrawal from treatment in the First Maudsley Study

The First Maudsley Study was a large study that compared family and individual therapies for each of the four distinct groups of patients. These were:

1. Patients who developed anorexia before the age of nineteen, and had it for less than three years.
2. Patients who developed anorexia before the age of nineteen, and had it for more than three years.
3. Patients who developed anorexia at age nineteen or later.
4. Patients with bulimia.

In each group, roughly half the patients were treated with family therapy and half with an individual therapy. It was only for the first group, the young patients with a short history of anorexia, that family therapy proved the more effective treatment. The clinical features of this group are typical of most patients with anorexia treated in CAMHS.

Szmuckler et al (1985) reported the findings about parental EE and withdrawal from treatment across all four patient groups. The crucial issue for the change of family therapy approach concerned parental critical comments and subsequent withdrawal from treatment. Ratings of parental EE were made before the beginning of treatment. Four out of nineteen patients with anorexia (including the adult patients) offered family therapy dropped out of, or failed to start, out-patient family therapy. For patients who were offered family therapy there was a significant relationship between their mothers' levels of critical comments, one aspect of EE, and drop-out from, or failure to start, out-patient family therapy. However, only one adolescent patient in the early onset, short history group (of ten who were treated) dropped out of family therapy at an early stage, although two others failed to complete one year of therapy.

Szmuckler et al (1985) offered a number of possible explanations for these findings. One was that critical mothers may have been those who already felt over-burdened by the task of caring for the symptomatic daughter, and rejected an offer of treatment in which they felt they were expected to do all the work. In other words, Szmuckler was suggesting that the critical mothers were psychologically unavailable for the task they were being asked to do. Another possibility was that the critical mothers felt they were being blamed for the illness. The implication would be that it was those mothers who were already critical who felt that way, or who responded to that feeling by dropping out of treatment. This second explanation seems to have been favoured by the therapy team. Le Grange et al (1992b) stated that the change in therapy model was made in response to the evidence on parental criticism and treatment outcome. The evidence from the First Maudsley Study appears to have been the only objective evidence that could have guided the decision to change the model at that stage. By implication the therapists concluded that they would have got even better results if they had not addressed family relationship issues early on, and, if they themselves believed and stated that family relationships were not relevant to the onset of anorexia.

Dare et al (1994) studied the families of anorexic girls. They argued from the low levels of EE found that the families of girls with anorexia were unexpressive and conflict avoiding. They suggested that this link reflected the fact that "Conflicts between parents and adolescents cannot be faced and negotiated unless the participants are prepared to show strong feelings", (Dare et al, 1994, p. 223) and that this would give rise to problems when families were forced, for example as a result of the anorexia, to face levels of conflict they would prefer to avoid. They thought that because of the families' lack of experience in dealing with conflict they had failed to developed skills in conflict resolution and that, trapped in unwelcome conflict that they could not resolve they would then pass the blame on to the patient. She would respond with resentment and blame her parents so that a vicious circle of blame might be setup. In the light of this sort of argument, the Maudsley therapists altered their approach to treatment in the direction of a less "confrontational" approach. They were afraid that addressing family relationship issues early on would elicit guilt and blame, endangering the therapeutic alliance and increasing resistance to treatment. This, they thought, could prevent progress or lead to the family dropping out of treatment.

Studies of Maudsley Model Family Therapy

No comparative trial has been made comparing the old model and the new. The next two studies were based on the current Maudsley Model. They were comparisons of treatment modality, but not of treatment approach. Some evidence from these studies was considered to justify the change of model. They were intended to be experimental investigations of the contents of treatment. They compared two treatment formats. In one, all sessions were conjoint and patient and parents were never seen separately, as in the family therapy in the First Maudsley Study. In the second, all sessions were separate, and the patient was never seen with her parents. The first of these two studies, Le Grange et al (1992a, 1992b) and Squire-Dehouk (1993), is usually referred to as a Pilot study for the Third Maudsley Study, while the last, Eisler et al (2000) and Eisler et al (2007) is the Third Maudsley Study itself. All these studies were based on the new model. In both studies, families were randomly assigned to treatment in one or the other of these treatment formats.

Unfortunately there is some confusion about exactly what was being compared with what in these two studies. Sometimes the description given indicates that conjoint treatment had more of a focus on family relationships than separated treatment had. Dare and Eisler (1995b) describe the conjoint treatment as maintaining more elements of family therapy than the separated therapy. They say that the conjoint therapy focused more on the style of the parental couples relationship and their relationship to their children. In it therapists concerned themselves with "the place the illness of the patient had come to play in the pattern of family life" and sought to change patterns that "tended to perpetuate the patient in the sick role, different from the position of her siblings", Dare and Eisler (1995b, pp. 339–340). By contrast they argued that many elements of family therapy were ruled out in separated treatment. However, this difference between treatments is not so clear in the descriptions given in the report of the Third Maudsley Study, by Eisler et al (2000). In a footnote they specifically noted that the treatments were "conceptually similar". However, some differences are clear. For example, siblings were not included in the separated therapy. Equally, of course, the therapist could not observe the communication between parents and daughter, and could not intervene directly in order to change it. In the separated treatment it was not possible to have a family lunch session. Family lunch sessions were included in the conjoint treatment in the Pilot study, but dropped from it in the main study (Eisler, 2004).

The Maudsley Model rejects family lunch sessions

Today there is a difference of opinion between the Maudsley Model Family Therapists in the UK and the Family-Based Treatment therapists in the USA about family lunch sessions. The Maudsley group no longer use family lunch sessions. In the UK, many therapists who claim to be following the Family-Based Treatment manual do not, in fact, use the family lunch session. In the Pilot Study, Le Grange et al (1992a, 1992b), eighteen patients were treated, nine in a conjoint family therapy, and nine in a separated family therapy format. The results seemed to confirm the Maudsley group's concerns about the use of "confrontational" techniques by the therapist, and about conjoint therapy itself. In the study there was a measure of critical comments by parents at the initial assessment and a reassessment after thirty-two weeks. Critical comments (from both mothers and fathers) reduced in the separated treatment but increased in the conjoint treatment. The differences were not statistically significant but the pattern was clear.

Dare and Eisler (1997) supported their decision to abandon the use of family lunch sessions by reference to unpublished research by Squire-Dehouk (1993). She followed up the eighteen families in the Pilot study two years after treatment. At two year follow-up fourteen patients were interviewed, face to face or by phone, as were parents of fifteen of the patients. Some further information was obtained by questionnaire. In only one case did the family refuse to give any information. The follow-up data suggest more strongly than the original report that the separated treatment modality was superior. Patients in separated treatment made more progress with weight recovery. These differences were reflected in statistically significant differences on measures of food intake and menstrual status. In addition they were asked to complete a self-report questionnaire, the Family Adaptability and Cohesion Scales (FACES III—Olson et al, 1979), about their perception of the family relationship, both as it was, and as they would like it to be, so that the comparison of the ratings provided a measure of family satisfaction or dissatisfaction with their relationships.

Parents who had experienced the separated family therapy were more satisfied with the treatment approach and with their marital relationship after treatment than were those who had experienced conjoint treatment. In general Squire-Dehouk (1993) found that parents did not feel misunderstood or blamed by the therapist, in either treatment modality. However, the patient was more likely to feel misunderstood or blamed in the conjoint treatment. This difference would not have been statistically significant given the small number of cases. Squire-Dehouk commented that usually parents and patients did not feel misunderstood or blamed, and attributed that to the therapist's intention to counteract blame by taking a neutral stance about the cause of anorexia, and using praise and positive connotation. She thought the fact that the patients in the conjoint treatment did sometimes feel blamed might have been the result of the lack of individual sessions with the therapist in their treatment.

In both treatments two-thirds of parents found it acceptable that they were asked to take charge of their child's eating, but some parents were strongly against this. This included two cases in which the parents rejected the diagnosis of anorexia, and one in which parents felt that the approach conflicted with their values. Parents were asked about their experience of taking charge of their daughters' eating, and their responses were categorised in terms of the degree of power struggle that had ensued. The families in the conjoint treatment had experienced a more intense power struggle and this difference was statistically significant. She noted that this might include physical fights, and spoke of "forced feeding", and commented that parents in the separated treatment "found ways of taking control without going into overt intensive battle with their offspring", Squire-Dehouk (1993, p. 44). She did not ask for specific feedback about the family lunch sessions, presumably because the research design required her to ask the same questions to family members from both treatments.

Squire-Dehouk concluded that family lunch sessions were unnecessary since families in the separated treatment had achieved more progress with the management of weight recovery, with less overt conflict, and were more satisfied with the treatment in general, than those in the conjoint treatment. Probably this conclusion was accepted, because family lunch sessions were dropped in both treatment conditions in the next study.

There has been no formal comparison of treatment that includes family lunch sessions and treatment that excludes them. However, in the Pilot study family lunch sessions were included in the conjoint treatment, but they were dropped from it for the substantive study. In the Pilot study parental critical comments increased with treatment in the conjoint therapy group (which had family lunch sessions), but reduced in the separated group, (which did not, have family lunch sessions) while in the Third Maudsley Study parental critical comments reduced in both groups, both of which now had no family lunch sessions. In the Third Maudsley Study improved family satisfaction, and reductions in family criticism, were achieved in both treatments. These findings as a whole could be interpreted as confirming the proposition either that family lunch sessions, or the way those were managed, had accounted for the increased parental criticism, and family dissatisfaction, arising in the conjoint treatment, reported by Le Grange et al (1992b) and Squire-Dehouk (1993), respectively, in their reports of the Pilot study.

Conjoint therapy versus separated therapy

Writing in 1997 Dare and Eisler argued that the results of the Pilot study indicated that the separated treatment modality was superior to the conjoint modality. The research had been designed to investigate the interaction between these different approaches to the family therapy, on the one hand, and different family atmospheres on the other. In both the Third Maudsley study, and its Pilot study, expressed emotion ratings were made to measure the number of Critical Comments (CC) made by family members at the initial assessment, and again at a much later stage of treatment. They found that although the levels of all three scales of negative expressed emotion were low, nevertheless relatively higher levels of CC made by the patient's mother predicted a poorer outcome. They concluded that separated therapy "which by its very nature made it impossible to use some of the more challenging and confrontational techniques characteristic of the Philadelphia group was just as effective as our customary conjoint therapy; in families where there were high levels of criticism or hostility, it was, if anything, more effective", Dare and Eisler (1997, p. 319).

Despite the fact that Dare and Eisler (1997) could not demonstrate any advantage to conjoint therapy in 1997, when they published the substantive report of the outcomes from the Third Maudsley Study (Eisler et al, 2000), they noted that a comparison of the full range of outcome measures provided a different picture. Outcome measures included the Morgan-Russell Global Outcome ratings, and five Morgan-Russell subscales (Morgan & Russell, 1975)—clinical ratings of the extent of recovery in the domains of nutrition, menstrual functioning, mental state, psychosexual and psychosocial adjustment. In addition they used various questionnaire measures of depression, and self-esteem, as well as the Revised Eating Disorders Inventory, (EDI-2) Garner et al (1983). They found that the separated treatment had produced superior results in all the eating disorder symptom measures. This difference was accounted for by a more positive treatment response in separated therapy in families in which the patient's mother had made more critical comments about her daughter with anorexia at the initial assessment. Families with lower levels of criticism did equally well in both treatments. Despite a lower recovery rate measured in terms of eating disorder symptoms, the conjoint therapy had produced superior outcomes in terms of all the other measures of pathology, with just one exception. The conjoint therapy group showed greater improvement on the clinical ratings of mental state, psychosexual adjustment, and psychosocial adjustment, and on measures of depression, obsessionality, tension, mood, self-esteem and on the ineffectiveness, interpersonal distrust, interoceptive awareness and maturation fears sub-scales of the EDI-2. With one exception, the perfectionism scale of the EDI-2, on which there was no difference between treatments, all measures of psychological features of outcome, apart from measures of eating disorder symptoms, showed greater improvement in conjoint therapy. Changes in ratings of both criticism and warmth were comparable in both treatments. Criticism directed by parents towards daughters was reduced in both treatments. Criticism directed by parents at each other was also reduced, and warmth between parents increased, in both treatments. Patients seen in the conjoint condition rated their families as having become more flexible at the end of treatment, while the adolescents in the separated condition rated families as having become more rigid. It can be argued that the greater improvement in weight and eating disorder symptoms in the separated therapy group reflected increased parental effectiveness and control. The broader psychological improvement in the conjoint therapy reflected the patient's experience that her parents had become more flexible in their approach to her, a change likely to facilitate increased autonomy and maturity in the adolescent patient. Dare and Eisler reported these results in two papers (Eisler et al, 2000; Dare et al, 2000) but subsequently they have not received much attention.

A possible interpretation of the Third Maudsley Study is that it tends to validate the family therapist's traditional flexibility in relation to the question of either meeting the family together, or, at times, meeting some family members without others. The study demonstrated that when therapists using this model were required to take an inflexible position, whichever position it was, something was always lost. From a family therapy point of view seeing people separately is a boundary making technique. It may be particularly useful when families are conflicted or over-involved. On the other hand there is a danger that the boundary becomes too rigid, limiting the opportunities for therapeutic improvement, if it is the only approach to treatment. Therapists who only met parents and daughter separately may have found it easier to join successfully and hence be more effective in helping them to negotiate the early stages of treatment in which weight recovery must be initiated. This may have been particularly true when family relationships were already stressed. However, the psychological benefits achieved by conjoint therapy were lost exactly because it was not possible then to work directly on the relationship between the patient with anorexia and her parents. This greatly reduced the quality of the outcomes as far as psychological improvement was concerned. Therapists who met the family only conjointly may not always have been able to surmount the initial difficulty of joining the parents and the patient in such a way as to succeed with the initial therapeutic task, refeeding. Despite this disadvantage they were in a better position to observe and intervene in the relationship between parents and daughter. This led to, on average, much more psychological improvement in daughters, even though, as a group, they showed less symptomatic improvement. Bearing these research findings in mind one could argue that therapists should maintain the traditional stance of flexibility. In the event, the authors of the study have continued to argue the case for flexibility rather than arguing that there are two distinct treatments, each suitable for a different kind of family. Eisler et al (2000) made it clear in a footnote that they continued to be flexible in their day-to-day practice. Drawing conclusions from the same evidence Paulson-Karlsson et al (2009) used an approach in which initial sessions would take place in the separated format, while later sessions were conjoint, and found that this approach produced good results.

The reason that the conjoint treatment at the Maudsley, as used in all the clinical trials, excluded any separate sessions was a scientific one. The researchers wanted to be sure that there could be no question that the "family therapy" was contaminated with individual therapy. The two research trials that compared the separate and conjoint treatment approaches were intended as experimental manipulations of the therapy with a view to gaining a better understanding of the process of therapy. There is no empirical evidence on this point but it seems most likely that flexibility should be the preferred strategy.

* * *

The research questions that remain are these: What is it that happens in the separated session that helps parents to take charge of the eating situation? What is it that happens in the conjoint sessions that helps the patient who is struggling to make the psychological adjustment she must make when her symptoms are challenged?

Are the changes made by Dare and Eisler justified by the evidence?

An observer might think it odd that in the early 1990s a research group that had just completed a therapy trial that produced a high recovery rate nevertheless felt it necessary to change their model. As we have seen Dare and Eisler (1997) expressed concern that structural techniques, including the so called "confrontational" techniques derived from structural therapy, would stand in the way of recovery and lead to families dropping out of treatment. A reader could understand Dare and Eisler (1997) to imply that the Pilot study could be seen as a comparison between traditional conjoint therapy, on the one hand, and a separated therapy that also took the view that parents do not cause anorexia on the other. However that is not the case. It is clear from Le Grange et al (1992a) that the attitude to the cause of anorexia was the same in both modalities of treatment in the Pilot study. In both treatments, parents were to be told at an early stage that they were not the root cause of their daughter's anorexia. In addition the same four therapists conducted both treatments, and it seems there was no intention to compare different approaches to treatment beyond the differences that were inevitable given the different (separated or conjoint) treatment modalities. As yet no study has been published comparing Structural Family Therapy for anorexia with Maudsley Model Family Therapy, or any other comparison of different family therapy approaches.

It is possible that, in the minds of the Maudsley therapists, the family lunch sessions came to stand for Minuchin's general approach. Despite the change to the Maudsley Model it seems clear from the discussion by Squire-Dehouk (1993) that family lunch sessions were intended to be high intensity. They were intended to induce a therapeutic crisis along the lines described in some cases by Minuchin et al (1978). Squire-Dehouk understood the treatment as one that was intended to change the family's ability to handle conflict. She says, "The family therapy starts with a family lunch session to which the parents are invited to participate in finding ways to make their child eat. This aspect in the therapy is considered to be very important because it allows the therapist to observe and intervene in the interactional patterns of the family. The therapist can focus his therapy on teaching the family to tolerate conflict and facilitate conflict resolution ..." Squire-Dehouk (1993, p. 57). She noted that Barcai (1971) had pointed out "the possible negative effects of such crisis inducing family therapy", Squire-Dehouk (1993, p. 57) that might lead to the family dropping out of treatment or to alarming reactions such as a suicidal gesture. Again this suggests that family lunch sessions were equated with the creation of therapeutic crises, because Barcai was addressing the issue of therapeutic crisis induction, not the issue of family lunch sessions. In his report Barcai describes an early piece of work he did with Minuchin. Minuchin (1970) described the same case. In it a strategic intervention was used in which the family members were instructed that for the duration of the weekend they should each only eat as much as the patient was willing to eat. This led to tension at home and to a suicidal gesture by the patient's father. The purpose of Barcai's paper was to argue that therapists needed to be careful to monitor the situation arising from therapeutic crisis intervention (not necessarily arising in family lunch sessions) and make themselves available on the phone if they used this kind of approach. Barcai and Minuchin were not arguing against crisis inducing interventions, only that the tensions created needed to be managed. Subsequently, Minuchin does not seem to have used this particular strategy in work with anorexia.

Dare and Eisler (1997) may have seen the findings of Squire-Dehouk about family lunch sessions as validating their developing opposition to the use of structural techniques. Against their conclusion it should be said that satisfaction with family lunch sessions, with conjoint therapy, and with subsequent family relationships are all likely to be influenced by the degree of success or failure in the therapy as a whole. Discomfort associated with the therapy, and with the family relationships, may abate quite quickly if the patient recovers. Hence the relative lack of success of the conjoint therapy, arising from some possibly unknown source, may have accounted for all the differences in the feedback about the two treatments. It is not obvious why the conjoint treatment had been less successful. In many respects it appears to have been the same as the treatment that was successful in the First Maudsley Study since in that too, the family therapy was a conjoint treatment in which the therapist only saw the family together and family lunch sessions were included. The only thing that had changed was the shift of thinking in the Maudsley Model itself.

* * *

It is interesting to consider the family lunch session as a paradigm of the treatment model. From the point of view of the Philadelphia group, the sessions served a function in restructuring the family, not simply in putting parents in charge of their daughter's eating, but specifically in removing the patient from her triangulated or detouring role in the parent's relationship at mealtimes. The intensity of the family lunch sessions was seen as sometimes necessary to achieve that result. In the lunch scenario comments could be made which were challenging to the family organisation. These presumably include the "confrontational" techniques that were criticised by Dare and Eisler (1997). Yet the fact that the therapists had a restructuring goal in mind may have helped them to maintain flexibility and not allow the sessions to become simply a battle for control from which one party or the other must depart defeated. Their comments on the need to change the relationships might offer something engaging for parents and patient. The high level of recovery achieved in the early studies (Minuchin et al (1978) and Russell et al (1987)) indicates that the tension created in these sessions was managed successfully at the time. Possibly when therapists lost their confidence in the psychosomatic family model, and found no family model to put in its place, they had much less to offer in these sessions. The sessions might well then have become simply a battle for control.

* * *

It seems unlikely that therapists today would regard the intensity of conflict as acceptable, especially the intensity of physical confrontation which Minuchin was willing to countenance in the consulting room or wherever it might take place. Anxiety on this account may have contributed to the general trend in the UK not to have these sessions. However, the authors of the FBT treatment manual offer a contrasting approach to family lunch sessions. This will be discussed in the next chapter.

How should we understand parental criticism?

Parental criticism, or, more accurately, maternal criticism of the patient, became a concern to the Maudsley therapists in the first instance because they noticed that it was related to dropout from family therapy. They thought that if the therapist made parents feel blamed, the parents would become more critical of the patient, and this would lead to poorer outcomes. They took account of this by changing their model in a way that was intended to avoid making parents feel blamed. Despite the change they noted that maternal criticism of the patient still predicted poorer outcomes, a finding which they took to validate their position. Within their new model they found that separated treatment was more effective than conjoint treatment when outcome was judged in terms of weight and menstrual recovery. The difference was accounted for by a differential effect in families with high criticism. Those families did better in separated therapy than they did in conjoint therapy. They also noted that criticism increased in a conjoint treatment case series in which family lunch sessions were included, and decreased in a separated treatment series in which they were excluded. This observation contributed to the decision to drop the use of family lunch sessions. The authors of the FBT treatment manual rejected this latter decision, but in other respects they accepted the thinking behind the change of approach to treatment. However, a crucial element in research is lacking. There has never been a comparative trial between one of the older models of family therapy for anorexia and the Maudsley Model.

An alternative way of thinking about the issue of parental criticism would be this. Parents vary in the extent to which they are willing and able to engage with the task of parenting in the context of a challenging crisis such as the development of acute anorexia in a daughter. Parents' own mental states, their background, and their ability to support one another are likely to be the initial factors determining this. Subsequently, their willingness to engage is likely to be affected by their experience of success or failure. This statement can be reframed in attachment terms. The development of anorexia can be seen as a signal by the patient that she needs parental care and attention. Seen from an attachment perspective, parents who are able to offer this wholeheartedly are caretakers who are available. Families in this state, in which the patient signals her need, and the parents signal their availability, succeed with the task that the therapist gives them. Refeeding proceeds successfully, and the therapist is able to help to improve the family communication. If, however, the parents are not initially available, or have become unavailable after a series of unsuccessful engagements in therapy, therapeutic engagement is less satisfactory. Occasionally the parents may refuse to engage in the therapeutic task. More often they do so, but critical comments directed at the patient inform her of their unavailability. In these circumstances the patient may escalate her resistance to eating as a way of demanding more commitment from her parents. Alternatively she may regain some weight, but fail to make the psychological transition to recovery. Her attachment needs may then be expressed through a range of eating disorder symptoms, low mood, and other problems. Eisler et al (2007) found that the impact of high maternal criticism could be accounted for by the fact that the patients with critical mothers had lower weights at initial presentation. This might be accounted for if behaviour is seen as a signal of the patient's need for parental care, then the patient's escalating weight loss could be understood as a marker of parental unavailability.

Whichever way you see it, the implication is that parents need to be given more support and attention for their own needs. Parents whose unavailability to their daughter is signalled by parental criticism may need to be given separate time with the therapist. Sometimes, this may need to be focused on the impact on the parents of their experience of previous unsuccessful attempts at treatment. In more serious cases separate work may be needed to target more significant areas of parental dysfunction, such as those arising from their early experiences with their own parents, or unresolved losses in their lives, or serious marital relationship difficulties between them.

Has the shift to the Maudsley Model improved outcomes?

Evidence does not indicate that Maudsley Model Family Therapy is superior to older models of family therapy for anorexia. It is interesting to note the decline in outcomes from conjoint therapy at the Maudsley over time. In the First Maudsley study, Eisler et al (1997) six (60%) of patients had a good outcome and only one (10%) failed to benefit. In the Pilot study, Squire-Dehouk (1993), three (33%) had a good outcome and three (33%) did not benefit, and by the time of the Third Maudsley Study, Eisler et al (2000), five (26%) had a good outcome, and ten (53%) did not benefit. This is not what we would expect to see if the new model was superior to the old. A possible interpretation is that as the model changed to the Maudsley Model therapists had less to offer in conjoint therapy.

One of the great strengths of the Maudsley studies is the success of the researchers in following-up the cohort of patients for as long as five years, with few patients lost to follow up. The data shows that between group differences were less marked at follow-up. By the time of the five year follow-up for the First Maudsley study patients had continued to improve, so that nine out of ten had a good outcome. In the five year follow up of the Third Maudsley study, Eisler et al (2007) found that the patients in conjoint treatment made remarkable further progress, with thirteen out of eighteen followed up having a good outcome. Nevertheless, patients in separated therapy still did better both at end of treatment and at follow-up, at least in terms of eating disorder symptom measures. However, a weakness of this follow-up information is that it does not address the issue of further treatment. This seems to be a particularly important issue in treatment series where the initial response to treatment has been relatively disappointing. The question is whether the subsequent recovery was partly the result of other treatments using different methods.

If we judge the Maudsley Model simply by reference to the three studies at the Maudsley then, whether we consider separated or conjoint treatment, the outcomes from the new Maudsley Model were inferior at the end of treatment, and still slightly inferior at five year follow up, compared to those produced by the original, pre-Maudsley Model approach. Eisler et al (2000) attributed the relatively poor end of treatment results to the presence of more treatment resistant cases. That is to say there were more patients who had had previous unsuccessful therapies. This would not have accounted for the differences between the separated and conjoint treatment modalities. In any case the data in Russell et al (1987) indicates that the treatment cohort in the First Maudsley Study had an even higher level of previous unsuccessful treatment.

If we compare across all studies, using an index of outcome based mainly on weight and menstrual recovery, little has changed since the earliest studies, at least by the time of the follow-up. The following tables present recovery rates, mostly reflecting weight and menstrual recovery. Where possible the Morgan-Russell Global Outcome Score has been used. It is based on a clinical interview. A "good" outcome is one in which the patients weight is in the normal range, she has recovered her menstrual cycle, and is free of bulimic symptoms. Clinical experience shows us that generally patients who fall into this category are doing well, but not always. Occasionally patients who fall into this category are struggling with eating disorders symptoms, feel fat and depressed and remain in this state for a long time. A patient who has developed severe obsessive-compulsive disorder or depression can still be classified as having a "good" outcome. Hence not all "good" outcomes are equally good, although in general the picture is a positive one. An "intermediate" outcome is one in which the patient has achieved a weight above the criterion for the diagnosis, but is not menstruating, or has recovered in respect of weight and menstrual criteria but has some bulimic symptoms, not more than once a week. Typically these patients are still preoccupied with the need to control their food intake, are struggling with a lot of eating disorder symptoms, and often have low mood. A "poor" outcome is one in which the patient continues to fulfill the weight and menstrual criteria for anorexia, or has bulimic symptoms more than once a week. As far as possible, recovery rates are presented as a percentage of cases on an intention to treat basis, so that the effectiveness of treatment is not exaggerated in the event that therapists fail to engage treatment resistant families, or if early drop-outs are excluded from the data analysis, or if unsuccessfully treated cases are lost to follow-up. Table 1 shows recovery rates based on data for five studies that depend on treatment approaches pre-dating the current Maudsley Model. This is the work of therapists who, broadly speaking, viewed anorexia as substantially the result of family processes. They did not tell parents that they were "not the root cause" of the problem. They used a range of family therapy techniques and addressed a range of family relationship issues.

Table 1. Outcome and follow up data from five early studies of family therapy for anorexia in adolescents.

Study by *N =*	*End of treatment outcome*	*Follow-up outcome length of follow-up*
Minuchin et al (1978) N = 53		81% Recovered 4% Fair 9% Unimproved or relapsed 6% Lost to follow-up Mean 2 years 8 months follow-up
Martin (1985) N = 25	45% weight recovered	95% weight recovered Mean 5 years 1 month follow-up
Russell et al (1987) Eisler et al (1997) N = 10	60% Good 30% Intermediate 10% Poor	90% Good, 10% Poor 5 year follow-up
Robin et al (1995) N = 11	55% Good	82% Good 1 year follow-up
Wallin et al (2000) N = 26		65% Recovered 27% Improved 8% Poor 2 year follow-up

Table 2 shows recovery rates for studies whose authors shared the current Maudsley Models attitude to the cause of anorexia. The therapists did tell parents that they were not "the root cause" of the problem or that "parents do not cause anorexia". Outcomes reported in studies based on the FBT treatment manual by Lock et al (2001), Lock and Le Grange (2013) will be described in the next chapter.

A comparison of the outcomes presented in the tables does not suggest that the Maudsley Model has led to improved outcomes, at least when outcome is judged largely in terms of weight and menstrual criteria. This being so it would be helpful to know whether there is a difference between treatments in regard to the acceptability of the treatment, or whether any approach is likely to be more successful with "treatment

Table 2. Outcome and follow-up data from five series of patients treated with the Maudsley Model.

Study by *N =*	*End of treatment outcome*	*Follow-up outcome* *length of follow-up*
Le Grange et al (1992) Squire-Dehouk (1993) Separated treatment N = 9		78% Good 11% Intermediate 11% Lost to follow-up Two year follow-up
Le Grange et al (1992) Squire-Dehouk (1993) Conjoint treatment N = 9		33% Good 33% Intermediate 33% Poor Two year follow-up
Eisler et al (2000), Eisler et al (2007) Separated treatment N = 21	48% Good 29% Intermediate 24% Poor	80% Good 10% Intermediate 10% Poor 5 year follow-up
Eisler et al (2000), Eisler et al (2007) Conjoint treatment N = 19	26% Good 21% Intermediate 53% Poor	72% Good 6% Intermediate 22% Poor 5 year follow-up
Paulson-Karlson et al (2009) N = 32		72% recovered at 18 month follow-up 78% recovered at 36 month follow-up

resistant" cases, such as those who have been unsuccessfully treated before.

Do approaches differ in acceptability to families?

Dare and Eisler (1997) had expressed concern that approaches to the family therapy of anorexia made parents, or more particularly mothers, feel blamed. Much of their rationale for the Maudsley Model focused on the need to prevent this. So is the Maudsley Model more acceptable to families? One rather concrete indicator could be drop-out rates, since drop-out is most likely to be a rejection of the therapist's approach. Drop-out rates have always been fairly low, ranging from the 6% reported by Minuchin et al (1978), to 25% reported by Loeb et al (2007) in a study of FBT, but usually reported to be in the order of about 10%. One out of ten patients dropped out within three months in the First Maudsley Study, four out of forty in the Third Maudsley study, so the change of model seems not to have made any difference. On the face of it there is no concrete evidence that the new approach is more acceptable.

Is the Maudsley Model more appropriate for more severe or treatment resistant cases?

Another way of thinking about this is that families who are more ground down by a chronic problem, or families that have more treatment resistant daughters, or families which contain more vulnerable members, might be more appropriate for a less assertive, more supportive approach such as the Maudsley Model. Such families might benefit from a slower pace as far as the question of tackling family relationship issues is concerned. They might benefit more from seeing a therapist who assumes that parents are "not the root cause of the problem" and tells them so. Alternatively, they might benefit more from working with a therapist who addresses family relationship issues openly and directly. One way to look at this is in relation to previous treatment. Eisler et al (2000) noted that of forty patients in the Third Maudsley Study only sixteen had not had previous treatment. These sixteen did better than those who had had previous treatment. Patients who had already had repeated treatment did least well. There is not much data to compare with this, except what can be taken from Minuchin et al (1978). Twenty-two of the fifty-three patients in that treatment series had

had previous treatment. Only four had had more than one episode of previous treatment. Table 3 compares outcomes across the two studies for the three different groups of patients; those untreated before, those who had one previous episode of treatment, and those with more than one previous episode.

Table 3 shows that the proportion of patients making a good or intermediate recovery in Maudsley Model therapy dropped off markedly for those patients who had previous treatment. The proportion of patients achieving both a "recovered" and a "good" outcome status dropped much less in the structural therapy approach. The data is not satisfactory because the outcome criteria are not exactly the same, and the intensity or seriousness of previous treatments may

Table 3. The relationship between previous treatment and treatment outcome in two studies, Eisler et al (2000) and Minuchin et al (1978).

Study N =	*Patients who had no previous treatment*	*Patients who had one previous treatment*	*Patients who had more than one previous treatment*	*Total*
Eisler et al (2000) Good or Intermediate Outcome/ Poor	13/16	9/13	3/11	25/40
% of group	(81%)	(69%)	(27%)	(62.5%)
N = 40				
Minuchin et al (1978) Recovered + Good Outcome/ Others	25/31	14/18	3/4	42/53
% of group	(81%)	(78%)	(75%)	(79%)
N = 53				

not be comparable either. It may be an unfair comparison because the data from the study by Eisler et al (2000) is from the end of treatment, whereas the data from the Minuchin et al (1978) study is from a variable length follow-up, averaging two years eight months, and we know that at that point more patients will have recovered and that effects due to treatment differences may be eroded with time. Despite that it is presented here because it has bearing on an important question. At the very least the evidence does not suggest that the Maudsley Model is a better treatment than Structural Family Therapy for treatment resistant cases, defined here by the fact of the patient having had previous unsuccessful treatment. The data in this table, for what it is worth, suggests the opposite.

The question is important because it is possible that CAMHS therapists in the UK, influenced by the prevailing ideology, give up family therapy quite easily when they face difficulties. Patients are admitted to hospital or are given individual treatments such as Cognitive Behavioural Therapy (CBT). This wastes the patient's time at a crucial point in their lives and does not lead to recovery. One interpretation of the data in Table 3 is that faced with difficulties family therapists should conduct their therapy more assertively, drawing on the whole range of family therapy skills available to them. Consider the case of Judy, described in the previous chapter. This is the girl who at age fourteen had already had three unsuccessful admissions and who was being fed through a surgically implanted tube. Which of us would not be daunted faced with this girl? To judge from the data we would be right to feel this. Judy and her parents had a very long and gruelling family meal session with Minuchin, after which she started to eat and made progress towards recovery. This family meal session was surely one of which our colleagues at the Maudsley would disapprove. Under their influence we would probably not have the courage to try this. Yet in fact the session initiated change in a very treatment resistant case when the therapist insisted on persevering in putting the parents in charge, while, at the same time, presenting Judy's resistance in a family relationship context, describing her as rude, and intervening to prevent her mother from comforting her and so on. The answer to the question "Do families with 'treatment resistant' daughters benefit more from Maudsley Model treatment?" may very well be no.

CHAPTER FOUR

Family-Based Treatment

In their treatment manual, Lock et al (2001) and Lock and Le Grange (2013) adopt the same stance as Dare and Eisler (1997). They express the view that "parents don't cause anorexia", and insist that families should be told this at an early stage. However, whereas Dare and Eisler present what can be seen as a systemic, neutral, reflective stance towards family relationships, this hardly appears in the manual. The manual gives more emphasis to interventions intended to modify guilt and blame. In addition, more prominence is given to the idea that the irrational aspects of anorexia are seen as held in place by the patient's self-starvation itself. Psycho-education about the effects of starvation is therefore seen as an important issue. The manual offers a normative approach, putting parents in charge of their daughters eating, but emphasises the need to hand control back to the patient at an early stage. It encourages the patient to make her own decisions in other areas of her life. This could be seen as the point at which the treatment manual comes closest to older family therapy approaches, since the intention is to support the adolescent's developing autonomy. The therapist influences the parents so that the parents will then be able to support the patient in achieving appropriate adolescent goals. Great emphasis is placed on the idea of separating the perception of the patient as a person, from the perception of her anorexia. Lock et al (2001) suggest that the anorexia can be thought of as a tumour, or as an alien presence, that has taken over the girl's mind. They advocate the use of the interviewing technique introduced by Serpell (1999, 2003), and used in adult services as part of motivational therapy approaches. In this the patient is encouraged to list the gains and losses arising from their eating disorder from their perspective. In addition, they advocate the use of a Venn diagram to illustrate the extent to which anorexia controls the patient's thoughts, as against the extent to which she can still be herself. This can be used to illustrate the declining power of the anorexia as therapeutic progress is made. All these techniques are used in order to help the patient to explain her state of mind to her parents. They argue that this in turn should help her parents not to be critical of her behaviour. Lock and Le Grange (2013) strongly emphasise the need for parents to be united in managing the patient's symptomatic behaviour. However, they eschew any direct reference to parental marital relationship difficulties that might stand in the way of success. The approach maintains a narrow focus on the management of symptoms until a very late stage in treatment. The last stage of the work, as in the Maudsley Model, is designed to help the families address adolescent issues, and any issues in the parent's marriage, in both instances in a normative way, rather than assuming that relationship difficulties exist. In the second edition of the manual Lock and Le Grange (2013) specifically de-emphasise these elements of treatment, arguing that this kind of attention to family relationships is unnecessary in many cases.

Phases of treatment

The FBT manual presents three phases of treatment: the first is the initial evaluation and the setting up of treatment; the second involves helping the adolescent eat on her own, and the third is dealing with adolescent issues.

The first phase is expected to last for ten sessions, probably over ten weeks, but sometimes over a longer period. It includes the engagement of the family, the family lunch session, and the initiation of refeeding of the patient under parental supervision. The central theme, modifying family criticism, is introduced at the beginning, and remains a theme through all the phases. Additionally the therapist in this phase starts to align the patient with her siblings, by encouraging them to take a supportive, non-critical position with her. The manual highlights the differences between the patient's real interests and her anorexia, and helps the patient to communicate her state of mind to her parents, for example by using Venn diagrams to illustrate the extent of the hold anorexia has on her mind. There is also a psycho-educational element about the effect of starvation on the body and mind. The therapist is encouraged to focus with the patient and her family on the patient's own wishes and goals, and the way that anorexic preoccupations and poor health arising from malnutrition stand in the way of achieving these.

The second phase, which is expected to last a further six sessions, is intended to help parents hand control of eating back to the patient safely. The intention is that the second phase of treatment begins when parents have been empowered to refeed their daughter. The expectation is that she now needs less intense supervision of her eating, and has achieved a weight of at least 90% of ideal weight for her height and age. They argue that at this stage the parents should be feeling more comfortable with their ability to manage the "illness", and the relationship between the therapist, the parents, and the patient, are likely to feel more comfortable. The goals of phase two are to continue to return the patient to physical health, to negotiate the return of control of eating to the patient herself, and to begin to focus on the individual and family issues of adolescence. Since the parents are now more confident in their control, and the patient is less challenging of it as far as eating is concerned, sessions are now scheduled at intervals of two to three weeks. A lot of change is expected in these six sessions. At the beginning the parents will still be in charge of their daughter's eating but at the end they will have handed control back to her. What is intended is a mutual negotiation between the parents and their daughter, and a gradual handing back of control over some meals and some decisions about what to eat. The therapist's role is to support the family through any setbacks which might lead to critical behaviour by parents, by reframing the behaviour on both sides as reflecting a shared wish to help the patient regain appropriate independence, even if that has not been achieved in a particular instance. Also, by the end of this stage the family will have started to think about adolescent issues, at least in so far as these affect eating, and about broader issues, such as the adjustments the parents may need to make in response to their daughter's adolescence.

The third phase, which is expected to last a further four sessions, addresses adolescent issues, and, to some extent, the parental marital relationship, insofar as this has implications for the patient moving into adolescence.

Modifying family criticism

Modifying family criticism is seen as a central issue throughout the work. Lock and Le Grange (2013) demonstrate various approaches to achieving this. One is the declaration that parents do not cause eating disorders. They also emphasise that the therapist must model uncritical acceptance of the patient. In addition they stress the importance of "separating the illness from the patient" which is to say that the therapist says that anorexia has taken over the patient's mind in a way that she cannot resist on her own. It is not really she who resists parental pressure to eat, but an "alien" pressure inside her. In their examples, Lock and Le Grange illustrate a stance in which the therapist intervenes whenever comments are made about the patient which could be taken as critical, and repeats the observation that the illness is not the patient herself, using phrases such as "this is anorexia talking". Also they emphasise discussion with the patient and the family in regard to ways the patient can or does try to counter the illness, and about her future healthy life goals, frequently modelling praise of the patient as a way of countering criticism.

The family lunch session in FBT

Unlike Maudsley Model Family Therapy, Family-Based Treatment maintains the use of the family lunch session but in a very different form. The therapist's role is to coach the parents in a specific way of managing the meal, and in what to say. Success becomes a joint enterprise for the therapist and the parents. There is no intention to observe parental failure in order to facilitate a relational reframe in the manner of the structural approach. In this form the session seems likely to be "safe", in that the therapist's leadership would be expected to prevent escalating conflict and the type of confrontation that caused concern to the Maudsley therapists. It is an approach that is unlikely to leave parents feeling criticised. It seems likely they would feel more effectively supported by the therapist than they are likely to feel if they are simply asked to achieve this task at home on their own. The therapist is seen as empowering parents, while at the same time aligning them with one another. Parents are told they should ensure that they are taking exactly the same line and that they have agreed the details between themselves without interference from their daughter. The approach is non-directive as to what should be eaten. The manual stresses that parents do know what healthy eating is. The therapist is not to provide meal plans, or arrange dietary advice, but would challenge the parents, and remind them about the patient's nutritional needs should it become clear, in the family lunch session, or subsequently, that parents were accommodating to the anorexic pressure to eat less.

Strengths and weaknesses of the manual

The treatment manual has a number of strengths. Its approach to the initial task of convening the family is more or less identical with that described in the structural approach by Sargent et al (1985), and would be acceptable to any family therapist who expected to work through the parental subsystem. It usefully emphasises the importance of maintaining the therapeutic alliance with the patient, her siblings and her parents, something that is easily overlooked during the initial stages of treatment when the therapist must help parents to overcome the patient's reluctance to eat. It places a value on direct communication. The manual retains the use of the family meal session, but in a form very different to the original. It presents an approach to the task of "putting parents in charge of their daughter's eating" in family lunch sessions in a safe way which will be useful for family therapists who are not used to doing that. It illustrates this with a transcript of a family lunch session. This demonstrates how the therapist can use the session to assess the families approach to eating, and the extent to which the parents have accommodated to the patient's pressure to eat less. The intention is to challenge the parents to take charge of the situation, to discourage the patient from making it too easy for them, and to reach a point where some progress has been made and the parents feel empowered.

Apart from the question of modifying criticism, the manual gives relatively little prominence to questions of family relationships or adolescent needs. In the 190 pages describing the three phases of treatment, 157 pages are devoted to the question of putting the parents in charge of their daughter's eating, and then handing control back again. In that context the relationship issues addressed are only those to do with modifying criticism of the patient, communicating the patient's state of mind about eating, and aligning her with her siblings. Issues to do with adolescent needs and parental relationships are to be tackled only in the last four sessions of a twenty-session treatment format. But, in the second edition of the manual Lock and Le Grange (2013) argue that even this may be unnecessary. They base this argument on the success of the very short form of the treatment (ten sessions) demonstrated in the outcome study by Lock et al (2005).

On the negative side much may be lost by excluding so much of family therapy technique. For example, although circular questioning is mentioned as a helpful technique early in the manual, it is an issue that is hardly returned to or illustrated. In so far as it is, it appears to be seen as a technique that helps the therapist to keep track of family members' opinions, rather than as one that facilitates family communication itself. Similarly, although Dare and Eisler (1997), faced with a parental difference of opinion about the management of refeeding could seek to explore the impact of the anorexia on the system in which parents took different positions, there is no indication that Lock and Le Grange would do this. The manual seems excessively avoidant of addressing family relationship issues, and this may well reduce its therapeutic impact, especially in relation to aspects of recovery over and above weight recovery. Perhaps this is the reason for the high level of continuing neurotic difficulties experienced by the patients after treatment is completed, which has been demonstrated in the outcome research.

The approach to treatment presented in the manual is very narrow. The limited focus on managing refeeding may help the patient achieve rapid weight recovery, but it does not necessarily lead to the most complete improvement in other respects. The manual contains transcripts of sessions, or extracts from sessions with two patients and their families. These are used to illustrate the work of the therapist during all three phases of treatment.

The style of therapy in FBT

The style of the work illustrated in the manual is very different to that of most approaches to family therapy. Reading the treatment excerpts used to illustrate the approach it is clear that the therapist whose work illustrates the manual takes a central position in conducting sessions.

Almost all the communication passes through the therapist, and takes the form of answers to questions. He keeps the family on task in relation to his own agenda, and operates to damp down, rather than to explore or deepen emotional expression. There may be a price to be paid for this in that families' tendencies to keep relationship issues superficial are not challenged, and this may stand in the way of therapy goals.

At the beginning of treatment, the manual discourages any kind of exploration of relationships or deepening of effect. Consider the transcript of the first session describing the initial engagement of the family (Lock & Le Grange, 2013, pp. 68–71). In this case Susan, a seventeen-year-old with anorexia, is met in an initial session with her mother, two younger brothers Dan and Paul, aged twelve and ten, and Tom, her stepfather of two years. In an initial, too brief, social phase to this interview, the stepfather speaks as the father. The therapist does nothing to address this question of the family structure. Where a family therapist would be almost bound to ask each of the children: "What do you call Tom? Do you call him dad?" and give weight to their replies, here the issue is ignored. Again, this could be an opportunity to comment on the different experiences of the siblings in relation to the stepfather. The therapist could say, perhaps to the mother "so Susan was fifteen when Tom joined the family, and Dan and Paul were ten and eight", and could have explored that issue with the stepfather and the rest of the family, marking the fact that the children may have had different experiences of this transition. Instead the issue is ignored, and the therapist interacts with Susan, her mother, and her brothers too briefly to achieve the goals of a social phase. Moving on to the Problem Phase, the therapist asks what it has been like for the family dealing with the eating disorder. The stepfather talks at some length until the therapist asks for the mother's views. She expresses distress, crying, saying that she knew how to look after a baby but doesn't know how to deal with this and so "I feel very frustrated, helpless, angry, guilty". The therapist responds with "Where does the guilt come from, as we know that parents don't cause eating disorders. Are there things you should have done differently?" To this the mother says "Things I should have done differently? I should have been there more." At this point the therapist shifts the focus to the question of how the parents have been trying to manage Susan's eating, and offers what seem pretty unsatisfactory reassurances that since the daughter is still alive "You're doing something right", Lock and Le Grange (2013, p. 71).

The point that Lock and Le Grange are making here is that the therapist responds to the mother's distress by insisting that "we know parents don't cause eating disorders", and finding ways of recognising the parents' efforts so far. This is all very well, but "I should have been there more" is a very powerful message to ignore. Probably a family therapist's preference here would be to stay with the mother's feelings for longer. The therapist would probably acknowledge the mother's desire to be more available for her daughter and to take responsibility for her daughter's mental wellbeing. There would be many possibilities for further exploration. The therapist could explore the mother's frustration, how this communicates itself to Susan, and how Susan understands it. It could be an opportunity to see whether a bridge could be built between mother and daughter and to frame that as something that could be addressed in the work. It would also be an opportunity to see whether the stepfather could tolerate that, and to be supportive of the mother's wish if, for the time being, it seems likely to be frustrated. While there are limits to how far you could go with this exploration in the Problem Phase of the initial interview it should be perfectly possible to acknowledge the issues, keeping them in mind for future discussion.

An illustration of the middle phase of treatment is intended to show that the therapist maintains a focus on food and on weight recovery. In this session Susan and her mother attend, without the stepfather. The family seem to be struggling since Susan has not regained any weight and is in a state of mind in which she is challenging the accuracy of the paediatrician's scales. Although the therapist certainly does maintain the focus on this issue through the session and praises Susan for her efforts, it is not apparent that any progress is made. Mother and daughter do not seem to leave the session with any new resolve, or new understanding with one another, or new energy or commitment for the task. The patient has not communicated anything new to the mother, or the mother to the patient. Perhaps the intention here is simply to communicate that the therapist maintains a focus in a supportive way.

Although the approach includes the idea that the patient should be helped to communicate about her mental state, in order to help parents not to feel critical, this seems to target only the most superficial and impersonal levels of communication. Perhaps this emphasis is adopted to protect parents. The therapist is there to help the patient explain her symptomatic behaviour to her parents. Such explanations can exist on several levels. At its simplest and most impersonal, the explanation could be "I behave this way (starve myself/make myself vomit) because I have intrusive thoughts that tell me I am fat and disgusting". This seems to be the level of communication that Lock and Le Grange are looking for. If the therapist sought a deeper level of communication the patient could be helped to say, "I feel this way because I hate myself and I feel I am never good enough". Although this does not directly address the patient's relationship to her parents many parents would begin to feel that such implications might exist. They might respond with curiosity or defensiveness. No such communication is illustrated in the manual, and it does not seem to be the sort of communication that Lock and Le Grange would seek to encourage. The next level of communication would be directly interpersonal, addressing the present "You make me feel ..." or the past "My school results were never good enough for you however hard I worked ..." a level of family communication that the treatment manual eschews. Yet it is exactly this level of communication that one might suppose is likely to lead to real and lasting psychological change, especially if the parents can be helped to hear it.

In the last phase, the FBT treatment manual approach to adolescent autonomy is very much focused on obtaining support for adolescent activities, rather than on the issue of the adolescent's ability to express difference from her parents. There is a danger that the therapist may take the role of standing up for the right of the patient to engage in such activities. The therapist's influence may then be to shift the parents from an authoritarian to a permissive stance. This may not facilitate the development of a secure and effective bond between the adolescent and her parents. It is interesting to reflect that patients who recover from anorexia often put themselves at risk, for example by engaging in ill-considered sexual encounters, or alcohol or drug use. Sometimes this behaviour is impulsive; sometimes it is a conscious attempt to make up lost ground, since the patient lags behind her age peers in relation to such matters. There are dangers in these activities, not least that the patient might be traumatised by her own behaviour. In some instances this trauma can lead to a full-scale relapse into anorexia. The therapist might be tempted to say "Well that's adolescence for you. We all did this kind of thing and it's nothing to do with me", but actually it is. No approach can entirely eliminate this kind of outcome. However, the therapist should seek to promote a secure bond between the adolescent and her parents, based on communication, one in which parents can be authoritative not authoritarian or permissive. Within such a secure parent–adolescent relationship the parents might assert influence that would help prevent such events or that might be used by the adolescent to consider her behavioural options, potentially preventing such risky behaviour. Failing that, the adolescent might be able to use her parent's support to process the resulting distress, rather than re-engaging in self-starvation as a remedy. In place of any such approach the manual takes a line that addresses adolescent issues in a superficial and impersonal way.

This superficiality is demonstrated in the transcript of the work with Rhonda (Lock & Le Grange, 2013, pp. 227–228), which illustrates phase three of treatment. This transcript is taken from close to the end of treatment. The therapist is trying to explore adolescent issues with the family. He seems to be encountering resistance. The patient remembers the time when she became ill, which, surprisingly, she sees as a time when she was "happy". The therapist delivers his talk on adolescence, commenting on physical changes and sexual development, the development of a social identity and independence, and how this can be a challenge for parents. Rhonda offers a glimmer of light, saying "… I'm not looking forward to going through it with my kids", (Lock & Le Grange, 2013, pp. 227–228). Her father immediately dismisses this, and the therapist acquiesces in this. The therapist continues to try to explore the challenge of adolescence, but the focus of the session reverts to symptoms and the therapist is not really able to develop the discussion. The authors, perhaps ruefully, observe "The therapist attempts to involve the family in an initial review of common issues for adolescents and their parents. In this case the family does not feel that there are problems of this sort in the family …", (Lock & Le Grange, 2013, p. 228). The therapist, having shaped a therapy process that has had a very narrow focus for sixteen sessions, fails to open up new ground here. A family therapist might draw the conclusion that if the therapist spends the first sixteen sessions of the work discouraging the discussion of feelings, relationship issues and developmental difficulties in a personal way, then it may be very difficult to revive such discussion at a later stage when, in any case, the work is about to be concluded.

Disadvantages of the FBT approach

The stance taken by both the Maudsley Model and FBT towards the cause of anorexia diverts attention from the real issues. The announcement to the family that the parents "are not the root cause of the illness" may seem to the patient and family to indicate that she, the patient, is the cause, so it may not reduce her sense of being criticised. Moreover, some of these patients certainly do come to treatment ready to express concern about difficulties for them in the family relationships and so do some parents. The approach taken by Dare and Eisler (1997), and illustrated by Lock et al (2001) and Lock and Le Grange (2013) may be quite disabling for them, since they are not encouraged to express such views. In addition, it is hard to see how Lock and Le Grange would respond to a therapeutic impasse. An impasse is often reached when parents fail to refeed their daughter to the point where she is safe or begins to show signs of improvement. The approach does not give the therapist a frame of reference to work with in such cases. The danger is that the therapist, trying to follow the manual, will simply go through repeated efforts to activate the parents by raising their anxiety. In these circumstances it is far from clear that the parents will feel less criticised than they would if the therapist explored the relationship issues that stand in the way of progress. Equally, an impasse can occur when the parents do succeed with the task, but the patient does not improve mentally, remaining profoundly alienated from the therapist and parents because she is deeply distressed to have reached a healthy weight. There is no automatic link between refeeding and psychological recovery. The FBT approach gives the therapist too little guidance as to the relationship issues that need to be addressed in such circumstances. In either of these situations, rather than tackling those issues, perhaps the therapist will give up and send the patient to hospital.

A further difficulty and one that applies to treatment manuals in general, is the prescriptive nature of the approach. Earlier generations of family therapists could calibrate their approach to different family relationship patterns. However the manual gives little guidance to the therapist facing the many different scenarios presented by the families of patients with anorexia.

How far is Family-Based Treatment supported by evidence?

There is now a series of outcome studies, Lock et al (2005, 2006a, 2006b) and Le Grange et al (2005) that specifically test the model outlined in the treatment manual by Lock et al (2001) and Lock and Le Grange

(2013). Two more studies, Loeb et al (2007) and Couturier et al (2010) report outcomes in dissemination studies. In these studies, therapists were trained in the approach in the manual, and treatment outcomes achieved subsequently were reported. Another study, Lock et al (2010) compared the outcome of FBT with those achieved by a largely individual focused treatment, Adolescent-Focused Individual Therapy. This provides further data on the outcome of FBT.

Le Grange et al (2005) reported outcomes for a group of forty-five children treated with FBT. They used the same broad outcome categories used in the Maudsley studies. Fifty-six percent had a good outcome and 33% an intermediate outcome. However, fourteen patients included in the series did not meet the weight loss criterion for the diagnosis of anorexia, and should be considered to be subclinical cases. If all the subclinical cases achieved a good outcome, as they did in the study by Loeb et al (2007), then the corrected outcomes for the thirty-one patients who did meet the diagnostic criteria would be 35% good, 48% intermediate, and 16% poor. Le Grange et al (2005) did not provide any other information about the quality of the outcomes.

Lock et al (2005, 2006a, 2006b) did not use exactly the same outcome criteria as those reported in the Maudsley studies and by Le Grange. This makes direct comparison of outcomes a little more difficult. Lock et al (2006b) reported a case series of children, average age eleven, using FBT, who showed significant improvements in weight and psychological symptoms. Lock et al (2005) compared a shorter, ten sessions, six month treatment format, with a longer, twenty sessions, one year format, for adolescent patients, both based on the treatment manual. They found little difference in outcome between the groups, although patients whose eating symptoms were more obsessive, and those from families in which parents were separated, did better in the longer treatment. Lock et al (2006a) followed up the patients seen in the 2005 study, mainly by collecting information from patients and parents on the phone. They reported that patients maintained the improvements made in treatment and made further gains.

Dissemination studies have demonstrated that results could be achieved by mental health workers given some additional training and following the manual in their work with families, such as the study by Loeb et al (2007). In a two day workshop, Loeb et al (2007) trained two psychologists and three psychiatrists in the use of the treatment manual (Lock et al, 2001). This group of therapists treated twenty adolescent patients with clinical or subclinical anorexia, and received supervision from one of the authors of the manual. Outcomes were assessed with the Morgan-Russell Global Outcome Score, and with the Eating Disorders Examination (EDE), Fairburn and Cooper (1993)—a semi-structured clinical interview for eating disorder symptoms. At the end of treatment, thirteen patients met the Morgan-Russell criteria for good outcome, three for intermediate outcome and four for poor outcome. However, the results are not so impressive if the subclinical cases are excluded, since all had a good outcome. For the patients who met diagnostic criteria for anorexia the outcomes were, therefore, six good, three intermediate and four poor. For the group as a whole there were clinically significant improvements on two subscales of the EDE. These were Restraint and Eating Concern. However the patients had not improved on the remaining two subscales, Shape Concern and Weight Concern, or on a measure of depression. So, in general, patients continued to experience symptoms, including eating disorder symptoms, despite their treatment. Couturier et al (2010) also reported a dissemination study in which experienced clinicians were trained in the FBT approach and achieved acceptable results.

Does FBT produce superior outcomes?

The strongest evidence for the approach in the FBT manual is the continuing good results achieved in these outcome studies. However, it does not appear that the shift from earlier models to the Maudsley Model, and then to FBT, has led to an improvement in recovery rates. Given the differences between early models and the FBT model it is remarkable that such different approaches should all produce such similar recovery rates. Perhaps we should see this as evidence of the underlying robustness of a family approach to treatment, so long as parents are helped to challenge the anorexic behaviours. However, questions need to be asked about the quality of recovery achieved by therapists using the FBT manual.

Table 4 presents the results of the FBT outcome studies for purposes of comparison with those summarised in Table 1 and Table 2 in the previous chapter. Unfortunately the study by Le Grange (2005) had to be omitted, as no information was available about the group of patients who did fulfill diagnostic criteria for anorexia, and inclusion of subclinical cases would almost certainly exaggerate the recovery rate. The study by Couturier et al (2010) has also been omitted, as the information in the report could not be fitted to a system of outcome categories.

* * *

Table 4 shows recovery rates for studies based on the FBT manual by Lock et al (2001). The Loeb et al (2007) studies report outcomes using the same criteria as the Maudsley studies. Lock et al (2005, 2006a, 2010) describe outcomes in terms of the following criteria. Patients whose weight recovery reaches 95% of their ideal weight, and whose scores on EDE, fall within one standard deviation of the published norms achieve "Full remission". This indicates their eating disorder concerns are only at the level that would be typical of many women in the community as a whole. Lock et al point out that although menstruation is not taken into account, nevertheless at this level of weight recovery it will usually have been resumed. Therefore this criterion is comparable to Good Outcome in the Morgan-Russell Scales. Those whose weight recovery brings them above the weight threshold for the diagnosis of anorexia, 85% of their ideal weight, irrespective of psychological symptoms, but fall short of the criteria for full remission, achieve "Partial remission". This may be regarded as comparable to Intermediate Outcome.

In the study by Lock et al (2006) outcomes were classified using weight criteria alone. Patients who achieved 95% of their ideal weight were classified as "Responders", those who did not but achieved weights above 85% of IW were classified as "Partial responders".

* * *

As in the other tables the figures are presented on an intention to treat basis to ensure that drop-outs from treatment and losses to follow-up do not inflate the overall results.

Despite the changes in approach when we compare the outcomes with those summarised in Table 1 and Table 2 in the last chapter, it is not possible to discern evidence that changes of model have led to improved outcomes when we consider outcome measures largely based on weight and menstrual criteria. This being so it would be interesting to know whether there are important differences in other aspects of outcome. For example, given that patients who have recovered from anorexia often have continuing psychological and social difficulties, is there a difference between treatments in this respect?

Table 4. Outcome and follow up data from four studies of Family Based Treatment.

Study by N =	*End of treatment outcome*	*Follow-up outcome length of follow-up*
Lock et al (2005) N = 86 Lock et al (2006a) N = 71	53% Full remission 23% Partial remission 3% No remission 10% Dropped out 9% Lost to study	73% Above 90% IW* 5% More above 85% IW* 5% Still in anorexic weight range 17% Lost to follow up Mean 4 year follow-up
Lock et al (2006b) N = 32	59% Responders 16% Partial responders 3% Non responders 22% Lost to study	
Loeb et al (2007) N = 13	46% Good 23% Intermediate 31% Poor	
Lock et al (2010) N = 61	34% Full remission 39% Partial remission 8% No remission 18% Not engaged or dropped out	36% Full remission 21% Partial remission 16% No remission 26% Not engaged, dropped out, or lost to follow-up One year follow-up

*IW = Ideal Weight. Follow-up outcomes are expressed in this way because too few patients completed the EDE at follow up to allow classification in the Full Remission category.

The quality of psychological recovery in FBT and in family therapy

It is difficult to compare the quality of psychological recovery demonstrated in different studies. Numerous different measures have been used and there has been no consensus on measures or criteria. Some studies, notably the Maudsley studies, have taken a much richer approach and taken a wide range of measures. These have already been discussed in relation to the differential outcomes demonstrated for conjoint and separated therapy within the Maudsley Model approach. Because the Maudsley Model studies compared separated and conjoint treatment, and demonstrated that conjoint treatment produced broader psychological recovery, it is not possible to generalise about the effects of the model as such. However, there is clear evidence for continuing psychological difficulties after FBT.

* * *

Lock and Le Grange (2013) acknowledge that roughly 50% of young people with anorexia are not fully recovered after FBT. The evidence suggests that a particular problem is the continuing psychological difficulties experienced by patients who may be seen as recovered in terms of weight and menstrual functioning. The outcomes from the FBT study reported by Lock et al (2005) illustrate the issue. Overall they considered that 67% of the patients treated could be considered to be fully remitted in terms of weight recovery and improved scores on the EDE. At follow-up Lock et al (2006a) obtained information from the patient or one her parents in person or by telephone interview on average four years after treatment. Some information was obtained about 83% of the patients who had been treated, and the EDE was repeated with 40% of the patients. To judge from this 40% sample, weight gains and menstrual recovery had been maintained at follow-up and improvements on the EDE had been maintained or further improvements had been made. Sixty-seven of the patients, or their parents, provided information about further treatments and about other psychological symptoms experienced by the patients. Of these, twenty-seven had had another diagnosis, with depression, anxiety and OCD being the most common problems. Forty-one had had further psychological treatment after completion of FBT. Thirty-five had had further treatment with medication. So at least two-thirds of patients for whom this information was available had had further neurotic problems severe enough to warrant treatment in, on average, the four years since completing their treatment. By contrast Minuchin et al (1978) reported that 81% of patients were fully recovered from the eating disorder, and 81% were functioning well in the spheres of family, academic or work, and peer relationships, at a follow up on average two years eight months after treatment. The measures are not directly comparable but it is possible that Structural Family Therapy and other early approaches that addressed a wider range of family relationship issues achieved better quality outcomes than FBT.

The FBT model may be so focused on the weight recovery goals of treatment, it is not surprising if weight recovery is the main change achieved. It potentially leaves many patients with substantial residual psychological symptoms and problems. This being so, the question can be asked whether both Maudsley Model Family Therapy, and Family-Based Treatment, achieve outcomes equivalent, in all respects, to those of the earlier studies.

Conclusion: we know very little about what makes treatment effective

Questions can be asked about the relative effectiveness of the Maudsley Model and FBT approaches, compared to earlier models that drew on a wider range of family therapy techniques. Some therapeutic efficacy may have been lost as a result of the elimination of so much family therapy technique from the model in the successive changes that ended in the FBT manual. The belief that families do not "cause" anorexia may stand in the way of therapeutic efficacy if it prevents therapists from drawing on their knowledge of the relationship between unhelpful family processes and the development of difficulties in the younger generation. It is not the case that the newer models have been shown to be superior. Family therapists who took the view that anorexia was the result of family processes do not seem to have been less effective than those later therapists who explicitly denied this. Such treatment has not been shown to be more acceptable than older approaches, for example to judge from drop-out rates. Newer approaches have not been shown to be more effective in treatment resistant cases.

A number of assumptions common to the Maudsley Model and to FBT are not strongly supported by evidence. Despite the therapists' conviction, there is no evidence that an approach that concentrates on supporting parents in refeeding their daughters while holding back from addressing relationship issues is superior. Therapists who approached the task with the opposite conviction appear to have done at least equally well in earlier studies. The finding that parental criticism of the patient leads to poorer outcome, which was so central to the change of approach, is not as securely established as was previously thought. It was not confirmed by Le Grange et al (2011) while Eisler et al (2007) observed that ratings of maternal criticism were correlated with the extent of the patients' weight loss and were no longer a significant predictor when this was taken into account. The techniques that Lock and Le Grange (2013) offer as effective in the management of guilt and criticism have not been shown to be superior to other possible techniques in any objective research. Although Dare and Eisler argued that the therapist's belief in family models of anorexia causes them to behave in ways that make parents feel guilty, this has not been demonstrated in research. Even the concern about the use of "confrontational techniques" is not rooted in unchallengeable evidence.

Notwithstanding Russell's claim in the foreword to the second edition of the manual that "The manual ensures an optimum sequence of treatment procedures" (Lock & Le Grange, 2013, p. xii), there is really no objective evidence about the staging of treatment. Of course the outpatient therapist has to tackle the patient's eating at the outset, one way or another. However, the question of how and when to address family relationship issues is a matter of opinion rather than evidence.

* * *

A factor that may have reduced family therapists' confidence in family models of causation in recent decades was the idea that anorexia was to a great extent a heritable disorder. This idea has not stood the test of time. It is the subject of the next chapter.

CHAPTER FIVE

Anorexia is not an inherited disorder

Current models of family treatment were developed by Dare and Eisler (1997), Lock et al (2001), and others, none of whom argued that anorexia was an inherited disorder. On the other hand, in the course of the last two or three decades many other leading researchers in the field of eating disorders, such as Strober et al (2000), have increasingly inclined to the view that anorexia is substantially an inherited condition. A number of authors have concluded that anorexia was highly heritable. For example, Kaye et al (2000) argued that studies indicate that inheritance accounts for 50–90% of the variance in the aetiology of anorexia, while Wade et al (2000) argued that it accounted for 58%, but with a substantial confidence interval, giving a range of estimates from 33% to 84%. The Maudsley Model denied the role of the family in the aetiology of the disturbance at much the same time that the case for genetic causation of anorexia was being argued most strongly. The issue is important because the more we think that anorexia is accounted for by genetic variables the less we may look for, and try to influence, environmental impacts. Scientifically, the assumption that anorexia is inherited discourages research on environmental, including family influences. It fits with the Maudsley Model claim that family influences do not "cause" anorexia. Clinically, the assumption may reduce our investment in changing these influences, for example, by conducting family therapy. An incorrect assumption that the cause is largely hereditary may leave us blind to the patient's real needs. Recent research evidence does not support claims that anorexia is determined by heredity.

The debate about the aetiology of anorexia is part of a much larger debate about the relative impact of genes and environment on the development of behaviour. Until relatively recently studies depended upon attempts to estimate the relative impact of genetic and environmental variables by comparing the behaviour of relatives, and particularly, of adopted children and of twins. A useful review of this kind of research is to be found in Fonagy et al (2004). In this study both sides of the question are discussed, and while Fonagy et al make the case for the significance of environmental, especially attachment, influences on development, they recognise the possibility of complex interactions between genes and environment affecting many kinds of outcome. However, the decoding of the genome is gradually rendering that kind of research and argument redundant. Increasingly it is possible to make direct observations of the relationship between a wide range of behavioural outcomes, including the development of anorexia, and variations in the form of genes, or of the genome as a whole.

There are two types of study that test the question whether anorexia is inherited. One group of studies seeks to establish the rate of anorexia among twins or relatives of people with anorexia. These studies are often called "genetic" studies. Twin studies have been the most influential studies within this approach. They are influential because many people believe that similarities between identical twins, over and above similarities between fraternal twins, can only be accounted for by the identical twins having identical genes. The assumption could be false. Other studies focus on the increased risk in the first degree relatives of people with anorexia. These are relevant to genetic explanations in that a lack of family aggregation would contraindicate genetic hypotheses. They cannot decisively differentiate between genetic and other explanatory models that also predict aggregation, such as systemic models. Family therapy assumes that families pass on the family culture. For example we know that children grow up speaking the same language as their parents and often practicing the same religion. We do not think of these as being genetic effects. Family therapists assume that families pass on many other things; values, relationship styles, and attachment security would be some examples, and these can be seen as parts of our social, not our genetic, inheritance. However, it is the specific way that the individual child experiences the family culture, and her place in the family's relationships, that determines the outcome. These factors in turn influence the development of psychopathology. The second type of study arises from the decoding of the human genome. This has enabled genuine genetic studies of anorexia. It is these genetic studies that are likely to finally demonstrate the extent to which anorexia is heritable.

Studies of family aggregation of anorexia

Twin studies

Bulik et al (2000) discussed twin studies. There are two possible approaches. In one approach, twins are identified in clinical situations as having an eating disorder and their co-twin is assessed for the disorder. The second approach relies on a twin register. In this design a register is kept of all twins born over several decades, and all the twins are asked to participate in the study. Bulik et al argued that the disadvantage of the first kind of study is that the clinical sample of patients with anorexia may not be typical, for example they may have more severe illness or more co-morbidity, and this may affect the results. They also expressed concern that in these clinic-based studies twins concordant for anorexia would be more likely to come to the notice of the investigators, so sampling could be skewed towards concordant twin pairs. They regarded the use of a twin register as a better design in that it could identify a wider range of cases and these would be more typical of the illness. However, there are also methodological problems for such twin register research.

Twin register studies

Klump et al (2001) studied 662 female twins drawn from the Minnesota Twin Family Study at age sixteen to eighteen years. He identified thirteen (1.9%) girls who had anorexia, all of whom were below 85% of Ideal Weight (IW). There were two concordant identical twins, and three discordant identical twin pairs. There were six discordant fraternal twins. He identified a further group of thirteen girls with subclinical anorexia. They had weight at or below 90% of IW and at least one cognitive symptom of anorexia. There were four concordant identical twin pairs, and no discordant identical twins in this subclinical group. There were five discordant fraternal twins. Hence the concordance rate for identical twins with anorexia was 29%, but rose to 40% when sub-clinical cases where included, while the rate for fraternal twins was zero, in both cases. The strength of this study is that diagnosis was established close to the time of the illness, and low weights actually observed, rather than being retrospectively reported long after the event, as has been the case in some other studies.

Walters and Kendler (1995) described a larger study and this was reported a second time by Wade et al (2000). They came to extraordinarily different conclusions from the same data. There were 1,033 female twin pairs. There were 590 pairs of identical twins, and 440 pairs of fraternal twins and ninety-seven individual twins whose sisters refused to take part. Participants were assigned to a diagnosis of anorexia, or an anorexia-like episode, according to three sets of criteria. The "computer narrow" criteria were closest to strict diagnostic criteria for anorexia, the "clinical narrow" criteria were more inclusive, while the "clinical broad" criteria included a wider range of sub-clinical cases. Concordance rates were reported for each set of diagnostic criteria. Using the "computer narrow" definition of anorexia the study found no identical twins concordant and one pair of fraternal twins concordant; using the "clinical narrow" definition there was one pair of identical twins and two pairs of fraternal twins concordant, while using the "clinical broad" definition there were two pairs of identical and four pairs of fraternal twins. There were no concordant identical twins that fitted strict criteria for the diagnosis of anorexia. Table 1 summarises the results according to Walters and Kendler (1995).

Walters and Kendler concluded that whichever set of diagnostic criteria were applied the ratio between identical twins and fraternal twins concordant for the diagnosis was the opposite of the ratio which a genetic explanation predicts. For this reason and because of the small number of concordant cases, they regarded it as impossible to use the data to estimate the heritability of anorexia or anorexia-like conditions. However, in a further analysis of the data from the study reported by Walters and Kendler, Wade et al (2000) came to quite different conclusions. They argued that the study demonstrated that the heritability of anorexia was 58%, albeit with a large margin of error, with a confidence interval ranging from 33% to 84%. The original conclusion drawn by

Table 1. Findings from Walters and Kendler (1995) concordant pairs and non-concordant cases.

Twins	*Computer narrow*	*Computer narrow plus clinical narrow*	*All criteria*
Concordant Identical twin pairs identified in 295 pairs	0	1 pair	2 pairs
Concordant Fraternal twins pairs identified in 220 pairs	1 pair	2 pairs	4 pairs
Non Concordant cases identified in 515 pairs and 97 individuals	9 Individuals	31 Individuals	68 Individuals
All cases	11	37	80

Walters and Kendler seems obviously correct and it is surprising that the estimate by Wade et al continues to be accepted.

Another study using a very similar approach to a large sample drawn from a twin register was reported by Raevuori et al (2008). Identical twins were no more likely to be concordant for anorexia, or for high scores on subscales of a measure of eating disorder pathology, than were fraternal twins (Garner et al, 1983).

The results of these studies seem to clearly contradict genetic hypotheses because, notwithstanding Wade's report, the data does not show higher concordance rates for identical twins. However, this may reflect methodological difficulties. We know that women with anorexia tend to opt out of research. Beglin and Fairburn (1992) demonstrated this. We also know that some women and girls give inaccurate accounts, substantially underestimating their weight. This has been demonstrated in research by Smith et al (1992), Dring et al (2004) and Meyer et al (2009). The studies show that a minority of women significantly underestimate their weight, to the extent that such self-reports should not be relied on in research. Accurate diagnosis in the study reported by Walters and Kendler (1995) and by Wade et al (2000) must have depended on participants accurately reporting their height and weight, typically twelve years or so after the events described. So the failure to report concordant twin pairs may reflect these two problems.

A twin study by Kortegaard et al (2001) is also sometimes regarded as providing evidence for the heritability of anorexia. This study, based on a postal questionnaire, also contains possible methodological problems. Kortegaard concluded that concordance for "diagnosis" between identical twins was roughly twice the level of concordance for fraternal twins.

Clinic based twin studies

The second approach to twin studies is to identify twins receiving treatment for anorexia in clinical settings, and to assess their co-twin for anorexia. Using this approach Holland et al (1984) found a concordance rate of 56% in sixteen pairs of identical twins, and 7% in fourteen pairs of fraternal twins. A second study, Holland et al (1988), that reported overlapping data found concordance of 56% in twenty-five identical twin pairs, and 5% in twenty fraternal twin pairs. By contrast Waters et al (1990) found no concordant pairs in a group of five identical and six fraternal twins identified in a small clinical series.

Although there are also potential methodological difficulties for the clinic based twin studies, they probably give a more realistic estimate of the extent of concordance between twins. This is probably between the 29% reported in the twin register study by Klump et al (2001) and the 56% reported by Holland et al (1984, 1988). Probably concordance rates for anorexia are far higher among identical than among fraternal twins, and much higher than they should be by chance.

Studies of first-degree relatives

Ross (2006) criticised studies that argued for a high level of heritability in anorexia on the basis of twin studies or studies of first-degree relatives of women with anorexia. Summing-up the results of studies by Lilenfeld et al (1998) and by Strober et al (2000) he was able to draw on data about thirty-six individuals with anorexia and 383 of their first degree relatives, and 225 comparison individuals, who did not have an eating disorder, and 508 of their first degree relatives. Ross argues that taken together these results indicate that the incidence of anorexia in the first degree relatives is 2.9%, while it was only 0.2% in the relatives of the comparison group. However, it seems to follow that if a girl has a first degree relative (other than a twin sister) with anorexia, then she is almost three times as likely to develop it as she would be expected to be by chance. By contrast if she has no first degree relative with anorexia her risk falls to one-fifth of the risk for the population as a whole. Pinheiro et al (2010), commenting on the same studies, argued that first-degree female relatives have a ten-fold greater lifetime risk of having an eating disorder, compared with relatives of unaffected individuals.

Studies of the Genome and Anorexia

During the course of the last decade, the technology available to decode the genome advanced rapidly, also becoming faster and cheaper. Early studies attempted to guess at target genes likely to contribute to anorexia, and focus the genetic analysis on those. As the technology improved, larger and more comprehensive studies became possible. These have now provided clear results. At first a number of genetic risk factors were proposed, but it proved difficult for different research groups to confirm one another's results. By 2010 Pinheiro et al (2010) were able to comment on thirteen studies of different genetic mechanisms and their association with anorexia. These studies had yielded "sporadically significant and typically non-replicated findings", Pinheiro et al (2010, p. 1071). They thought this might be attributable to the inadequate size of the studies. In addition, they were able to comment on five studies that had provided more consistent evidence for the influence for four genes, HTR1D, OPRD1, SLC6A4 and BDNF. Shortly after this Calati et al (2011) and Lee and Lin (2010) both published meta-analyses of a number of research studies of one variation (5-HTT) in gene SLC6A4 that had produced variable results. Both these meta-analyses concluded that the overall evidence for that observation was positive. The study by Pinheiro et al (2010) was designed to test most of the associations between genes and anorexia that had been proposed up to that point in a larger sample that would provide greater statistical power. The genes were chosen for study because of possible association with eating disorders demonstrated in previous studies. It examined 5,151 Single Nucleotide Polymorphisms (SNPs), variations in the form of the gene, in 182 genes, including the variations in gene SLC6A4 which were the subject of the meta-analyses by Calati et al (2011) and by Lee and Lin

(2010). The subjects were 1,085 females with a history of anorexia, and a comparison group of 677 healthy women with no history of eating disorder. Data analyses compared all the women with anorexia and the comparison women. Further analyses were made in order to compare two sub-groups of patients with anorexia, those with no history of bingeing, and those who fitted a narrower definition of restrictive anorexia. No relationships could be demonstrated between any gene or SNP and anorexia or anorexia sub-group. Pinheiro et al (2010) did not confirm previous findings of association of any genes with anorexia.

In a further analysis of data from the same study, Root et al (2011) examined the association of these genetic factors (the 5,151 single nucleotide polymorphisms in 182 genes) with seven "quantitative phenotypes" associated with anorexia. These were: lowest illness related BMI, age at menarche, drive for thinness, body dissatisfaction, trait anxiety, concern about mistakes (an aspect of maladaptive perfectionism) and anticipatory worry and pessimism. Again, no significant relationships could be demonstrated. Pinheiro et al (2010) argued that there are a number of alternative approaches to finding genetic links to anorexia of which one would be a genome wide association study. Such a study could identify associations with genes that had not been studied up to that point.

Wang et al (2011) reported such a genome wide association study. Genomes were successfully analysed for 1,033 patients with anorexia, almost all of whom were female, and 3,773 comparison subjects. Wang reported a limited relationship between anorexia and SNPs. There were over 598,000 SNPs. He confirmed the associations with HTR1D and OPRD1, but no other relationships with any gene or SNP. In the meantime, Nakabyashi et al (2009) in another genome wide association study had identified another two genes associated with anorexia in a sample of Japanese patients. Wang et al (2011) did not find evidence to confirm those findings in the largely European descended participants in their study.

Boraska et al (2012) carried out another Genome Wide Association Study. The study sought to establish associations between SNP's and scores on psychometric tests. Of these the Drive for Thinness and Body Dissatisfaction subtests of the EDI-2 seem most obviously relevant for the study of anorexia. The study design was complex. Groups of individuals with high and low scores on the psychological tests were compared and results of interest were re-tested in successive data sets from different centres. Boraska et al identified six genes that may prove to have some association with eating disorders, as well as others that may be associated with problems such as obsessive-compulsive personality disorder, but the effects were not large enough to allow this to be established with any certainty. They concluded that larger studies were needed.

Wade et al (2013) conducted a genome wide association study. Subjects were 2,564 female twins. The research tested the relationship between genes and variables derived from scores on measures of eating disorder concerns derived from a questionnaire. One of these variables was considered to represent a specific anorexic spectrum of problems, while another represented a general factor of eating disorder concerns. Wade et al found no statistically significant relationships between any SNP and either of these variables. She did not replicate the findings of Wang et al (2011) in relation to HTR1D and OPRD1, or those of Nakabyashi et al (2009). In common with the other researchers, Wade et al argued that larger samples are required to find genes each of which would have a very small relationship to anorexia.

How large are the genetic effects?

A number of genetic influences in the development of anorexia have sometimes been demonstrated, but each is very small. Wang et al (2011) reported that variation in gene OPRD1 was found in 21.7% of anorexic cases, and in 18.6% of the comparison group, and reported a weaker relationship between HTR1D and restrictive anorexia only. The small size of these relationships is interesting. If we assume that between 1% and 2% of women experience an episode of anorexia in their lives then the risky form of the gene OPRD1 increases risk by about 0.5%. That is 0.5% of 100%. Hence it is hard to argue that a gene like OPRD1 can have much impact on the development of anorexia. Yet this is the largest association between a gene and anorexia reported in this genome wide association study. Although Wang et al did not quantify the difference for HTR1D the report indicates that it was smaller than that observed for OPRD1. Hence the two genes that have been shown to be related to anorexia, in the study by Wang et al (2011) and in some previous studies, but looked for and not found by Pinheiro et al (2010) would not account for much more than 1%. Similarly, Lee and Lin (2010) published data from studies of 5-HTT in gene SLC6A4, including data from five studies of European populations. From this data we can calculate that the riskier form of the gene accounts for an increase in risk of 0.5% in females in European populations if we assume a lifetime risk of 1%, or 1% if we assume a lifetime risk of 2%. But, of course, this finding was not confirmed by either Wang et al (2011) or Pinheiro et al (2010).

Wang et al (2011) noted that research on neuropsychiatric disorders had found evidence that variations in genes could have important causal effects, but that another kind of variation in DNA, Copy Number Variations (CNVs), could also have an important influence. CNVs are larger differences in DNA arising when whole sections of DNA, including multiple genes, are either omitted or duplicated. Wang et al (2011) noted that CNVs have been found to be associated with conditions including schizophrenia, autism and bipolar disorder. However, they found that, unlike patient populations with those disorders, the anorexia group did not have a significantly larger number of CNVs in general. In addition, the frequency of relatively rare and large CNVs did not distinguish between patients and the comparison group. Twenty-one women with anorexia, out of 1,033, had specific CNVs that have been linked to mental illnesses in other studies. Hence, such CNVs were few in number and if they are clinically significant in specific instances they nevertheless could only account for a very small proportion of cases.

* * *

As we have seen, because most of the studies take their material only from female subjects they do not draw attention to what may be the largest single biological risk factor. The fact of being female is thought to increase the risk of anorexia, compared to males, ten times. We do not know to what extent this reflects the impact of upbringing and female socialisation or biological factors.

Wang et al (2011) concluded that still larger studies are needed to identify genetic factors to test the possibility that a number of other genes may have low levels of association with anorexia. Pinheiro et al (2010) argued that of the many genetic factors they studied the two that came closest to being significantly associated with anorexia were genes that find expression in the gut. They argued that if these associations held they would have become significant in a larger study if that study had 3,430 to 4,270 participants. It follows that the association of these genes with anorexia may exist but must be very slight indeed.

Discussion

Despite substantial research efforts, results to date do not support the view that anorexia is highly heritable. The genetic impact that can be demonstrated on the development of anorexia is negligible. Although it is possible that a number of additional genetic factors will be demonstrated to have low levels of relationship with anorexia, there would need to be a very large number of these if they were to account for the claims made in the light of some studies of twins. The relatively high concordance rates observed in identical twins may be accounted for by some other factor such as the relationship between the twins, not by their genetic similarity. The relationship between identical twins may often be very intense and feelings both of competition and identification may put both at risk if one of them develops anorexia. Anyone who works as a therapist working with a patient who has an identical twin with anorexia, whether the pair is concordant or discordant, can hardly fail to notice the intense impact of this relationship. Sokol et al (2009) provided an interesting perspective on this in a paper describing twelve-year-old identical triplets concordant for anorexia. They commented that the triplets had an overly close relationship and encouraged each other and competed to lose weight. Managing this relationship was crucial to therapeutic work. Sokol et al were not writing about the origin of anorexia but described qualities of the relationship between the triplets that might drive them in the direction of concordance, in the context of a relationship dynamic that may only occur in identical twins, or, of course, identical triplets. Therapists who have not had this experience may well have encountered situations in which a patient with anorexia latches on to another and competes with her to lose weight. While these relationships are not equally intense, and can be brought to an end in a way that relationships between twin sisters cannot, the experience will give the therapist some idea of what is involved here. It is also possible that family and societal pressures tend to influence identical twins in the direction of similarity, but do not create the same pressures for fraternal twins.

Conclusions

It now seems unlikely that genes account for the tendency for anorexia to run in families. Instead, environmental factors, especially family factors, are likely to be a far more significant influence. In that case, the family aggregation would reflect social, not genetic, inheritance. If so, more attention should be given to the question "What are the family factors which give rise to the kinds of psychopathology which underlie anorexia?" Clinicians should be wary of suggesting to patients or their families that anorexia is substantially due to genetic influence. The evidence no longer favours that conclusion. Such a suggestion would be misleading. It might also promote undue passivity in the face of what could be experienced as biological inevitability, carrying the idea that the patient has some intrinsic fault that may be impossible to overcome.

CHAPTER SIX

How should we understand anorexia?

Girls and young women develop anorexia because they are unhappy. The unhappiness that gives rise to anorexia is not so different from the unhappiness that gives rise to bulimia, or depression for that matter. The girl who develops anorexia has extremely negative self-esteem, and high anxiety. To many clinicians, these difficulties in the mind of the girl suggest serious difficulties in the relationship between her and her parents. These difficulties are not sufficient to account for anorexia. To respond to these difficulties with anorexia, rather than with, say, depression, it is necessary to have an unusual degree of self-control, and a cognitive style that subjects the self to constant scrutiny. These qualities are reflected in the patient's perfectionism and obsessionality. To many clinicians these two problems suggest over-socialisation. That is to say that the girl has internalised too great a degree of inhibition of impulses. Such difficulties are often seen as associated with causal factors such as contingent parental love and approval. Arising from these two underlying difficulties we see that the person with anorexia usually has certain characteristic behavioural patterns: a marked tendency towards self-censorship that researchers have labelled "silencing the self", and a tendency to orient themselves towards meeting the needs of others within the family and peer group, sometimes referred to as excessively nurturing behaviour or as "selflessness". Many clinicians associate this pattern with family experiences in which the child experiences one or both carers as vulnerable, and seeks her own security by developmentally inappropriate attempts to meet parental needs. Feminist therapists have described these self-silencing and selfless patterns as representing the stereotype of the "good woman" in a patriarchal society. In addition, in western culture, girls with anorexia are generally excessively oriented towards dieting and towards thinness as a sign of attractiveness and may have distorted perceptions of their own body weight and shape. This western pattern reflects excessive cultural preoccupation with appearance, weight and diet. Clinical impressions are that these excessive preoccupations are often shared with one or both parents. Cultural pressures are probably mediated by family culture and family values.

Clinical discussions of anorexia have often focused on developmental aspects of the situation. Casper (1983) proposed that children who fail to develop a stable self-concept and secure self-regard are at risk of developing anorexia. She commented that the parents of patients with anorexia remember these children as exceptionally good. However, "Patients remember themselves in a different light: Their goodness, they say, was not happy contentment, but a disguise; it was rather shyness and refraining from creating trouble through action. What was interpreted as 'goodness' by their parents, patients experienced as compliance and yielding submission, a wish to please and to feel accepted in a world they thought was critical of them", Casper (1983, pp. 388–389). She comments that Bruch (1974, 1981) thought that these early tendencies towards compliance and submission led to an excessive denial of inner feelings. The way in which feelings and wishes are expressed defined the self. Suppressing them stood in the way of the development of a secure sense of self. This continuing lack of security in the sense of self made the child vulnerable to emotional challenges and set the scene for breakdown when confronted by the challenges of adolescence. Then, as she puts it, "When in such children self-induced dieting meets with success and affords them an occasion to feel competent through their own action, they seize this opportunity to feel competent to direct their weight with unusual determination in the erroneous belief that thereby they can win control over themselves and their lives", Casper (1983, p. 389). In other words, the development of anorexia serves a function, creating a fragile false sense of self-control and self-worth, but only so long as the anorexic behaviour goes unchallenged, and only so long as it can be maintained. Therapists from a wide range of schools regard anorexic behaviour as driven by the experience that successful control of eating and weight have a reparative function in relation to internalised difficulties.

Schmidt and Treasure (2006) comment that "People with AN, even with severe emaciation, may insist on the benefits of their highly compromised physical state for their well-being, and are reluctant to contemplate change", Schmidt and Treasure (2006, p. 344). They comment that anorexia may be valued because it makes the patient feel in control, and because starvation numbs those emotions that the person with anorexia finds it difficult to deal with. They comment that a study by Serpell et al (1999) confirmed that adults with anorexia saw it in a positive light because it made them feel safe, communicated distress and stifled unwelcome emotions. Serpell (2003) found a somewhat similar pattern in children and adolescents with anorexia, but with less emphasis on control and the stifling of emotions.

The function of anorexia can be described in intra-psychic terms, as it was by Schmidt and Treasure (2006) and by Serpell et al (1999, 2003). It can also be seen in inter-personal terms. For example Dallos and Vetere (2009) noted that researchers considering anorexia from the point of view of attachment theory have seen it as symptomatic of certain attachment strategies. They argue that sometimes it has been seen as the persons attempt to "distance themselves from the negative feelings about the lack of emotional availability of their parents …" so that anorexic thinking and preoccupation is seen as distracting from more fundamental concerns, and protecting the patient from overwhelming feelings both of loss and abandonment. However, they continue, it has also been seen as reflecting that the young person is "entangled with their parents, in need of care, attention, medical intervention and support. … It can be seen as a form of implicit coercion of care and attention from the parents", Dallos and Vetere (2009, pp. 169–170).

Psychoanalytic, feminist-psychoanalytic, and attachment theory explanations see internalised difficulties as arising from the child's early experiences, beginning in infancy, and continuing through childhood, giving rise to the personality that succumbs to anorexia as a solution to the problems arising from an insufficiently secure sense of self.

Bachner-Melman et al (2007) reviewing the gender psychology argued that women in general are highly oriented to attend to others emotions rather than their own, and that this leads to four characteristic patterns of behaviour. Women tend to inhibit their self-expression to avoid conflict, put others needs first, judge themselves according to the standards of others and present outer compliance while inhibiting expression of anger or resistance. This combination can be seen as representing the stereotype of the "good woman". Such behaviour has been shown to be even more characteristic of women with anorexia than of women in general.

Research on anorexia, personality and personal style

The interaction between self-esteem, ineffectiveness and depression

Low self-esteem is regarded as a contributory factor in the development of internalising disorders in general. It contributes to the development of depression and eating disorder. However, in anorexia successful control of weight and eating serves a protective function, so that the patient experiences less challenge to her fragile self-esteem. Hence patients with anorexia who successfully control their weight by restricting have higher self-esteem than those who also binge. Patients with anorexia, whose control over their eating is challenged, for example in an in-patient refeeding programme, also experience a challenge to their self-esteem.

Button et al (1996) found that low self-esteem in girls aged twelve predicted eating problems at age fifteen. Low self-esteem at age twelve was associated with an eight-fold increase in incidence of eating problems at age fifteen. Casper et al (1981) found high levels of shame and self-criticism in teenage girls with anorexia. Leung et al (1996) in a large study of adolescent girls found that both low self-esteem, and family attitudes to weight and appearance, contributed to the development of both body dissatisfaction and eating disorder symptoms. Leung et al argued that problems in family functioning had an effect on reducing girls' self esteem, and hence, indirectly, to the development of eating disorder, and also to other psychiatric symptoms.

Self-esteem can be seen as having two components, self-liking and self-competence (Tafarodi & Swann 2001). Drawing on this model Paterson et al (2007) compared an adult in-patient group with anorexia with a comparison group of female students, using questionnaire measures of both self-liking and self-competence, as well as measures of eating disorder pathology and of problem solving style. As would be expected the group with anorexia scored lower on both components of self-esteem than the comparison group. An interesting finding was that, within the group with anorexia, severity of self-reported eating disorder pathology was predicted by the measure of self-competence, but not by the measure of self-liking. This is consistent with the idea that anorexia serves a defensive function in regard to self-worth, that is that those patients with anorexia who felt themselves to be competent in being in control reported less distress. By contrast, in a student comparison group the much lower level of eating disorder pathology would rarely be associated with success in controlling weight. In that group eating pathology was predicted by self-liking but not self-competence.

Self-competence can be seen as the opposite of ineffectiveness. Troop and Treasure (1997) interviewed women with eating disorders and a control group of healthy women about childhood experiences of adversity and about feelings of helplessness, versus feelings of mastery during childhood. Women with eating disorders reported lower levels of mastery, and more feelings of helplessness. However, this was reported less by women with restricting anorexia (AN-R) than it was for those with anorexia and bulimic symptoms (AN/BN) or bulimia. Lyon and Chatoor (1997) compared forty-three teenage patients with anorexia with eighty-five comparison girls without any eating disorder, and also collected information from parents. Patients with anorexia reported feelings of ineffectiveness, and low interoceptive awareness. This is to say they did not feel able to control their lives and did not think they were good at understanding their own feelings. There was a high level of depressive illness in the family histories of the girls with anorexia. They argued "Feelings of inadequacy and lack of control may have their origin in reliance on external rather than internal cues. Control of the body through culturally reinforced dieting may in turn alleviate feelings of ineffectiveness", Lyon and Chatoor (1997, p. 106). However, such a defence is only partially effective and only effective at all if the patient's control is complete. Patients with anorexia who binge would be expected to be more likely to be depressed and self-critical. Fennig et al (2008) compared levels of self-criticism and eating disorder symptoms in a group of eighty-one female adolescent psychiatric in-patients in an eating disorder treatment programme. As would be expected higher levels of self-criticism were found in patients with bulimia, whose self-esteem is not protected by successful control of weight and eating.

These studies provide evidence that low self-esteem is a risk factor for anorexia, and other eating disorders, and that the successful control of weight and eating achieved by restricting patients with anorexia serves to ward off self-criticism and shore up self-esteem, up to a point.

Anorexia and anxiety

Anorexia is closely related to anxiety. It has been demonstrated that patients with anorexia have high anxiety levels and that the onset of anxiety usually occurs before the onset of anorexia. Therefore, there is likely to be overlap between the causes of anorexia and of anxiety. For the population as a whole from puberty on there is an increase in anxiety symptoms. Davila et al (2010) reported that there is both an increase in the incidence of these symptoms, and a change in the pattern. Whereas separation anxiety is relatively common in childhood it is less common in adolescence. From puberty onwards it is replaced by specific phobias, social phobias and generalised anxiety disorder. The gender difference also increases at this time. Girls have higher rates of anxiety disorders than boys. Older adolescents have higher rates than younger adolescents. Girls also have much higher rates of post-traumatic stress disorder. The same is true for depression, which also increases greatly after puberty and is much more common in girls. This is the context in which anorexia develops. Obsessional disorders are regarded as anxiety disorders. Evidence demonstrates that anxiety and obsessionality develop in the individual before she develops anorexia.

Anorexia appears with increasing frequency from puberty onwards. It is accompanied and usually preceded, by anxiety. Kaye et al (2004) compared ninety-seven patients with anorexia, 282 with bulimia and 293 who fulfilled criteria for both conditions, with 694 healthy women for a lifetime history of anxiety disorder. They used both clinical interviews and questionnaire measures of anxiety symptoms. They found that 64% of patients with eating disorders had a history of anxiety disorder, 41% suffered from Obsessional-Compulsive Disorder (OCD), and 20% from social phobia. In roughly two-thirds of cases the onset of the anxiety disorder preceded the onset of eating disorder. Typically anxiety conditions preceded the eating disorder by three years or more. They noted that even patients who had recovered from the eating disorder, and had never met diagnostic criteria for anxiety disorders, "reported higher levels of anxiety, harm avoidance (avoidant behaviour driven by anxiety), and perfectionism, than the healthy women in the community" (Kaye et al, 2004, p. 2220).

Raney et al (2008) analysed data from structured clinical interviews with women who had a history of anorexia. Of these, 39% had suffered from one anxiety disorder, Over-Anxious Disorder of Childhood (OADC). Where it existed, the onset of OADC preceded the development of the eating disorder in almost all cases.

Obsessionality

The observation that anorexia is related to obsessional problems goes back a long way. Stonehill and Crisp (1977) obtained data from a group of forty-five women with anorexia receiving treatment either on an in-patient or out-patient basis. Compared to a healthy student control group, the patient group with anorexia reported more anxiety, obsessional, somatic and depressive symptoms. These problems were less severe after weight restoration. Rastam et al (1996) compared fifty-one adolescents with anorexia and a healthy adolescent comparison group. Obsessional-Compulsive Disorder (OCD) and avoidant personality (that is to say a personality in which behaviour is driven by the need to avoid situations giving rise to anxiety) were much more common in the adolescents with anorexia. A study by Halmi (2005a, 2005b), and a review by Truglia et al (2006) confirm the relationship between anorexia and obsessionality.

Strober (1980) observed that it could be argued that data that demonstrated this kind of personality difficulty in patients with anorexia might be accounted for by the duration of the anorexia, by long periods of poor nutrition and by the emotional distress the illness had caused. To test this he obtained data from a group of twenty-two adolescent female patients at the time of their first admission to treatment and again six months later when all the patients were within 4% of their ideal body weight. Strober used questionnaires measuring a wide range of symptoms and personality traits. Strober's findings confirmed those of Stonehill and Crisp (1977). Like the adult patients in that study the adolescent patients with anorexia were introverted and neurotic, and rated highly on obsessional symptoms and traits. Again, like the adult patients, these symptoms and personality traits were less severe after weight restoration. Strober observed that after refeeding patients were less socially withdrawn, demonstrated greater interpersonal sensitivity, sociability and psychological mindedness, but with a diminished sense of well-being. He concluded, that "As the patient's psychobiological regression is reversed … developmental issues pertaining to self identity, interpersonal communication, compatibility, and influence come to be seen in a more objective light, though now overshadowed by the anxieties and self-doubt that normally attend adolescent turmoil", Strober (1980, p. 358). Here again we see evidence that anorexia serves a protective function against difficult feelings.

In a retrospective study of patients' accounts and the accounts given by a healthy comparison group Anderluh et al (2003) demonstrated that there was continuity between a number of traits reported in childhood and the development of OCD in patients with anorexia. The traits were "perfectionism", "inflexibility", "being rule-bound", "doubt and cautiousness" and "drive for order and symmetry". All these traits, but especially the first three, were reported by most of the patients with anorexia, but by very few of the comparison group. The analysis of the data suggested that the larger the number of these traits that were present in childhood, the greater the risk of developing anorexia or bulimia in adolescence or in adult life. By contrast Waters et al (1990), in a smaller study, based on mothers' retrospective accounts, did not find that patients with anorexia had presented perfectionistic, obsessive or compulsive traits prior to the development of anorexia, when compared to their sisters. So, at least according to the patient's account, obsessional types of behaviour in childhood preceded the development of anorexia in many cases. Taken together the studies indicate that obsessional symptoms and traits are not secondary to anorexia, although they may be exacerbated by it.

Perfectionism

The evidence points to a close relationship between anorexia and perfectionism. Perfectionism is seen as a major risk factor for the development of anorexia, highly characteristic of the disturbance itself, and remains characteristic of those who have recovered. Some researchers have speculated about the relationship between these difficulties and the patient's experience of upbringing.

Perfectionists fear making mistakes, getting things wrong, or seeming to do so in other people's opinions. Their self-esteem is constantly threatened by these fears. Perfectionism is the characteristic that has been shown to discriminate most strongly between patients with anorexia and those with other diagnoses. Perfectionism has been seen as a major driver of anorexia. Goldner et al (2002) observed that anorexia runs in families and that one possible reason is that parents' perfectionistic expectations of children's behaviour may lead to perfectionism in the younger generation, who seek to ward off criticism by "perfect" behaviour. This may become internalised as self-oriented perfectionism, that is, as an attitude that comes to be experienced as self-imposed. Goldner et al proposed another link through a common genetic factor but acknowledged there was no positive evidence for this. She thought that cultural pressures to achieve a slim body build might be incorporated by the young person with low self-esteem, and, if she was also perfectionistic, an escalating pattern of weight loss aimed at achieving an increasingly unrealistic body ideal could result in anorexia. In addition, Goldner et al argued that distressing events might cause the person to invest in such a body ideal as a response to insults to self-esteem. Perfectionism may contribute to vulnerability because, by setting unrealistic goals for achievement and conduct, it may increase the frequency of occasions for distress when the person fails to live up to her standards.

The term Maladaptive Perfectionism is used to distinguish it from what can be called "Personal Standards Perfectionism" or "Adaptive Perfectionism" which is a drive to do one's best, but without the neurotic, driven and self-defeating aspects that we see in some clinical populations. In addition distinctions are often made between types of perfectionism, depending on the person's attitude to the source of the judgement about their perfectionistic behaviour. "Socially prescribed perfectionism" is the drive to achieve high standards in the context of feeling one has to meet other's standards and that nothing one does is ever good enough for them. "Self-oriented perfectionism" can be seen as the internalisation of this drive, so that the person now sets impossibly high standards for herself. "Other oriented perfectionism" is the attitude that other people must do their best and come up to the highest standards for us.

Halmi et al (2000) reported a study of 322 females with anorexia and a comparison group of forty-four women who were free of eating disorder symptoms. They used interview and questionnaire measures of perfectionism, obsessionality and eating disorder symptoms. Three subgroups of anorexia patients were identified, a purely restricting group, a restricting and purging group, and a bingeing and purging group. Each subgroup of patients had higher scores on both measures of perfectionism and on obsessionality than comparison women who were free of eating disorders. In the discussion they commented that "subjects with anorexia nervosa were distinguished from healthy comparison subjects by their more strenuous efforts at, and preoccupation with, avoidance of mistakes in daily life, and of parental criticism, doubts over the correctness of actions, and a more extreme adherence to personal and parental standards of excellence", Halmi et al (2000, p. 1803). They commented that these findings were consistent with previous findings in studies by Hewitt et al (1995) and Srinivasagam et al (1995) respectively. Perfectionism was correlated to drive for thinness even in the non-clinical subjects, and remained a significant problem for weight-recovered patients after treatment.

Castro-Fornieles (2007) conducted a study comparing a group of patients with anorexia or bulimia, with a mixed psychiatrically ill group and with a well comparison group, with all the participants in the study being female. The study compared the three groups in terms of perfectionism and diagnosis using questionnaire measures of perfectionism and of eating disorder symptoms. Although both the anorexia and the bulimia patients had higher total perfectionism scores they did not have higher scores on socially prescribed perfectionism. So unlike the other studies, this found that the eating disorder patients reported self-imposed perfectionism, but not the same sense that they had to be perfect to meet other people's demands.

Higher levels of perfectionism have been shown to predict more severe illness, longer duration of illness and higher levels of non-suicidal deliberate self-harm in eating disordered patients, Claes et al (2012). Nilsson et al (2008) demonstrated that higher levels of perfectionism were related to longer duration of illness in a long-term follow-up of adolescent patients with anorexia.

Perfectionistic self-presentation

Cockell et al (2002) identified an additional factor in perfectionism, the need to present a perfect image of oneself to others, which they described as "perfectionistic self-presentation". They argued, "... this desire to hide flaws and shortcomings reflects an interpersonal style ... that is a defensive extension of the social self", Cockell et al (2002, p. 746). Cockell reported a study of all four kinds of perfectionism. They compared three groups of women matched for age and educational level. The first group was patients with anorexia in treatment, the second a comparison group of psychiatric patients who had no history of eating disorder and the third group was made up of hospital staff, excluding any who had a history of eating disorder. Both questionnaire and interview measures of perfectionism were used, including a questionnaire measure of perfectionistic self-presentation. Women with anorexia were found to have higher levels of self-oriented and socially prescribed perfectionism, as well as higher levels of perfectionistic self-presentation. By contrast the comparison group of psychiatrically ill women did not differ from the well women in regard to perfectionism. There was no difference between the three groups on other-oriented perfectionism, indicating that the patients with anorexia did not set high standards for other people. Cockell et al suggest that patients may have acquired perfectionism as a result of their family experiences, in that clinical descriptions of the families of patients with anorexia describe the families as striving to present a public image of perfection and psychological health, with unacknowledged needs and problems. They conclude "In such a family environment, women with AN may have learned to maintain a facade of domestic tranquility by promoting a picture of perfection and concealing any hint of imperfection", (Cockell et al, 2002, p. 747).

Perfectionism and social anxiety

Perfectionism is also known to be associated with social phobia. Juster et al (1996) found that patients with social phobias scored higher than control subjects on a measure of perfectionism. Within that patient group more severe illness was associated with higher perfectionism scores. They summarise a number of studies that showed that patients with social phobias tended to report their parents as having been excessively concerned about the opinions of others and as having used shaming as a disciplinary technique. They argue that that these practices could be seen as sensitising the child to develop social anxiety.

Anorexia and internalising symptoms

Internalising symptoms include anxiety, depression, social withdrawal, and somatic problems. By contrast externalising symptoms are aggressive, oppositional and "delinquent" behaviours. In a retrospective study of adolescent girls with anorexia or bulimia Adambegan et al (2012) obtained parents' reports of girls internalising and externalising symptoms in childhood. The girls' sisters were the comparison group. They found that girls who developed anorexia had internalising symptoms prior to the development of the eating disorder, while those who developed bulimia had both internalising and externalising symptoms.

Depression is associated with anorexia but is less likely to pre-date the onset of anorexia itself. Fernandez-Aranda et al (2007) reported data from a large study of patients with severe eating disorders. Systematic clinical interviews allowed diagnoses to be established retrospectively for 1051 women who had, or had had, a diagnosis of anorexia. More than 60% of these women had also had a diagnosis of major depressive disorder. This rose to 80% or more for those women who also had bulimic symptoms. About one-third of these depressive episodes happened before the onset of the eating disorder, usually in the year before the onset. The remaining two-thirds occurred within three years of the onset of the eating disorder.

Jordan et al (2008) obtained information from clinical interviews with fifty-six women with anorexia. Sixty-three percent had experienced a major depressive disorder, and 55% had experienced an anxiety disorder, with obsessive-compulsive disorder, panic disorder/agoraphobia, social phobia and simple phobias all roughly equally represented among the anxiety disorders.

Overall the evidence about anxiety and depression suggests that anxiety can be seen to precede the development of anorexia and often remains a serious problem for the patient through life, irrespective of the question of recovery from anorexia itself. By contrast depression is less commonly experienced prior to the development of anorexia. However, it often becomes a problem for patients in later stages of anorexia. This supports the argument that the pathway into both anorexia and depression shares many features, but that the development of anorexia serves, to some extent, to protect the patient from dysphoria and depression, at least in the early stages. At a later stage this effect may break down when the patient begins to perceive that the illness is out of her control, that it alienates her from family and friends, and stands in the way of the development of relationships and the achievement of life goals.

Silencing the self and suppressing anger

A behavioural pattern that is highly characteristic of anorexia is "silencing the self". This means the use of self-censorship, not being assertive, not expressing one's own feelings, needs or ideas. Geller et al (2000) point out that the pattern has been highlighted as a particular characteristic of behaviour in women arising from their socialisation. They argued, "... despite being open communicators, women are socialised to suppress negative feelings and needs in order to preserve close relationships" Geller et al (2000, p. 9). They commented that women with anorexia have often been seen as suppressing negative feelings. Geller commented that since Strober (1991) summarised evidence that women with anorexia tend towards extreme harm avoidance, reward dependence and low novelty seeking. Geller suggested they might suppress expressions of negative feelings in order to avoid distress and discomfort, because they exaggerated others sensitivity, and because they preferred to keep their relationships predictable. Geller collected data in the same study reported by Cockell et al (2002) on perfectionism. Measures in the study were the Eating Disorders Examination, which is a standardised clinical interview, and eight self-report questionnaires. Two questionnaires measured the suppression of feelings; the Silencing the Self Scale (STSS), Jack and Dill (1992), and the State-Trait Anger Expression Inventory (STAXI), Spielberger et al (1985), a measure of the expression and suppression of angry feelings. The STSS yields four sub-scales: Externalised Self-Perception (judging the self according to how others see you), Care as Self-Sacrifice (putting others needs first), Silencing the Self (inhibiting expression in order to avoid conflict or possible loss of relationship) and Divided Self (outer compliance concealing hidden anger and resentment). High scores on the STSS are seen as indicating conformity to the stereotype of the "good woman". Other measures addressed depression, self-esteem, illness severity, perfectionism and perfectionistic self-presentation.

As they expected, Geller et al (2000) found that the women with anorexia had significantly higher scores on all the subscales of the STSS than both the psychiatrically ill and the well comparison groups. The difference could not be entirely accounted for by different levels of global self-esteem among the three groups. In the discussion they argue that one possible way of understanding this is that women with anorexia suppress expression because they fear negative outcomes. Both perfectionism and self-silencing might reflect the need to avoid expected criticism or rejection. Both relate to low self-esteem, since fragile self-esteem is one factor creating such vulnerability, but so are real life experiences. Geller et al commented on the real lack of power in relationships experienced by many women. They suggested that self-silencing by girls and women with anorexia may reflect a real need to keep the peace in the context of relationships that they cannot control or alter.

Buchholz et al (2007) studied silencing the self, anxiety and the severity of eating disorder symptoms in 149 adolescent girls diagnosed with eating disorders. They studied self-silencing in the context of peer relationships using a modified form of the STSS, Sippola and Bukowski (1996). Both social anxiety and self-silencing were associated with greater severity of eating disorder symptoms. The STSS subscale Externalised Self-Perception was strongly associated with both the Body Dissatisfaction and the Drive for Thinness measures of the EDI-2. Buchholz et al argued that "adolescent girls who closely monitor their thoughts and feelings in order to maintain their friendships were more likely to report greater body dissatisfaction and higher drive for thinness". Social anxiety was also associated with body dissatisfaction, as well as with self-silencing. Buchholz concluded, "... these girls may be less likely to express negative thoughts or feelings while struggling to maintain a socially desirable ideal of the good woman", Buchholz et al (2007, p. 162).

Silencing the self has also been found to be characteristic of adult women who report eating difficulties in community samples. Zaitsoff et al (2002) argued that "silencing the self" could be a characteristic of women with anorexia as a result of a long period of disturbance. If not it should be characteristic of adolescent girls with less severe levels of eating disorder concern. They studied a group of fourteen to fifteen-year-old schoolgirls in the community, using a number of questionnaire measures. Of these the Stirling Eating Disorder Scales (SEDS), Williams et al (1994) was a measure of eating disorder symptoms and concerns, and the Silencing the Self Scale (STSS) and the State-Trait Anger Expression Inventory (STAXI) were used, as were measures of self-esteem and of shape and weight-based self-esteem. They compared two groups of girls, those who scored above the eightieth centile for the SEDS, and those who scored below. High scores indicated the presence of eating disorder symptoms and concerns. Results were similar to those Geller (2000) had obtained with adult patients. Girls who scored high on SEDS had low self-esteem; their self-esteem depended on their estimation of their shape and weight. There was one difference; the teenage girls with eating disorders concerns did not score significantly higher than other girls on the care subscale of STSS. Zaitsoff et al suggest that putting others first may be less characteristic of adolescent girls than of adult women.

Smolak and Munstertieger (2002) confirmed the relationship between self-silencing and eating concerns in female, but not in male, college students mostly aged eighteen to nineteen. As with the younger teenage girls in the Zaitsoff study (2002), there was no relationship between eating problems and the care subscale of the STSS. Perhaps, therefore, the care subscale discriminates between the more disturbed clinical population and people with less severe eating disorders identified in community studies. Those whose eating disorder is more severe may be more likely to see themselves as remaining silent as a way of putting other peoples' needs first.

An interesting finding of both the Geller et al (2000) and Zaitsoff (2002) studies concerns the findings from STAXI. Both the patients with anorexia and the symptomatic schoolgirls' results indicate that they both express anger and that they suppress it. Both groups seem to be saying that they have a lot of anger, and both suppress and express it.

Self-harm is one feature associated with anorexia that is often thought to be associated with the suppression of anger by the patient. Truglia et al (2006) argued that one sign of this is the relatively high level of self-harming behaviour in patients with anorexia. She reported data from four studies of self-harm in anorexia that show a prevalence ranging from 16% to 68% in clinical samples.

Another approach to the study of interpersonal problems in eating disorders uses the Inventory of Interpersonal Problems (Horowitz et al, 1988; Alden et al, 1990). Using this measure, Hartmann et al (2010) demonstrated that patients with severe eating disorders, including those with anorexia, have a predominantly submissive, unassertive interpersonal style, and were typically distressed about their social inhibition, unassertiveness and overly nurturing behaviour. They concluded that "our findings confirm empirically what has repeatedly been reported in clinical descriptions: AN subjugate themselves in relationship in order to avoid the loss of another person", Hartmann et al (2010, p. 625).

Meyer et al (2010) used yet another questionnaire, the Attitudes Toward Emotional Expression Scale Laghai and Joseph (2000) and a measure of eating disorder symptoms, the Eating Disorder Examination Questionnaire, Fairburn and Beglin (1994), with a group of 122 women recruited in the community. They found that negative attitudes towards the expression of emotion were associated with higher levels of eating disorder symptoms. They noted that "those women who are concerned about their eating, shape and weight believe that to display emotion is a sign of weakness, that they should keep their emotions under control and that others might be rejecting or damaged should they themselves express their emotions", Meyer et al (2010, p. 189).

Anorexia and selflessness

The term "selflessness" is used to describe a related issue. It is the tendency to sacrifice one's own interests for the sake of others. Bachner-Melman et al (2007) argued, "eating disorder patients feel and behave like selfless souls serving others' needs and cannot imagine others would be willing to meet their needs", Bachner-Melman et al (2007, p. 213). They used the Selflessness Scale developed by Bachar et al (2002) to compare four groups of women, those currently suffering from anorexia, those who were partially recovered, those who were fully recovered, and a control group who had never had an eating disorder. As they expected patients who currently had anorexia had the highest levels of selflessness, while recovered women and controls had the lowest. The partially recovered group had intermediate levels. They argued that becoming able to assert one's own needs is an important aspect of recovery and should be a focus of therapeutic work.

Problems continue after recovery

Follow-up studies typically find that recovered patients continue to suffer from high levels of eating difficulties, anxiety, depression, and interpersonal difficulties. Clearly therefore not all recoveries are equally good, and outcome studies have gradually shifted focus to include more information about the quality of the patients recovery, and the quality of the patients life after treatment, as well as on diagnostic issues. For example Yackobovitch-Gavan et al (2009) attempted to follow up 152 patients five to eleven years after they had been treated for anorexia in an adolescent eating disorder department. Only sixty agreed to take part. Of these, thirty-six (60%) had recovered in that they had maintained normal weight and eating, and had regular menstrual cycles in the previous twelve months. Recovered patients had higher anxiety levels and higher levels of obsessional concerns about eating than a comparison group of healthy women. Milos et al (2005) found that many patients who had been treated for anorexia developed bulimia or continued to suffer from a less severe eating disorder. Smith et al (1993) followed up twenty-three patients who had been treated for anorexia as adolescents. Two (9%) still had anorexia, and 17% had developed bulimia, 2% had less severe eating disorder, 30% affective disorders and 43% an anxiety disorder. Eddy et al (2008) followed up 216 women with anorexia (AN) or bulimia (BN) over seven years. More than half crossed over between restricting anorexia (AN-R) and anorexia with bingeing and purging (AN-BN) subtypes, and one third crossed from AN to BN. Those patients were at risk of crossing back to AN, but patients who initially had BN were less likely to develop anorexia.

Conclusions

The purpose of this chapter has been to illustrate the wide range of difficulties that patients with anorexia experience, and to suggest that anorexia cannot be understood other than through the perspective of the symptomatic, personality and relationship difficulties that invariably accompany and precede it. Anorexia is a very severe personal disturbance associated with anxiety and other forms of distress, and with a highly characteristic psychological and interpersonal style. These features reflect difficulties in the sense of self. Anorexia develops in adolescence in young people who have pre-existing difficulties. In stressful circumstances anorexia begins when the person discovers that control of food and weight can lead to the temporary alleviation of distress caused by low self-esteem and a deficient sense of self. It is maintained because it is at least partially successful. It is preceded by, and accompanied by, high levels of anxiety. Low self-esteem and low confidence in self-efficacy are characteristic, as is maladaptive perfectionism. People with anorexia are excessively concerned about how others see them. Patients censor the expression of their own feelings and needs, and see themselves as self-sacrificing. They are unusually concerned for the welfare of others and seem to be caught between idealising their parents and feeling let down by them. Such difficulties are seen in the psychological literature on child development and family psychology as arising from the child's upbringing. It is notable that while some of the authors of this research attributed the patients' psychological difficulties to heredity; others drew attention to childhood experiences, and the quality of family relationships, as the probable source of these difficulties. The older literature on the family and anorexia, Minuchin et al (1978), paid little attention to these issues because it was concerned with the concurrent function of anorexia in the family, not with developmental issues. The literature attached to the Maudsley Model, and Family-Based Treatment, largely ignores these psychological difficulties, except in so far as it sees them as being exacerbated by starvation. However, outside that school there is a near consensus that anorexia should be seen as a form of perverse self-control which is driven by distress, distress arising from difficulties in the person's sense of self. This in turn is often, but not always, attributed to the patients' experiences of upbringing.

So far as it goes this model is consistent with models advanced by leading figures in the field such as the "cognitive-interpersonal" maintenance model proposed by Schmidt and Treasure (2006). However, there is one important difference. Schmidt and Treasure use the term "phenotype" when discussing the personality vulnerable to anorexia. This carries the implication of biological, and substantially genetic, explanation for the vulnerability. Seen from this point of view the anxiety, obsessionality and perfectionism characteristic of people with anorexia can be seen as arising as a result of inherited temperament, or the interaction between that and environmental factors. As we have seen this is no longer a likely explanation. Instead we need to think about the vulnerability as arising in the context of the child's socialisation in her family. It follows that we need a family model to understand the onset of the disorder. This would account for the family circumstances that produce the potential vulnerability in the child, and those that are in play at the time, usually in adolescence, when the child develops anorexia.

CHAPTER SEVEN

Family interaction research

Research on family interaction and anorexia started out with attempts to test the Psychosomatic Family Model. That was an ambitious goal. At an early stage it proved difficult to achieve an operational definition of the concepts in the psychosomatic model, such as "enmeshment", "over-protection", and "rigidity". It is far from clear that all authors use these terms in the same sense. A less ambitious goal would be to test the question "Are the families of patients with anorexia a random sample of families in general at this stage in the life cycle?" That is to say do these families appear different, or more "pathological", than other families? Subsequently, as we have seen Eisler (2005) proposed that the apparent psychopathology in the families of patients with anorexia reflected the effect of the "illness" on the family, and that this impact would have much in common with the effects of other long-term illnesses on the family. Two studies have addressed this by testing the hypothesis that the families are similar to other families who have a teenager with a long-term illness.

A small number of research studies are based on direct observation of interaction between family members in interviews or experimental family tasks, or statements made by family members in clinical or research interviews. A larger number of studies have been based on self-report questionnaires provided by one or more family members. Some of these questionnaires concern family relationships in general. Others focus specifically on parenting, usually, specifically, on the patient's experience of her parents. Some studies have used more than one approach.

Early studies mostly attempted to test the Psychosomatic Family Model. In general research does not confirm that all families with a child with anorexia fit the model. Other studies approached the question in the light of different theoretical perspectives. No consensus emerged about an alternative family model, although a number of researchers, such as Leung et al (1996) and Laliberte et al (1999) have put forward useful propositions about the impact of family factors on the development of the psychological vulnerabilities that culminate in the development of anorexia.

A substantial body of research exists which illuminates aspects of the relationship between the family and anorexia. These include observational studies, self-report studies based on questionnaires completed by patients and other family members, and studies of life events and risk factors. These will be briefly summarised here and discussed in relation to a series of key findings.

Studies of clinical populations

At least thirty-seven studies compare aspects of family relationships in the families of patients with anorexia, with relationships in comparison families of girls and women who are free of anorexia.

Observational studies

Eight observational studies: Minuchin et al (1978), Kog and Vandereycken (1989), Humphrey et al (1986a) Humphrey (1989), Blair et al (1995), Latzer and Gaber (1998), Wallin and Hansson (1999), and Lattimore et al (2000a, 2000b) confirmed at least some differences in interaction between families with a daughter with anorexia, and non-clinical comparison families. All observational studies that made this kind of comparison found at least one significant difference. However, the only part of the Psychosomatic Family Model to stand up to repeated test is Minuchin's observation that the patient's parents are unsuccessful in a conflict resolution task conflict when she is present, Minuchin et al (1978). Three observational studies, Kog and Vandereycken (1989), Blair et al (1995), Latzer and Gaber (1998), confirm Minuchin's results.

Observational studies of family conflict

Minuchin et al (1978) described a study of the quality of expression of conflict within the families of young people with anorexia as part of the original presentation of the Psychosomatic Family Model. In this research Minuchin et al observed each family's interaction in a two-phase experimental situation. In the first phase the parents engaged in discussion of areas of disagreement between them, while their daughter watched the interaction through a one-way screen. In the second phase the daughter came to join her parents and the task of discussing the conflict continued. Minuchin and his colleagues were able to compare the behaviour of the families of patients with anorexia in this two phase task with that of four other groups of families. These were families with a child who was free of illness; families with a child who presented with stable diabetes; families with a diabetic child who had behavioural problems; and families with a diabetic child who failed to achieve stability in the management of diabetes so that there were repeated hospital admissions of the child in a crisis. The findings of this study in relation to conflict were that the parents of the patients with anorexia seemed very uncomfortable with conflict. Sometimes they started by denying that they ever had disagreements, or they used general language, avoiding direct difference with their partner. When they did discuss differences they changed the subject and avoided intensity. In the second phase, when their daughter joined them in the task the parents immediately detoured the conflict task through their daughter, or shifted their attention entirely to talking to her, so that little further direct communication between the parents was attempted despite the task being to talk about a disagreement between them. In all these respects Minuchin et al reported that the families of the patients with anorexia had greater difficulty focusing on conflict than any of the other groups. The parents' behaviour was in marked contrast with that of parents in the comparison groups who were able to talk directly with each other about real differences.

Another aspect of this study was that in the diabetic groups a physiological measure was also taken from both the diabetic child and the parents. This measure was a measure of the level of Free Fatty Acids in the blood. The levels were monitored throughout the experimental task and for a period after it was completed. The children in the uncontrolled diabetes group had a rapid increase in Free Fatty Acid levels throughout the task, and the levels continued to rise while the task was completed. This was not true for the diabetic patients in any other group. The inference is that the uncontrolled diabetic children were involved in their parents' relationship in a different way than the other diabetic children, and that this, in one way or another accounted for the families' failure to help their child achieve diabetic control. It seems that Minuchin and his colleagues would have expected similar results from psychophysiological measures of stress levels in the patients with anorexia had such measurements been available.

Kog and Vandereycken (1989), in the course of a complex study of family interaction, found that the families of girls with anorexia were more conflict avoiding than non-clinical comparison families, using a measure derived from another experimental task in which the family discussed disagreements.

Latzer and Gaber (1998) replicated these findings, in relation to anorexia, in a study that compared the performance of families with a daughter with anorexia, and comparison families, in the context of a similar experimental task. Two groups of forty families were compared. One group had a daughter with anorexia in the age range twelve to twenty-six. The comparison group was families with daughters matched for age, and matched for socio-economic status and for the family's country of origin. The parents and daughters were asked first of all to choose two areas of disagreement or conflict between the daughter and one or both parents. They were asked to keep off the topics of food and eating as far as possible. Then they discussed a topic chosen by the daughter, and then a topic chosen by the parents. The discussions were recorded. Although some families in both groups did discuss food issues these were by no means the dominant topics of discussion. The discussions were then coded to determine to what extent the family chose an appropriate topic; the speed and ease of the choice of topic; how far they stuck to the chosen topic; how much they developed the discussion and the extent to which they achieved resolution. There were substantial differences between the two groups on all variables. Families with daughters with anorexia had more difficulty choosing topics, remaining focused on them and developing the discussion and moving towards resolution.

Blair et al (1995) compared the families of patients with anorexia with two groups of comparison families. These were families of young people with cystic fibrosis, and families of young people in which no family member had an illness. The study examined various aspects of family functioning related to the Psychosomatic Family Model. The capacity to achieve conflict resolution was studied in an experimental task. In this task the families were asked to discuss two areas of conflict for up to ten minutes. Conflicts arising directly from the daughter's illness were not the focus of these discussions. Families with daughters with anorexia were less able to achieve conflict resolution. Blair et al observed that this was not because they did not engage with the task, but because having engaged with it they were less able to negotiate and achieve resolution.

A study of parent–child conflict in anorexia

One study focused on conflict between adolescent girls with anorexia and their mothers. Lattimore et al (2000a, 2000b) studied the interaction of girls with anorexia and their mothers engaged in a similar conflict task, without the father, and compared it with similar interaction between girls with other psychiatric disorders, but no eating disorder. Video-taped interaction was analysed for nineteen girls with anorexia and their mothers, and fourteen comparison patients. In addition, psychophysiological measures were collected from both the girls and their mothers. The experimental task had two phases. In the first phase the girls and their mothers were asked to talk about things they liked to do together and why they enjoyed them. In the second phase they were asked to talk about a number of predefined sources of conflict. For the girls with anorexia and their mothers these included issues to do with food and weight and appearance, as well as general issues likely to be associated with conflict in adolescence. In the second phase the comparison mother–daughter dyads discussed only the general conflictual issues. Findings did not confirm the expectation of conflict avoidance between mother and daughter in the second phase task. In the high conflict task the daughters with anorexia and their mothers showed more disagreement, more blaming, more mindreading (by mothers), less positive affect, and more negative affect than the control dyads. The girls with anorexia more often responded with silence, criticism, and negative feelings, and disclosed feelings more than their mothers. There was more destructive communication than constructive communication, and each partner was more likely than the comparison dyads to respond to the others' destructive communication with a destructive communication. In the comparison group mothers made more frequent requests for clarification and offered more support. Lattimore (2000b) did not attempt to assess the achievement of conflict resolution. However, the description of the conflict between the girls with anorexia and their mothers suggests that they were not moving towards resolution, as Lattimore (2000b) noted.

In this study the patients and their mothers had completed a self-report measure of family functioning, the McMaster Family Assessment Device (FAD) (Epstein et al, 1983). Within the anorexia dyads increased heart rate during the high conflict task was associated with self-reported poor problem solving and poor communication in the family. The psychophysiological measures indicated that the heart rates of girls with anorexia speeded up during the high conflict task to a greater extent than the comparison patients. By contrast the heart rate of their mothers slowed down during this task, while that of the comparison group mothers did not. While the girls' increase in heart rate would be expected in an angry, emotional exchange, their mothers' slower heart rate in the conflict is not what would be expected. Lattimore (2000a) suggests that it might be accounted for if the mothers felt worn down by their interactions with their daughters, and were responding by emotionally withdrawing and not allowing themselves to become upset. On the other hand it is not clear why this might not have been equally true of the mothers of the other young psychiatric patients.

Minuchin (1978) assumed that the reason for the conflict avoidance in the situation with parents and daughters was that in the triad of mother, father and daughter, detouring through the daughter regulated her parents' conflicts. From that point of view the results of the Lattimore study are not at variance with those of Minuchin et al (1978), Kog and Vandereycken (1989), Latzer and Gaber (1998) and Blair et al (1995), since detouring of conflict arising in the parents' relationship could not have occurred in the two-person situation between mother and daughter.

Observational studies: enmeshment, over-protection, rigidity and failure to resolve conflict

From an early stage it proved difficult for researchers to achieve operational definitions of these four central components of the Psychosomatic Family Model. Kog et al (1985) argued that the concepts overlapped with each other and that Minuchin's Model, Minuchin

(1978) could be reduced to three dimensions: the degree of intrafamilial boundaries, family adaptability, and the families' style of handling conflicts. Kog et al (1987) attempted to validate a number of constructs they had derived from the Psychosomatic Family Model in an experiment in which fifty-three families with a daughter with an eating disorder took part. They used three different kinds of approaches to measuring these constructs. These were observer ratings of family interaction in experimental tasks, behavioural indices derived from family tasks, and a self-report questionnaire. They argued that they could demonstrate a degree of validity for three constructs, conflict, boundaries, and adaptability, using indices derived in one way or another from the family tasks. The term "adaptability" was applied to a construct that had to do with the degree of variability in coalition formation, and in the affective atmosphere of the family. The term "boundaries" was used for a concept that represented the degree of differentiation between subsystems, or the degree of individuation versus coordination of family members' behaviour and attitudes. The self-report questionnaire failed to discriminate the three constructs because family members' self-reports converged into a single evaluative dimension. This seems to have been more influenced by the families' perceptions of levels of conflict than by the other dimensions. The family evaluative dimension was one that placed a warm, supportive relationship at one pole, and conflict and lack of support at the other. Kog and Vandereycken (1989) applied the research methods that had been developed in the Kog et al (1987) study to the comparison of thirty families with daughters with severe eating disorders, ten with a daughter with each condition, AN-R, AN-BN and Bulimia, and a comparison group of thirty families with daughters free of eating disorders. However, behavioural measures that had been designed to measure the same construct showed little relationship with one another, except for the behavioural measures of conflict. As in their previous study there was considerable overlap between the three self-report measures, which should have been independent of one another. The study did not provide impressive support for the Psychosomatic Family Model as a whole, but did confirm that the families with daughters with eating disorders tended to avoid conflict. Kog and Vandereycken (1989) concluded that the small group of patients with bulimia had a negative perception of their families' interaction, while the patients with anorexia generally saw their families in a positive light as cohesive and non-conflictual. Kog and Vandereycken

(1989) noted that the families of patients with anorexia, and the patients themselves, valued that cohesiveness and lack of conflict. They did not see it as a problem for them.

* * *

In another attempt to test concepts drawn from the Psychosomatic Family Model, Blair et al (1995) made ratings of observed "enmeshment" and "weak boundaries" across three groups of families, families with daughters with anorexia, families with young people with cystic fibrosis, and families with young people with no illness. Families with daughters with anorexia were considered to demonstrate higher levels of enmeshment, but not more problems reflecting weak boundaries.

Wallin and Hansson (1999) researched the quality of family interaction in the families of adolescent girls, average age fifteen years, presenting for treatment typically only six months after the onset of anorexia. The research material was collected before treatment was started, and would not have been influenced by the families' experience of accommodating to a daughter with anorexia over a long period of time, or by their experience of treatment. Ratings were made using five dimensions describing the level of: adaptability, cohesion, hierarchical organisation, competence and style. The data was compared to similar ratings of family interaction in the families of children who had no clinical problems. Significant differences were found on all scales except adaptability. According to Wallin and Hansson (1999) most families with daughters with anorexia were seen as being "enmeshed", generally having weak boundaries between the generations and being more dysfunctional than the comparison families. Of all the studies this is the one whose findings are most favourable to the Psychosomatic Family Model. Nevertheless, Wallin and Hansson (1999) observed that there was a range of patterns in the families and they concluded that it could not be argued that all the families with daughters with anorexia fitted the Psychosomatic Family Model. The main weakness of this study is that the comparison families had children with an average age of eight years. The observed differences could conceivably be accounted for by the age difference and not by the anorexia.

Studies using Benjamin's Structural Analysis of Social Behaviour

Another approach to the study of the association of qualities of family interactions and eating disorders uses Benjamin's Structural Analysis of Social Behaviour. This is a coding system allowing analysis of communication between two people. Humphrey et al (1986a) described the use of this system in a study that compared the families of girls with anorexia with bulimic symptoms (AN-BN) with comparison families who had daughters of similar age and who presented no psychological problems. In another study, Humphrey (1989) used the system to compare and contrast the families of girls with restricting anorexia (AN-R), girls with AN-BN, those with bulimia (BN), and non-clinical comparison families. Seventy-four families took part in the study by Humphrey (1989). Of these sixteen had a daughter with AN-R, sixteen had daughters with (BN), eighteen had AN-BN, while eighteen families of students and school-girls without a psychiatric disorder constituted the non-clinical comparison group. The girls with eating disorders were recruited through a hospital based treatment programme where they were described as "new to treatment or hospitalisation", but no information was given about the duration of illness prior to their participation. The girl and her parents took part in an experimental task which was video recorded. First they talked together about the girls' separation from the family arising from her admission, and then they talked for ten minutes following the prompt "Daughter has been withdrawn, and keeping a lot to herself, lately. She doesn't really want to talk to anyone in the family. The parents want to find out what is going on", Humphrey (1989, p. 208). Trained coders coded first typed transcripts of the content, and then re-coded while watching video of the conversation to code the process. Coders were blind to the diagnostic category or control status of the family.

Humphrey found that there were significant differences in the patterns of communication between the eating disorder families and the controls, as well as differences between the eating disorder groups themselves. These differences were not accounted for by the content of the discussions, but by the process.

In relation to their daughters the mothers of girls with AN-R were more nurturing and comforting than mothers of controls, but also more ignoring and neglecting than the mothers of the other eating disordered patients and the controls. They communicated less assertion and separation in relation to their daughters. Like the mothers, the fathers of girls with AN-R were both more nurturing and comforting and more ignoring and neglecting to their daughters than, in this instance, the fathers of girls with bulimia and of controls. The fathers of all three eating disorder groups showed both more "watching and managing" but also more "belittling and blaming".

The daughters with AN-R were more "deferring and submitting" in relation to both parents than any other group of daughters, but like all the daughters with eating disorders were more "sulking and appeasing" towards their fathers than were the control daughters.

In the families of patients with bulimia, mothers were more "belittling and blaming" towards their daughters, and also more "sulking and appeasing", and "belittling and blaming" was reciprocated in the relationship of daughter to mother.

Compared to all the eating disorder families the control families displayed a number of positive communication themes to a significantly greater extent. The cluster "help and protect" was more common for all relationships, "approach and enjoy" was more common for mother–daughter dyads and "trust and rely" more common in daughters' communications to both mothers and fathers, and in fathers communications to daughters.

* * *

Humphrey (1989) also noted that all the eating disordered patients parents scored higher on the cluster "affirm and understand", which at first sight appeared a very healthy sign, but that further analysis indicated that these communications were far more likely to be parts of complex, ambiguous, communications. This being so she thought this did not represent healthy communication.

Complex codes, indicating statements that were ambiguous and coded as expressing two clusters simultaneously, were more common in the families of girls with eating disorders than in the comparison families. They were a significant issue in the relationships between daughters with eating disorders and their fathers. Differences did not achieve statistical significance for the relationship between mothers and daughters. Fathers in all the eating disorder families were more likely to use complex messages combining "nurturing and comforting" with "watching and managing"; "helping and protecting" with "ignoring and neglecting"; and "watching and managing" with "ignoring and protecting". For this last combination the fathers of girls with AN-R had significantly higher levels than all other groups. The fathers of girls with bulimia used more complex communications to their daughters combining "affirming and understanding" with "watching and managing" than comparison fathers, but fathers of girls with anorexia did not. Daughters with restricting anorexia communicated more complex statements combining "disclosing and expressing" with "deferring and submitting" than daughters in all other groups, but all the eating disordered patients combined "asserting and separating" with "sulking and appeasing", more than the controls.

In all the comparisons made in the study the combined anorexia/bulimia group AN-BN was never found to be significantly different from the AN-R or BN groups, and these patients, and their families, seemed to show communication patterns midway between those associated with restricting anorexia on the one hand, and with bulimia on the other.

Humphrey (1989) summarised these findings by saying that the parents of patients with anorexia were found to be both too nurturing and too neglectful, which she took to confirm clinical impressions that these families were often nurturing in a way that undermined the daughters ability to individuate, while at the same time ignoring and negating her self-expressions and developmental needs. The daughter with anorexia was seen by Humphrey to mirror this situation in her communications, in that, "she cannot seem to disclose her true self and feelings without also submitting to her parents' opinions and expectations. It may well be that this pattern of parental control and negation of the anorexic's true, separate self leads to the development of her 'false self' and to her restrictive and destructive attitudes towards her body", Humphrey (1989, p. 213). By contrast there was a much more open conflict, involving sulkiness and mutual blaming in the relationship between women with bulimia and their mothers, and their efforts to separate were undermined by their hostile submission. She also observed that this picture differs from the picture that the families of patients with anorexia themselves communicate, which she characterised as an idealised version of family relationships, in which the families present a picture of "perfection and psychological health while underneath the facade are many unacknowledged needs and problems", Humphrey (1989, p. 213).

Humphrey (1989) regarded her findings as consistent with theories about the relationship between family dynamics and anorexia, including the Psychosomatic Family Model. However, it is not really clear how these observations relate to the Psychosomatic Family Model. They do seem to indicate that the families have more difficulty with closeness and with conflict than other families, and that the girls with anorexia had difficulty asserting themselves with their parents, especially with their fathers.

Studies of Expressed Emotion

Studies of Expressed Emotion (EE) have usually been focused on the impact of the quality of family relationships on the outcome from treatment. Most of these studies have not had comparison groups of families with a well adolescent. However, observations made by researchers using this approach have sometimes influenced the debate about anorexia and the family. Hodes et al (1999) noted that the study of EE had its origins in studies of family relationships and relapse in schizophrenia. The studies had their origin in concern with ways in which families' responses to psychiatric illness might have the effect of making the patient's prognosis better or worse. Studies collected data from information with family members individually or in family sessions. The interview and associated ratings yielded five measures, two of these, Critical Comments (CC), and Positive Remarks (PR), were based on frequency scores, while three, Emotional Over-Involvement (EOI), Warmth (W) and Hostility (H) were global ratings.

Early research on EE demonstrated its predictive validity in relation to relapse in the treatment of schizophrenia. Subsequently it was applied to the study of a wide range of other problems, including eating disorders. Hodes et al (1999) described the process by which the EE ratings were made. The study demonstrated that two quite different ways of obtaining interview material nevertheless achieved broadly similar results. The first, the Camberwell Family Interview, was the format described by Vaughan and Leff (1976) and used in studies of schizophrenia. In this approach, one member of the family was interviewed and the focus was on the presenting problem and how the family was dealing with it. In the second, the parents and children were interviewed together using the Standardised Clinical Family Interview (Kinston & Loader, 1984), and the focus was primarily on the question "What are you like as a family?" and not on the presenting problem. This second approach was adopted in the UK based studies of eating disorders (Le Grange et al, 1992a, 1992b; Eisler et al, 2000).

It is clearly the case that the level of critical remarks demonstrated by the parents of adolescents with anorexia, in all studies, was lower than that demonstrated by families of schizophrenic patients. This is sometimes taken as corroboration of the idea that the families of patients with anorexia are "conflict avoiding" or even that the family patterns demonstrate a low level of relationship problems. Le Grange (1992b) who reported the lowest levels of parental criticism in any of the studies of anorexia up to that point argued that "The families in this study can be described as generally having a low-key pattern of affective expression and a muted response style (low levels of EE)", Le Grange (1992b, p. 186). Dare et al (1994) also argued from the low levels of EE, that the families of patients with anorexia were generally unexpressive and conflict avoiding. However, clinical experience had led them to think that there was also a subgroup of families in this population who were in a state of constant, unresolved conflict. They thought this group of families was more difficult to engage and to help in the treatment of a daughter with anorexia or bulimia. This they associated with these families' higher levels of guilt and blame.

Hodes (1999) compared the levels of EE demonstrated in his study with ratings made in other studies and with other groups of patients. He observed that Vostanis et al (1994) measured EE in the parents of three groups of children, children with Conduct Disorders, children with Emotional Disorders, and non-clinical controls. Hodes (1999) argued that the parents of adolescents with anorexia fell in the mid-range of the levels reported in the study by Vostanis et al (1994). Hence they could not be seen as indicating exceptionally low levels of criticism. Since Vostanis et al (1994) found the level of critical remarks in control families to be intermediate between the level found in families with a child with conduct disorder (relatively high) and children with emotional disorder (relatively low) it would be hard to draw conclusions about the absolute level which would indicate healthy family functioning. To compound this difficulty, a study by Asarnow et al (1994) found high levels of EE associated with depression in children, which is an internalising disorder. The families of depressed children had high levels of EE, especially critical remarks, when compared both to control families whose children were problem free, and equivalent age children who had been diagnosed as having schizophrenia. This was even more the case when the children had both depression and behavioural problems. It is difficult to draw conclusions about how families compare, simply from the levels of EE or CC. In the Vostanis et al (1994) study the comparison families, whose children did not present behavioural or emotional disorders, were distinguished from clinical families by their higher levels of warmth and positive remarks.

It is perhaps worth adding here that one should be wary of equating CC with conflict. Criticism does not lead to conflict unless it is reciprocated or argued about. Blair (1995) found no relationship between ratings of levels of CC and a self-report measure of family conflict.

Questionnaire studies comparing clinical populations with comparison groups

Twenty-nine self-report studies have used questionnaire measures of qualities of family interaction and compare the families of patients with anorexia with non-clinical comparison families, or, in a few instances, with normative data. Some studies obtain data from both patient and parents, but many have only collected patients' reports.

Studies using the Family Environment Scales

Nine studies use the Family Environment Scales (FES) Moos and Moos (1980). Humphrey (1986) compared the families of girls, average age eighteen years with AN-BN, and the families of girls with Bulimia, with those of girls with no disorder. She used two questionnaires, the FES, and the Family Adaptability and Cohesion Evaluation Scale (FACES) developed by Olson et al (1978). Parents and daughters reported the family characteristics in much the same terms. Humphrey concluded that the family members of the AN-BN girls experienced more isolation, detachment and conflict, and less involvement and support, than family members in the comparison families. Parents of girls with bulimia reported more family conflict, but their daughters did not.

Stern et al (1989) compared the families of girls with AN-R, AN-BN and Bulimia, with the families of age matched controls. All the eating disorder patients' families reported low levels of expressiveness. This was described as the extent to which family members are able to act openly and to express their feelings directly. On "cohesion", a measure of the level of concern, commitment and supportiveness between family members, patients with AN-BN and Bulimia rated their families as less cohesive, compared to controls, but girls with AN-R did not.

Strauss and Ryan (1987) compared patients with AN-R with those with AN-BN and with controls. Both the anorexia subgroups reported low levels of expressiveness, and both reported less family cohesion. The AN-R group reported more problems with conflict in the family, compared to the comparison group, but the AN-BN patients did not.

Shisslak et al (1990) compared twenty-four patients with bulimia and thirteen with AN-BN with a comparison group of young women. The patients were young adults with several years' history of eating disorder. No information was collected from parents. Women with AN-BN reported their families as low in cohesion and expression, high in conflict and discouraging of autonomy. In another questionnaire, the Family Dynamic Survey, they reported a low level of closeness in their families, a lack of emotional support, and a poor quality of family communication.

Hodges et al (1998) found that low levels of family cohesion and expressiveness, were reported by the AN-BN and BN subgroups, while AN-R reported only low expressiveness.

Latzer et al (2002) compared patients with anorexia, bulimia and non-clinical comparison subjects on the FES. Both eating disorder groups scored their families lower on cohesiveness and expressiveness.

Laliberte et al (1999) used the FES and developed additional Family Climate scales to measure "Family Achievement Emphasis", "Family Social Appearance Orientation", and "Family Body Satisfaction". They regarded these three additional scales as providing a measure of the "Family Climate for Eating Disorders". They also measures of eating symptoms and of self-esteem. Subjects were 324 female students and 121 of their mothers. The additional Family Climate measures were found to be independent of the general FES Scales. The measures were then used again in the second wave of the study to compare patients with AN-BN or bulimia with a comparison group of women who scored low on a measure of eating disorder concerns, and another comparison group of patients with depression. They found that the family climate measures had a more specific relationship to eating disorders than the FES measures of cohesiveness, adaptability and conflict, which were associated with depression as well as with eating disorders.

* * *

Some studies using the FES did not find differences between families with a daughter with anorexia and those with a well daughter. Thienemann and Steiner (1993) found differences between the FES subscale results of different eating disorder subgroups only on the Independence subscale, compared to the normative data.

Sim et al (2009) used three subscales of the FES: cohesiveness, expressiveness and conflict, with the mothers of twenty-five girls with anorexia, but not with the fathers or the patients. They compared the results with those of mothers of girls with diabetes, and a well comparison group. There were no significant differences between groups on cohesion or expressiveness, but the mothers of daughters with anorexia reported high levels of family conflict and lower levels of cooperation with their partners in managing their relationship with their daughters. The mothers of girls with anorexia were also more depressed.

* * *

Overall, eight of nine studies using the FES with clinical populations found some significant difference between the families of women with anorexia and comparison families. However, only three of the studies included patients with AN-R, and one of these found no difference for that group. The main finding was that the patients with anorexia reported low levels of expressiveness and of cohesion in their families. This finding was completely consistent for patients with AN-BN. Families of patients with AN-BN, and of those with Bulimia, also reported more overt conflict.

Studies using the Family Assessment Device

The Family Assessment Device (FAD), Epstein et al (1983) is a questionnaire that produces measures of the family Problem Solving, Communication, Roles, Affective Responsiveness, Affective Involvement, Behaviour Control and General Functioning. Steiger et al (1991) noted that there has been a historical tendency to associate diagnostic subgroups of eating disorder with different family characteristics. For example AN-R has been associated with "well-meaning enmeshment" whereas bingeing has been associated with "hostile-interdependency". He noted that an association has also been suspected between the different diagnostic groups and different personality disorders. AN-R has been seen as associated with anxious-fearful personality disorders, and Bulimia and AN-BN with "dramatic-erratic" personality disorders, including borderline personality disorder. Steiger et al (1991) compared four eating disorder subgroups with a comparison group of women without eating disorders. The patients were twenty with AN-R, twelve AN-BN, twelve who had bulimia and had had anorexia in the past, and eleven who simply had bulimia. The patients were mostly in their mid to late twenties, so many would have had relatively long histories of eating disorder. There were twenty-four comparison women. All the eating disorder subgroups reported more difficulties in family functioning on the General Functioning, and the Problem Solving, Communication, and Affective Responsiveness Scales. They found no relationship between eating disorder subgroups and different types of personality disorders.

Waller et al (1990a) found that adult women with both anorexia and bulimia reported family difficulties on all six subscales of the FAD, while their parents did not. It was the daughters' perception of family functioning that differentiated the clinical families from the comparison families, whereas parents' perceptions did not. They argued that the daughters' perceptions were the more valid because they were related to the existence of the eating disorder.

North et al (1995) compared thirty-one girls with anorexia, and four boys, and their mothers, with two comparison groups. These were: age-matched girls with other psychiatric disorders and their mothers, and aged matched girls without disorder and their mothers. The girls in the two clinical groups were patients referred to a Regional Adolescent Unit and the research procedures were completed usually within three weeks of their initial assessment. The average age of the patients with anorexia was fourteen years nine months. Measures were the FAD and ratings of family functioning derived from a clinical interview, the McMaster Structured Interview of Family Functioning (MCSIFF), Bishop et al (1987). The interview and the FAD produced ratings of comparable aspects of family functioning. The FAD ratings provided by the girls with anorexia, and their mothers, were very similar to those provided by the problem free comparison group, and generally significantly lower than the comparison group of young people with other disorders, and their mothers. This would have been a negative finding, had the analysis of results ended there. However, North then divided the anorexia group into two on the basis that some patients had purging behaviour (self-induced vomiting) while others did not. The scores on the FAD now appeared in a very different light. The purging subgroup, both mothers and daughters, reported more family problems than the restrictors and their mothers. The purging group, and their mothers, scored in or above the range of the young people with other disorders, while the restrictors and their mothers scored below the range of the problem free comparison group. In other words the restricting patients and their mothers reported the families as having fewer family relationship problems than the non-clinical controls, while the purgers reported their families as having slightly more family problems than the comparison group of families with girls with other psychiatric problems. For this reason the anorexia group as a whole scored like the problem free group, because the subgroup differences cancelled each other out. North (1995) noted that the MCSIFF ratings derived from interviews correlated closely with the adolescent patients FAD scores, and less closely with those of the mothers. However, the MCSIFF ratings classified the families in the clinical range according to norms, implying that although the clinicians agreed in many ways with the self-reports, especially by patients, yet they saw the family functioning in a more serious light than the patients and their mothers did.

McDermott et al (2002) used a short form of the FAD with children and adolescents in the age range nine to eighteen years, and their parents, during their initial assessment at an eating disorder clinic. More than half had anorexia and the remaining participants had subclinical eating disorders or bulimia. Both groups reported more family relationship difficulties than the community norms.

* * *

In summary, three studies using the FAD found significant differences between the patients' families and the comparison families, at least from the point of view of the patient. Findings from the study by North et al (1995) are more complex and more interesting. None of these studies justify the view that there are no differences between the family of the patient with anorexia and non-clinical comparison families.

Questionnaire studies of family structure

A number of studies have attempted to test family theories of anorexia relating to family structure. The question at issue is whether families report "enmeshment" and reversals of family hierarchy in which the younger generation are burdened with meeting the needs of the parents, an inverted parental hierarchy.

Studies using FACES

Seven studies have used the Family Adaptability and Cohesion Evaluation Scale (FACES), Olson et al (1978), and the later versions,

FACES II and FACES III, Olson et al (1985). These questionnaires are measures of the family's perceived "cohesion", a dimension of separateness versus connection, and of their "adaptability", that is their ability to change to meet changing circumstances.

Waller et al (1990b) compared a mixed group of patients with major eating disorders, of whom thirty-three out of forty-one had a history of anorexia, with a comparison group of women, using FACES II. The eating disorder group reported lower family cohesion and lower family adaptability scores than the comparison women.

Rastam and Gillberg (1991) used a Swedish language version of FACES III with mothers, but not fathers or daughters, to compare families with and without a teenage daughter with anorexia. Overall, the questionnaire results did not distinguish between groups. Although there were significant differences on some items of the questionnaire they did not consistently tend to suggest that the families of daughters with anorexia were more cohesive or less adaptable. Drawing information from the FACES data and an in-depth interview with the mother they noted that the families did not seem to conform to the Psychosomatic Family Model. Instead they tended to have the same kinds of family problems generally associated with other mental disturbances in the younger generation. Families with daughters with anorexia were more likely to have divorced or separated parents. They more often had major family problems, such as those arising when one parent has drug or alcohol problems, were more common in the families of girlswith anorexia. These difficulties predated the patients' anorexia and did not seem to be a response to it. Mothers of girls with anorexia reported more disagreements between parents about parenting, and more overly strict discipline. Rastam and Gillberg (1991) commented that this pattern of difficulties did not fit with common clinical perceptions that girls with anorexia usually came from "intact" families with successful and high-functioning parents. A possible explanation for this is that the patient population was unusual in having been recruited as a result of an assertive screening study in one Swedish city. This was thought to have identified all the cases in the target age group. The implication could be that girls with anorexia whose families have such problems do not always get referred to treatment centres. Those who do get referred may not represent the whole population of girls with anorexia.

Cunha et al (2009) used FACES II and other questionnaires to compare a group of thirty-four patients with anorexia (twenty-eight AN-R, six AN-BN), with thirty-four comparison girls and young women.

The age range of both groups was thirteen to twenty-three years. No information was collected from parents. They found that patients with anorexia reported lower levels of family cohesion than controls.

Using the same measure Vidovic et al (2005), found that patients with eating disorders saw their families as less cohesive and less adaptable than controls, but the subgroup of patients with restricting anorexia did not report this.

Cook-Darzens et al (2005) used FACES III and compared the families of forty-two patients with anorexia aged twelve to nineteen, with a comparison group of families with adolescents in the same age range. Patients, parents and siblings completed the FACES III questionnaire. Patients with anorexia and their families reported lower cohesion, and this was especially the case for the patients' siblings. Overall there was no difference between the families on the adaptability dimension. Cook-Darzens et al (2005) also noted that the families of patients with anorexia were more dissatisfied with the level of closeness in the family than the comparison families.

Dare et al (1994) used FACES III with the families of a mixed group of eighteen adolescent girls with anorexia and eight with bulimia, but there was no comparison group of families with symptom free daughters. There was a wide range of different scores by family members. The patients tended to report the family as less cohesive than the parents did. This was not what they found most interesting. They had also asked the family members to score the questionnaire to indicate how they would like the family to be. By comparing the scores on the family as it was with the scores of how they would like it to be it was possible to obtain an index of satisfaction or dissatisfaction with the family functioning. In this respect the family members showed a marked degree of similarity, with most fathers, mothers and daughters with anorexia reporting a sense of being isolated and excessively constrained. Ratings of EE had been made from initial interviews. Members of low EE families saw the family as closer and more adaptable than did members of high EE families. Parents who were more critical of their daughter were also the most dissatisfied with the level of closeness in the family.

* * *

In all five studies using the FACES with the patient herself the patient reported low cohesion, although that did not hold for patients with AN-R in one study. There was no comparison group in the Dare et al

(1994) study, but the patients seem to have reported lower cohesion than their parents did.

Studies using the Parent–Child Boundaries Scale

Barber and Buehler (1996) argued that enmeshment has sometimes been seen as an extreme form of family cohesion. This had often led to conceptual difficulties in that some measures, for example the FACES measures, were based on the assumption that "closeness" can be seen as a single variable. Very low and very high levels can be seen as unhealthy, while mid-range levels would be healthy. By contrast they thought that some other measures, such as the cohesion scale of the Family Environment Scales were simply measures of supportive family interaction. They argued that cohesion should be seen as supportive interaction in the family. By contrast, enmeshment is an unhelpful, intrusive aspect of relationships. It could be compared to the concept of "parental psychological control" in the literature on parenting. Understood in this way, enmeshment as parental psychological control, would be seen as a quality of relationship that impedes the development of autonomy in the adolescent. By contrast, cohesion is a supportive relationship but one that is consistent with the adolescents' need to be free to have and express her own thoughts and feelings. Barber and Buehler (1996) demonstrated that cohesion was correlated with low levels of internalising disorders (not eating disorders), while enmeshment was correlated with high levels, in a group of early to mid-adolescents.

Kerig and Brown (1996), responding to this argument, produced the Parent–Child Boundary Scale (PBS). This scale is focused entirely on the intrusive, parental psychological control aspect of closeness, not on the aspect of warmth and support. Rowa et al (2001) used this scale with a group of women with anorexia and their parents, and a comparison group of young women and their parents. The PBS yielded measures of five subscales: "enmeshment", that is, a lack of individuation between parent and child; "role-reversal/care giving", that is parental dependency on the child in a way which is not age appropriate for the child; "role-reversal/confidante", in which the parent uses the child as a confidante; "intrusiveness", which is to say over-control and "hostile-spousification", which is the transfer of negative feelings by a parent from the other parent to the child. They also used the FACES III and predicted there would be no relationship between the two measures.

The women with anorexia reported boundary problems to a much greater extent than the comparison women. This was much more the case with regard to the patients' relationships with fathers than with mothers. With both parents the patient reported role-reversal in that she felt herself to be in the role of the parents' carer, but not in the sense of being their confidante. Women with anorexia experienced their fathers as intrusive, and felt themselves to be on the receiving end of paternal hostility redirected from the marital relationship, but did not have the same experience of their mothers. However, the women with anorexia did report "enmeshment", which in this context means a lack of differentiation, with both parents. The parents, on the other hand, did not report any of these things. As expected there was no relationship between the PBS and FACES-III, confirming that the argument of Barber and Buehler (1996) holds true for the families of patients with anorexia.

Family system implicit rules about emotional expression

Systems theory sees families as organised by systems of implicit rules that govern emotional expression. Gillett et al (2009) compared the families of patients with eating disorders with matched comparison families with a daughter who had no mental illness. They used a questionnaire called the Family Implicit Rules Profile, Harper et al (2007). This provided a measure of the families' use of constraining rules or facilitative rules. Constraining rules include such items as "Don't feel or talk about feelings" and "Don't identify, talk about, or solve problems". Facilitating rules include items such as "Share your feelings" or "Be affectionate". Taken together these measures of facilitating and constraining rules can be seen as a measure of the extent to which the families act as if they have a "meta-emotion" philosophy. The study confirmed the expectation that the families of patients with anorexia would report fewer facilitative rules and more constraining rules than did the comparison families. The report of the patients themselves presented a more negative picture of the families' rules than parents and siblings reported.

Other questionnaire studies of family relationships

Garfinkel et al (1983) compared the families of girls with anorexia with a comparison group of families of girls who were well using the Family

Assessment Measure (FAM) by Skinner et al (1983). Fathers, mothers and daughters completed this measure as well as questionnaires measuring eating disorder symptoms and various personality measures. Mothers and daughters, but not fathers, reported more family problems on various subscales of the FAM. Parents did not score higher than comparison parents on various measures of their own individual psychopathology.

Casper and Troiani (2001) used the FAM with seventeen adolescent girls with anorexia and their parents, and non-clinical comparison families. Patients with AN-BN and their mothers reported more difficulties in family functioning than controls, but patients with AN-R did not.

Harding and Lachenmayer (1986) did not find any difference between groups when comparing patients with anorexia with a student comparison group using a questionnaire designed for the study to tap the constructs of the Psychosomatic Family Model.

Waller and Hartley (1994) developed the Parental Style Questionnaire as a measure of parental approval or disapproval of behaviour, and of parental expectations, distinguishing parents with high and low standards for behaviour and achievement. They used this questionnaire with a large group of female students, and with thirty-three women with anorexia and fifty-nine with bulimia. Both groups of patients reported feeling disapproval from both mothers and fathers, and the more they felt this, the lower their self-esteem and the more severe the eating disorder.

Blair (1996) and Blair et al (1995) developed the Edinburgh Family Scale, which was another measure designed to test the concepts of the psychosomatic model. It yielded measures of enmeshment, conflict and rigidity. They used it in a study comparing the families of adolescents and young adults with anorexia, with the families of young patients with cystic fibrosis, and of young people who were well. No significant differences were found between the families of the patients with anorexia and those of the well comparison group using this measure.

Szabo et al (1999) used the Family Relations Scale (FRS), Barbarin (1992), with two small groups of families, ten with a daughter with anorexia, seven with a daughter with bulimia, and twenty comparison families. The FRS yields measures of differentiation, the similarity or difference between family members feelings and attitudes, family support, flexibility, boundary maintenance (in relation to the social world outside the family), and family hierarchy (the existence of an authority structure providing leadership and setting limits). In addition they had a measure of family idealisation. Families with daughters with anorexia reported less family hierarchy and idealisation, and more rigid boundaries with the social world, than did the comparison families.

Wallin and Hansson (1999), in the same study described previously collected questionnaire data from the parents and daughters with anorexia, and from the comparison families. They used two questionnaires, the Family Relations Scale and the Family Climate Scale. The Family Relations Scale is a Swedish language scale developed originally from FACES III but now substantially different according to their account. They used two of its subscales, measuring Chaos and Cohesion. High scores indicate dysfunction, so Cohesion on this measure presumably meant intrusiveness rather than support. Both mothers and fathers of patients with anorexia reported higher levels of cohesion than did the parents of non-clinical comparison families. The patients with anorexia did not. The patients with anorexia and their fathers rated their families lower on Chaos, but mothers did not. It is unclear what this means. On the Family Climate Scale mothers reported lower levels of closeness (which on this measure means supportiveness) but fathers and daughters with anorexia did not. On this measure the patients reported higher levels of Chaos (which on this measure meant confusion and instability), while parents did not. In all, seven of the twelve pairs of comparisons of variables between the patient and her parents and the comparison families, yielded statistically significant differences, but these findings are hard to interpret.

Guttman and Laporte (2002) used the Self-Report Family Inventory (Beavers & Hampson, 1990) and the Parental Bonding Instrument, in a study of women with anorexia and their parents. The patients with anorexia and their parents reported family functioning in much the same way that non-clinical comparison families did, except that there was a much higher level of agreement between parents, and a higher level of agreement between each parent and their daughter, than could be demonstrated in the comparison families. The families of the women with anorexia agreed with one another about the description of the family to an abnormal degree, compared to the families of women with borderline personality disorder and the families of non-clinical comparison women. The only exception was that the women with anorexia differed from their fathers in their reports of family conflict.

Karwautz et al (2003) used another approach to studying families, the Subjective Family Image Test. This was completed by thirty-one adolescent patients with anorexia and by a sister who had no eating disorder. The patients saw themselves as having less autonomy in relation to both parents, but especially in relation to their mothers, than did their sisters.

Community studies of the family and eating disorder

Community studies address the question of the relationship between family relationships and the development of eating disorders in community populations, typically of teenage girls and young adult students. In these studies eating disorders, eating psychopathology or eating concerns are identified using questionnaire measures. The severity of these disorders and concerns is usually much less than that found in clinical populations referred for treatment of eating disorders. The studies are important because we should expect to see continuity. The family factors that give rise to major eating disorders would be expected to be present, probably in a less extreme form, in the families of young people with less severe eating disorders and eating concerns.

Brookings and Wilson (1994) used the FES and two measures of eating disorders symptoms and related psychopathology, the Eating Disorders Inventory (EDI), and the Eating Attitude Test (EAT), Garner et al (1982) with a group of female college students. High conflict on the FES was associated with all the measures of eating disorder symptoms and associated pathology. Low cohesion on the FES was associated with the EDI subscale "Drive for Thinness", while expressiveness was not. Low cohesion and low expressiveness were associated with four sub-scales of the EDI that measure psychopathology commonly occurring with eating disorders, measures of ineffectiveness (a sense of powerlessness about one's own life), perfectionism, interpersonal distrust, and interoceptive awareness (difficulty understanding one's own feelings). They argued that family relationship factors were more likely to contribute to the development of general psychopathology than to the development of eating disorders as such.

Leung et al (1996) used the subscales of family cohesion and adaptability from FACES III as measures of family relationship difficulties, and rating scales as measures of family attitudes to weight and appearance. Subjects were 918 students, aged twelve to seventeen years, and their parents. Leung et al argued that there were both direct effects and indirect effects of family relationships on the development of eating disorder concerns. Direct effects reflected family attitudes to eating and weight, and indirect effects via the impact of the family attitudes on daughters' self-esteem. Family dysfunction had indirect effects, through its effect on self-esteem, and this indirect effect lead to an increase in general psychiatric symptoms, including, but not only, to eating disorder symptoms.

Kent et al (1999) in a questionnaire study of female psychology and nursing students found that eating psychopathology in general was associated with abuse and neglect in childhood. The strongest association was with emotional abuse. Their data analysis indicated that it was the impact of emotional abuse on the development of depression, anxiety and or dissociation that led ultimately to the development of eating psychopathology.

A small study by Ogden and Steward (2000) found that teenage girls and mother's reports of the mother–daughter relationship were predictive of the daughter's levels of body dissatisfaction and restrained eating. They found that the daughter was more likely to be dissatisfied with her body and to diet if the mother had a low level of belief in her own autonomy, and if both mother and daughter reported a lack of clear boundaries in their relationship. Another small study, Byely et al (2000) found that girls who reported negative family relationships in early adolescence were more likely to engage in problematic dieting one year later.

Questionnaire studies of parenting

Questionnaire studies of family relationships enquire about family relationships in general. Questions will say something like "In our family we …". By contrast questionnaire studies of parenting are usually focused specifically on the younger generations account of their parent's relationship with them. A large group of questionnaire studies are focused on parenting, rather than on family interaction as a whole.

Parenting and eating disorders in clinical populations

Numerous studies compare retrospective accounts of their parents by patients with anorexia, collected using questionnaires such as the Parental Bonding Instrument (PBI) Parker et al (1979), with accounts given by women without eating disorders. The PBI is a short questionnaire which was designed to measure two dimensions of parenting behaviour, High Care *vs.* Low Care, which contrasts warmth and affection with coldness and rejection, and Low Protection *vs.* High Protection, where low protection implies support for autonomous behaviour, while high protection indicates the opposite and is often referred to as over-protection. Tetley et al (2014) concluded from a systematic review of twenty-four studies of parental bonding in clinical populations of people with eating disorders, that eating disorders are associated with low parental care, and high parental protection, but not necessarily more so than is the case for other people with psychiatric disorders. Thirteen of the studies compared the reports of people with anorexia using the PBI with a comparison group of well women. Roughly half of these studies found lower levels of maternal and paternal care in this population, and roughly one third found higher levels of maternal and paternal over-protection. There was a tendency for these findings to be stronger in better designed studies.

Parenting and eating disorders in community studies

Community studies focus on the relationship between eating disorder concerns reported in non-clinical populations and reports of parenting. A number of studies, Turner et al (2005), Perry et al (2008), Cella et al (2014), demonstrate links between reported poor parental care and low levels of self-esteem, or psychological schemas associated with eating disorders, and the eating disorders themselves. These studies are consistent with the expectation that poor parenting leads to a troubled sense of self, and that this in turn leads to eating disorder. For example, Tata et al (2001) found high parental protection on the PBI related to low body satisfaction in young men and women, and to high scores on a measure of eating disorder symptoms in the women. One study, Romans et al (2001), used the PBI in a study of the development of eating disorders in a group of women who had experienced sexual abuse before age 16. As expected there was a high level of eating disorders in the group. High levels of paternal control predicted eating disorders in general, while anorexic (restricting) symptoms were predicted by low maternal care.

There are also some negative findings in community studies. Furnham and Adam-Saib (2001) for example did not confirm the relationship between the PBI and scores on a measure of eating disorder symptoms in any one of a number of different ethnic groups of young people.

The parental marital relationship

Given the central position of this relationship in family theories, such as Minuchin et al (1978) it is surprising how little research specifically focuses on this. Sim (2009) found the mothers of patients with anorexia reported "reduced parental alliance" when compared with reports by comparison mothers whose daughters were well. Espina et al (2003) found poor marital adjustment in the parents of girls and young women with major eating disorders, and this still applied to the self report by the mothers, but not the fathers, after the effect of concurrent depression and anxiety were taken into account. Both Espina et al and Sim considered that these marital difficulties could reflect the burden on the family arising from the eating disorder.

Attachment studies

Attachment approaches to anorexia will be discussed in the next chapter. In the main they use a different approach to the study of relationships based neither on the observation of interaction, or self-report. Instead they depend on systematic clinical inference using material from structured interviews. Almost without exception these studies provide support for the notion that eating disorders arise from difficulties in early, and in adolescent relationships, with parents and carers.

Prospective studies of community samples

As we have seen it can be argued that the family pathology found in numerous studies may be accounted for by the patients' and the families' experience of the "illness". If these family relationship difficulties can be shown to have predated the onset of anorexia then that could not be the case. Because anorexia is a rare condition prospective studies are virtually impossible. However, there are some prospective studies of the development of eating disorder symptoms in relation to family relationships. For example, Calam and Waller (1998) found that mothers' reports of poor communication within the family when their daughters were twelve years old associated with their daughter's scores on measures of restrictive attitudes to eating, dieting and oral control, five years later.

Early relationships, life events and risk factors

Early life events prior to the onset of a disturbance like anorexia can be established retrospectively with a reasonable expectation that such information will be accurate. These provide information about relationships long before the onset of anorexia. Shoebridge and Gowers (2000) used information from interviews with the mothers of patients with anorexia, and obstetric records, and a comparison group of mothers of age matched girls, to test the theory that patients with anorexia had been raised in an atmosphere of "high concern" parenting. Mothers of patients with anorexia were very much more likely than the comparison mothers to have experienced a miscarriage, stillbirth, or cot death prior to the birth of the daughter who developed anorexia. They were also more likely to have engaged in exclusive child care, to report infant sleep difficulties in the patient, severe distress in the infant at first separation, and that their daughter first slept away from home at a later age. These reports are unlikely to have been shaped retrospectively as a result of the mothers' experience of their daughters' anorexia.

* * *

Research on risk factors often includes information about family background, family and marital conflict and the quality of parenting. Pike et al (2008) found a variety of risk factors for anorexia that were common to psychiatric disorders in general, but that family discord and higher parental demands were specific risk factors for anorexia. They argued that exposure to negative comments about shape and weight could be seen as triggering factors.

Horesh et al (1995) found increased levels of negative life events in the histories of adolescent girls with anorexia, and, specifically, more negative events affecting parents and other family members than were reported by psychiatric patients with different diagnoses. Rastam and Gillberg (1991) found more parental marital breakdown in the families of patients with anorexia, and more losses arising from deaths of fathers and siblings. By contrast Webster and Palmer (2000) did not find increased levels of negative life events in childhood and adolescence in the retrospective accounts of adult patients with anorexia.

Discussion of research findings

Differences between families with AN-R, AN-BN and daughters with bulimia

Some studies find differences between families with daughters with different eating disorders. The observational study by Humphrey et al (1989) demonstrated differences between family interaction in families with daughters with restricting anorexia and those with daughters with bulimia. The style of interaction in families with daughters with anorexia and who also had bulimic symptoms was midway between the two groups. The observational study by Kog and Vandereycken (1989) also demonstrated differences between these two groups of families. Some questionnaire studies, Stern et al (1989), North et al (1995), Casper and Troiani (2001) and Vidovic et al (2005) identify differences between AN-BN families and controls, but not between AN-R families and controls. However, other authors emphasise considerable similarities between the families of patientswith anorexia and bulimia. Some, such as Steiger et al (1991) and Erol et al (2007), found no difference between diagnostic subgroups. One possible way of making sense of these different findings would be that there is no difference in terms of the general family background factors reported by Stieger et al, and by Erol et al (both using the FAD), but there are differences between diagnostic groups regarding the expression of conflict and overt family mistreatment. The evidence is consistent with the possibility that the families of patients with AN-BN or bulimia express conflict and related family difficulties more openly than do the families of patients with AN-R, while the families of patients with AN-R are more idealising of family relationships.

Patients have more negative views of the family than parents and siblings

In some self-report studies for example, Waller et al (1990a), patients report family functioning in more negative terms than parents or siblings. Rowa et al (2001) found patients with anorexia reported more boundary problems in relationships with both their mothers and fathers than did comparison women, while the patients' mothers reported fewer boundary problems than comparison mothers.

Clinicians' views agree with patients' views

In the study by Gowers and North (1999) clinicians' and researchers' perceptions of family functioning were more like those of the daughters with anorexia than they were like the perceptions of their parents. That is to say, the clinicians, like the patients with anorexia, saw family functioning in a more critical light than parents did.

Patients' views change with treatment or stages of recovery

Patients' views may change systematically in line with their clinical state. Gowers and North (1999), North et al (1997) reported further information derived from the study reported by North et al (1995). Mothers and daughters completed the Family Assessment Device (FAD) again after one year, and then after two years. They found that patients' perceptions of family functioning were less positive after one year and less positive than mothers' perceptions, although there was some improvement in the patients' clinical condition. Gowers and North correlated the MCSIFF ratings of family functioning, and FAD data from mother and daughter, with clinical ratings derived from the Morgan-Russell, the ratings of Nutrition, Weight, Menstrual function, psychosexual adjustment, and social adjustment. Patients who were rated as functioning better in terms of psychosexual attitudes and nutrition, and to a lesser extent also in terms of menstrual functioning and weight, reported more family problems. There was also a slight tendency for the mothers of the girls who were less underweight and recovering menstrual functioning to report more family problems. This is consistent with the possibility that as the patient begins to recover she presents more challenges in the direction of autonomy, and this activates family difficulties that are not experienced by her or perceptible to her parents so long as anorexia continues.

Although Gowers and North (1999) found the patients' perceived family functioning in more critical terms at one-year follow-up, after two years the patients perceived an improvement. Mothers did not perceive any change over time. Dare and Key (1999) suggested this change in patients' perceptions might reflect the break down in the defensive function served by anorexia that occurred in the course of treatment. This may have made it more difficult for the patient to keep unhappiness about her family situation out of consciousness. Another way of saying this would be that it made it difficult for patients to maintain an idealised view of their families. This is consistent with the possibility that the patient may need to see her family's functioning in a more critical light, and become more challenging in the family, during the process of recovery. Since research data is usually collected from patients at some stage in treatment this shift in the patient's perception according to the stage of treatment or recovery complicates research based on self-report. So far that has not been taken into account in the design of studies.

Is family "pathology" a response to, not a cause of, the "illness"?

It is now argued, for example by Whitney and Eisler (2005), that the family difficulties described in the families of girls with anorexia are the result, not the cause, of anorexia. Two studies have designs that control for the possibility that apparent family pathology in the families of patients with anorexia arises as a response to the illness and has much in common with family reaction to other illnesses.

Sim et al (2009) compared mothers with daughters with anorexia with mothers with a daughter with a chronic illness, diabetes, and mothers with a daughter who had no illness, using the FES as a measure of family functioning. Only the mothers completed the FES. They also used questionnaire measures of mothers' and daughters' psychological symptoms. Mothers of girls with anorexia reported greater family conflict, reduced parental alliance, and increased feelings of depression. Once the emotional impact of the illness on the mothers was statistically controlled, group differences were no longer significant. Sim et al argued that the mothers' reports of family distress and dysfunction might be accounted for by the mothers' emotional response to the illness. They argued that "Although the cross sectional nature of this research precludes drawing causal conclusions, this study does suggest that disruptions in family dynamics and emotional distress common in families with AN are secondary to the nature of the illness rather than factors in its genesis. This has great implications for the mistaken tendency to blame family dynamics …", Sim et al (2009, p. 537). Against this argument it must be said that the family difficulties reported by the mothers are not the ones reported on the FES, mainly by the patient herself, in other studies, since the patients tend to report low cohesion and, sometimes, low emotional expressiveness. The family difficulties reported by the mothers of the patients in the study by Sim et al may indeed be secondary to the families' experience of coping with a daughter with anorexia. This need not be taken as having any bearing on the question of family influence on the development of anorexia derived from other studies using the FES, or other studies in general. However, the study failed to find differences between the reports of the mothers of patients with anorexia and those of diabetic patients, and that, so far as it goes, is consistent with the idea that differences that were reported in this instance were accounted for by the experience of illness. The only exception in this study was that the mothers of women with anorexia experienced lower levels of "parental alliance" than did the mothers of the diabetic patients. This could have been either a contributory cause or an effect.

Blair et al (1995) attempted to control for the effect of illness on perceived family functioning by comparing the families of patients with anorexia with those of families of patients with cystic fibrosis. This comparison group was chosen because cystic fibrosis is another condition that is life threatening, causes high concern to parents, and makes the patient underweight. There was also a comparison group of families without an illness. Data was collected using a self-report questionnaire, the Edinburgh Family Scale, Blair (1996), an interview rated for expressed emotion and direct observation of a family problem-solving task. The self-report questionnaire found no differences between the different groups of families but the observational data did. They found that over-involvement increased with the severity of illness, irrespective of whether the illness was cystic fibrosis or anorexia. However, more families with a daughter with anorexia were rated as enmeshed, over-protective and poor at problem solving. Therefore, the study does not support the proposition that apparent family psychopathology is the result of the families' response to an illness.

Should the accounts of patients be discounted because they are "ill"?

It has been argued that the family pathology discovered in the research might be accounted for by some common aspect of anorexic pathology or by co-morbid conditions such as depression.

Thienemann and Steiner (1993), using the FES, found no differences between eating disorder patients and depressed patients, and none between any of these groups and the normative data for the population as a whole. However, FES scores were correlated with depression. Young people who were more depressed scored their families as having more problems on the FES. Wonderlich and Swift (1990) also found that negative aspects of eating disorder patients' reports of family relationship might be accounted for by the patients' depression. However this result was far from clear and they acknowledged that it might equally be the case that those patients who experienced more difficult family relationships were also more depressed.

Fornari et al (1999) also proposed that the perceptions of poor family functioning reported by patients with anorexia were accounted for by their co-morbid depression. What these studies show is that patients with anorexia who give negative accounts of the family are also depressed. However, this observation might also be accounted for by the sort of shift in the patients' perceptions occurring during and after treatment that was described by Gowers and North, and, indeed, by those changes reported by Strober (1980).

Dancyger et al (2006) compared the perceptions of family functioning reported by adolescent girls with eating disorders and their mothers. The girls also completed a measure of eating disorder symptoms and underlying psychopathology, the Eating Disorders Inventory (EDI). Self-reports of family functioning were collected using the Family Assessment Device (FAD). Daughters had more negative perceptions of family functioning on four subscales of the FAD, Problem Solving, Communication, Affective Responsiveness and General Functioning. Dancyger et al thought that the level of Interpersonal Distrust reported in the EDI could account for the patients' perceptions. They concluded "Differences in viewpoints between mothers and daughters regarding the family environment may be understood in terms of the daughters' level of distrust of people in general and their overall feelings of inadequacy" (Dancyger et al, 2006, p. 283). However it is not clear why this explanation should be preferred. The patient's experience of family relationship difficulties may account for both her interpersonal distrust and her negative account of family relationships.

Interpretation

Evidence on anorexia and the family should not be dismissed

None of the studies based on *observation* of family interaction failed to find at least some difference between the families of patients with anorexia and comparison families. The twenty-eight self-report questionnaire based studies of family relationships produced mixed results. Only six failed to find any difference between the reports of people with anorexia and their families and those of people without a disorder. This fact would be less striking if we considered only the AN-R patients, because in some studies they do not report family problems. It would be even less striking if we relied entirely on parents' accounts, because many studies collected data only from patients. Moreover, it seems clear that parents report family difficulties less frequently. In addition we have seen that the balance of evidence about parenting and anorexia favours the view that patients with anorexia have experienced less effective parenting than have comparison women. However, some studies that have produced negative findings will have been missed from this review. Overall, the balance of the evidence indicates that differences do exist between the families of patients with anorexia and families in general.

* * *

It is generally agreed that the evidence does not support the Psychosomatic Family Model. The authors of some observational studies that found differences between the families of girls with anorexia and comparison families, Kog and Vandereycken (1989), Wallin et al (1996), Wallin and Hansson (1999) have argued that a range of family patterns are found. So have the authors of some questionnaire studies such as Dare et al (1994).

* * *

We have seen that many studies of the family have found real differences between the families of the patient with anorexia and the families of young people without a disorder. The main findings are that the patient with anorexia often sees the family as less caring and more distant than the typical family. However, these differences may not be specific to the families of people with anorexia. They may reflect differences that can contribute to the development of internalising disorders, or to any neurotic or behavioural disorder for that matter.

What are the differences between the families of girls with anorexia and other families?

The evidence does not suggest that the family relationships are particularly close. In general when "cohesiveness" is defined in a positive sense as *supportive* closeness the patient herself reports that she experiences her family as unsupportive, while all family members tend to wish for a greater degree of closeness. The distinction made by Barber and Buehler (1996) between closeness in a supportive sense, and closeness in an intrusive sense, is an important one. Confusion about this distinction has created difficulties for the research, but the available evidence is consistent with the view that the families of girls with anorexia are often experienced as intrusive.

* * *

We have seen that four studies found that the families have difficulty in engaging with conflict and bringing it to a satisfactory conclusion. This can be seen as consistent with the pattern of communication described by Humphrey (1989) in which girls with anorexia were submissive and sulky, especially with their fathers. None of this suggests closeness since genuine intimacy is not possible without the capacity to engage in and resolve conflict. Those observations seem consistent with the questionnaire and observation studies that indicate that the predominant pattern is one in which family members do not feel close, and with evidence that the most typical pattern is one in which expressions of emotion are low key.

* * *

The one aspect of the Psychosomatic Family Model that has stood up to experimental test is the observation that conflict resolution is not achieved in the triangular situation in which parents and daughter discuss together. The detouring mechanism proposed by Minuchin et al (1978) as the explanation of this behaviour does seem to exist. For example, it was demonstrated by Kerig (1995) in a study of non-clinical families. This study indicated that parental "togetherness" can indeed be bought at the price of developing a shared, excessive preoccupation with a child. However, the price paid by the child is that the parental concern leads to low self-esteem and to the development of internalising disorders. That may indeed be a feature of the relationship between girls who develop anorexia and their parents, at least in some families. Minuchin et al (1978) attributed this observation to the "use of the child in the parental relationship", specifically in that the parents used their daughter as a conflict regulator. Kog and Vandereycken (1986) noted that the families of patients with anorexia were generally comfortable with the lack of conflict they experienced. The issue could be understood in attachment terms. For example, perhaps this pattern reflects attachment difficulties, and problems about emotional expression arising from them, causing parents to avoid conflict in order to avoid emotional arousal, perhaps specifically because they associate it with fear of separation and loss.

Are research findings valid?

Two observations seem significant here. The first is that within these families it is the patient who is most likely to report the family in an unfavourable light. Moreover, the probability that she will do so depends to a considerable extent on her clinical state. Some evidence suggests that patients who are successfully restricting their food intake, and have no bulimic symptoms, are much less likely to see the family in a critical light than those who have a mix of symptoms. In one study restricting patients even reported the families in a more favourable way than symptom-free women, so that their families were seen as more "normal than normal". Yet, since we know that diagnostic categories based on the question of restricting and purging are unstable we have to be wary of concluding that different sorts of families produce different sorts of eating disorder patient. The family of the AN-R patient will often be the family of the AN-BN patient, and the BN patient, because the same girl or woman will fit more than one of those diagnostic categories from time to time. The explanation may be that patients' perceptions change as they recover or proceed through treatment. We have already seen that patients who are successfully restricting protect their self-esteem. It seems that they also see their families in a more favourable light. The more their food restriction is challenged the more fragile their self-esteem and the more critical they are likely to be of their family situation. This in itself has no bearing on which perception is valid. However it is interesting that Gowers and North (1999) found that clinicians' views agreed with those of patients with anorexia to a much greater extent than with the patients' parents. This could be seen as validating the patients' views. Critics of family models of anorexia might take the view that the findings of the Gowers and North study indicate that clinicians indoctrinate patients with anorexia with a critical view of families. However, since the data was collected at an early stage, when little indoctrination would yet have been possible, this seems unlikely. In addition, the clinicians' views of the patients' family relationships agreed with the patients' views in detail, differing only in that the clinicians took a graver view of the matter. Moreover, the clinicians' and patients' views of the family were validated in another way. They proved to predict outcome.

* * *

Critics of family models of anorexia may also discount the findings of some studies on the grounds that some findings, such as the report of low levels of family cohesion, are common to families presenting young people with a wide range of problems. On the other hand there seems no reason why this should not be so. Young people who develop anorexia have low self-esteem, as do those who develop depression. They are insecure in much the same ways that other young people with internalising disorders are insecure. The proposition by Laliberte and others that anorexia arises in the context of general factors that impact on self-esteem, factors that can contribute to a wide range of difficulties, and specific factors that determine the form of the disturbance, seems very likely to be true. There is no reason to doubt that young people who develop anorexia are likely to have had family experiences similar, in some respects, to those of young people who develop other eating disorders, and other internalising disorders, such as anxiety states and depression, problems that, as we have seen, the patients with anorexia generally share.

* * *

As we have seen some authors argue that the evidence that the family of the patient with anorexia differs in some respects from families in general should be understood to arise as a result of the effect of the anorexia on the family. There is little reason to suppose that this is the case. Evidence from prospective studies of eating disorders, and of life events studies such as Shoebridge and Gowers (2000), and Horesh et al (1995) indicate that it is not. The demonstration of similar effects in community studies, with populations with less severe eating disorders, likewise supports this view. In those families the impact of the girls developing eating concerns are unlikely to have much impact on family relationships. Often other members of the family will not have known about them at all. Of course there must be an effect of anorexia on the family. It may be helpful for the clinician to understand what that is, but that question is not the subject of this chapter.

* * *

Attempts to explain disorders by reference to family qualities have not proved very useful. Broad categories, such as "the psychosomatic family", or attempts to describe families by using dimensions such as the centrifugal versus centripetal dimension, have little predictive validity. Probably a more useful approach to the understanding of anorexia will address the issue of the development of the individual through childhood and adolescence by the study of developmental pathways, especially the family relationships of that individual. We have seen that clinicians from many schools of thought propose that the final common pathway in these cases is that anorexia fulfills a function in resolving difficulties and distress arising from the patient's sense of insufficiency in herself. Such a set of pathways would need to account for that sense of insufficiency, and for the development of an orientation towards weight control as a solution, as well as for the development of the pathological capacity for self-control that is an essential component of the disorder. Factors that have been identified so far include specific aspects of attachment behaviour and emotional processing, parental styles bearing on the control of children's behaviour, and aspects of family attitudes to eating, weight and appearance, as well as the relationship of those attitudes to more general attitudes to acceptable self-presentation. These issues are the subjects of the next three chapters. We will see that a substantial body of research links various aspects of family relationships to the development of problems in the younger generation.

Conclusion

Although there remains much room for debate about this complex body of research, many studies find differences between the families of patients with anorexia and comparison families. The statement that "we know that parents do not cause eating disorders" is not a reasonable summary of the current state of the evidence.

CHAPTER EIGHT

The emotional life of the family

The emotional life of the family; a range of influences

We have seen that anorexia occurs in girls and young women who have a characteristic pattern of vulnerabilities. Psychological theories propose various links between the child's experience, the quality of her experience with her family and her developing sense of self. These in turn reflects the parents' own experiences of upbringing and their ongoing relationship with one another. This chapter is about the families' influence on the developing child, seen through a range of theories about the development of attachment, the impact of parents on the child's developing life narrative and sense of self, and the development of a secure sense of self. This in turn has implications for the development of an autonomous self at adolescence. The chapter concludes with a discussion of the research evidence linking these issues with internalising disorders, eating disorders and anorexia.

Given the pattern of difficulties that are associated with anorexia, difficulties that we can see as accounting for anorexia in the individual, we would expect certain characteristic difficulties in their families. We would expect that they should have less attachment security and more complex difficulties with attachment reflecting intergenerational transmission of insecure attachment. This is likely to be reflected in lower levels of parental care and attunement, poorer narrative support in childhood, and lower levels of autonomy support in adolescence. Evidence can be found for at least some of these propositions in relation to internalising disorders in general, and sometimes in relation to anorexia itself.

Numerous studies of attachment have contributed to our understanding of the development of children and adolescents, and the continuing influence of attachment processes in adult life. Other studies illuminate the positive role of parents in supporting the child in the development of a life story. Studies demonstrate that parents play a significant role in helping children process emotion and develop a positive sense of self. Research shows that with very young children parents provide the scaffolding for the development of the life story. With older children and adolescents the child takes the lead in providing meaning, and parents support this process by attending to the child's individual views, even when they differ from those of parents. By doing so parents provide autonomy support. Both processes can be seen as crucial to the child's developing sense of self. Katz et al (1999) demonstrated the efficacy of parental "meta-emotion philosophy" in contributing to children's developing ability to process emotions and general adjustment. Taken together these studies demonstrate that parents play a very important role, in a positive sense, in supporting the child's developing sense of self, and the ability to manage emotions in the context of relationships. Deficits in these areas, as much as or more than negative experiences like abuse and neglect, are likely to contribute to the development of a negative sense of self, and hence lead to internalising disorders. These processes in turn have been shown to be linked to the development of eating disorders, including anorexia. The quality of the parental marriage is likely to be an important modifier of attachment security. It can provide a positive model of relationships, but also, potentially, a series of significant stressors that impact on the emotional security of the child.

Another factor in the emotional life of the family, one that cuts right across the issues arising from the relationship the growing child has with each parent individually, is the relationship that the parents have with each other. Family therapists are accustomed to thinking about and addressing the interaction between these different factors all the time. Researchers, on the other hand, try to tease out the effects of each type of influence separately. There are two bodies of research highly relevant to outcomes, one about the relationship of the child with the parent, the other about the relationship of the parents to each other, and the impact of that relationship on the child. There is really no logical order in which to discuss these two areas. For the purposes of the discussion here it is most convenient to deal with the parental marriage first, and move on to issues about attachment, meta-emotion philosophy, and autonomy support after that.

The impact of the parental marriage on the developing child

The impact of the relationship

Cummings and Wilson (1999) use the expression "emotional security" to describe the outcome of the child's active process of monitoring the parents' relationship. Just as attachment theory sees children as actively monitoring the carers' availability, so this emotional security hypothesis sees children as actively monitoring the effect of the parental relationship on that security. Attachment theory sees insecurity impacting on the child's internalised model of attachment relationships. Children may monitor the marital emotional atmosphere and respond to the early signs of tension by behaving in ways to distract the parents. Equally they may respond by distancing themselves and withdrawing from emotional engagement. Either pattern can be harmful in the long term. Cummings and Wilson argued that marital discord has been seen as linked to children's adjustment problems and that this link has been demonstrated in many studies. However, they argued that conflict is intrinsic to relationships and also has positive results. All kinds of difficulties and tensions might build up in a marital relationship in which conflict was never expressed. Children might therefore benefit from their parent's ability to engage in conflict more than they would from an upbringing in a household in which it was constantly avoided. In addition, conflict is linked to the expression of emotions such as anger. A conflict avoiding household was likely to be one in which this emotion is suppressed or misdirected. Viewed from a positive point of view, children benefit from witnessing parental conflict. Parents who demonstrate an ability to manage conflict and the strong feelings it evokes are providing a model for their children of how they may manage their own relationships and emotions. Such parents are seen to be passing on to their children a model of relationships that values the expression and working through of differences. They also model behaviours that can lead to conflict resolution. Cummings and Wilson argue that children are always distressed by exposure to conflict between parents. However, when parents explain the situation and show children that the issues have been resolved, or, if not, that they are committed to working towards resolution, distress is moderated. In this kind of situation children benefit from learning that their own and their parents distress can be coped with and is a part of positive relationships. They also benefit from the modeling of emotional expression and problem solving skills used in the context of conflict resolution. In these respects exposure to parental marital conflict is helpful. By contrast, repeated exposure to destructive conflict, by which they mean conflict that is intense, escalating, violent or unresolved, causes anxiety and distress to build up.

Cummings and Wilson (1999) reviewed the evidence that children are distressed by parental conflicts and often seek either to escape the situation, or to get involved by mediating or offering comfort. Destructive parental conflict is linked to a range of negative outcomes. Physical violence in marriage is related to high levels of negative outcomes for children as are severe forms of verbal hostility or emotional withdrawal in the context of conflict. On the other hand some experiences of parental conflict are constructive and can have positive effects on children. Although children who observe parental conflict are distressed and anxious, two factors have been shown to determine the implications of this for emotional security. The first is parental conflict resolution. If children are aware that the difference between their parents has been resolved then their emotional reaction to the conflict is largely resolved. If children are aware the difference has been partially resolved, then likewise the emotional reaction is partially resolved. Parental explanations are important. Even if a difference is not resolved parents who explain that conflict is a part of relationships, and that the parents are committed to finding a resolution, reduce children's anxiety and distress. However, explanations that attack one party in the marriage or indicate a lack of belief in the possibility of resolution have the opposite effect. They argued that children's emotional security depends on the children's interpretation of the longer-term implications for the security of family relationships. Cummings and Wilson provided evidence that younger children are more upset by conflicts if the conflicts are about them, while older children and adolescents are more likely to try to intervene in their parents' conflicts.

Subsequently, Cummings and Merrilees (2010) provided a developmental psychopathology perspective on the relationship between parental conflict, children's emotional security and the development of both internalising and externalising symptoms. They pointed out that research demonstrates that it is not divorce but marital conflict that consistently predicts children's internalising and externalising symptoms, peer relationships and competence. Evidence suggests that destructive conflict between parents makes them less available. They argued that two distinct pathways exist with the potential to impact on the child. In one pathway one parent's hostility towards their partner may spill over on to and be directed at the child. In the other, one or both parents may respond by emotional withdrawal, becoming unavailable to the child. One way that this may happen is that parental behaviours associated with depression, including withdrawal, sadness and fear, impact on children's emotional security. Cummings and Merrilees (2010) referred to three studies that provided evidence that brief interventions can improve outcomes. These brief interventions targeted parents' ability to manage conflict constructively rather than destructively.

Cummings et al (2006) showed that emotional security was a key intervening process between marital discord and internalising and externalising problems in children and adolescents. Marital conflict was a stronger predictor of internalising problems than externalising problems, and a stronger predictor for older than for younger children.

Cummings and Merrilees (2010) argued that the experience of destructive marital conflict, which is to say especially conflict characterised by high levels of hostility, and/or conflict that remains unresolved and/or conflict that is child related, activates the emotional security system. Children become sensitised by repeated experiences of distress arising from these conflicts and overtime develop behavioural patterns that serve to reduce their discomfort. Such strategies may include behaviours that distract parents from conflict, such as challenging or fighting for example.

Even children as young as five years old can detect covert conflict between parents and respond to it in the same way as they do to overt conflict. Ablow and Measelle (2010) demonstrated that for these young children conflict in the parental relationship readily leads to self-blame and to attempts to intervene, and that it is the distress arising from the conflict, and the tendency of such young children to blame themselves, which leads to the development of internalising symptoms in these children.

The effect of the child's involvement in parental marital issues

Kerig and Swanson (2010) discussed the development of thinking in this area. They argued that hostility expressed between the parents could spill over into the behaviour of the child as a result of the direct modeling of the behaviour by the parents. Equally parents might be distracted from their children's needs because of their preoccupation with the marital conflict. Disagreements between the parents about parenting might exacerbate this. Another factor would be detouring, in which the parents allow themselves to be distracted from the need to resolve their differences by the behaviour of the child. Kerig and Swanson made a distinction between two types of detouring. One they called "detouring-attacking", in which the child is attacked, rejected or seen as a problem. The second they called "detouring-supportive", in which parents united around caring for a child who is seen as specially needy or vulnerable. This may create a relationship that is too close. However, another possibility is that the relationship is too close with one parent, to the extent of excluding the other parent. This, as they say, is what Minuchin et al (1978) described as "triangulation". Kerig and Swanson (2010) describe a variety of different ways in which a child may be, or may feel themselves to be caught up in the parent's relationship difficulties in ways which could impinge on the child's development.

One clear research finding is that the greater the degree of conflict between parents, the greater the likelihood that the child will be, or see themselves as being, caught up between their parents. Grych and Fincham (1993) found that children's perceptions of triangulation accounted for the link between the experience of parental marital conflict and the development of both internalising and externalising problems. Kerig and Swanson (2010) point out that such instances of triangulation do not always look conflictual. They may appear either warm and supportive, or hostile and rejecting. Detouring may place the child in either an infantilised, or a parentified position in relation to her parents.

Kerig and Swanson (2010) expand on the question of how children may be caught up in parental relationship difficulties, and the impact on the children expressed through internalising and externalising symptoms. They point out that the issue is seen as important in all three of the dominant models explaining the relationship between parental marital distress and the development of psychopathology in children. They quote studies that demonstrated that the more children and adolescents felt caught up in parental relationship difficulties, the more they reported both internalising and externalising problems.

Kerig and Swanson (2010) reviewed a number of slightly different descriptions of "triangulation" and conclude that the central issue is boundary dissolution. This is the "failure to acknowledge the psychological distinctness of the child". They proposed three types of boundary dissolution: intrusiveness, parentification (role reversal, the child inappropriately taking care of the parents' needs), and "hostile spousification" (directing hostility that arises in the relationship with the other parent at the child). They were interested in the interrelationship between these parenting phenomena and the interaction between the sex of the parent and that of the child. They argued that research on marital unhappiness shows that unhappy couples typically differ over issues relating to sex roles. They also tend to devalue one another's adequacy in performing sex roles. In addition they point out that the transition to parenthood generally increases the distinctiveness of the roles played by men and women. This often becomes a source of dissatisfaction or distress to the couple. They describe a study of couples and their children in the age range eight to eleven. They used measures of parental conflict, and measures of parents' perceptions of their partners and their children's sex role characteristics. They confirmed their expectation that partners who were unhappy with their marriages saw both their partners, and their opposite sex children, in negative terms in relation to sex roles. Those children who were on the receiving end of the negative perceptions of the opposite sex parents had lower self-esteem and higher levels of internalising disorders. This illustrates what they meant by "hostile spousification".

Kerig and Swanson (2010) described a study of young adults' perceptions of inter-parental conflict in their families of origin and its impact on internalising and externalising symptoms. As expected young people who reported high levels of parental conflict also reported high levels of boundary dissolution. Boundary dissolution in turn predicted both internalising and externalising problems. The relationship between inter-parental conflict and internalising symptoms was mediated by maternal intrusiveness, maternal hostile spousification and maternal parentification, and not directly by any of the paternal relationship variables. Paternal relationship factors did impact on both the development of externalising disorders and the development of relational aggression with partners.

* * *

Studies of the effect of parental conflict on children inevitably tend to focus on overt conflict since this is what parents acknowledge and it can be measured using self-report. This being so there is a danger that the impact of covert conflict may be overlooked. A possible solution is to incorporate assessments of family structure with studies of conflict and its consequences. Kerig (1995) obtained information from seventy-five children in the age range six to ten years and their parents, in families where both parents and the child lived in the same household. She used the Family Cohesion Index as a measure of family structure. In this the child and each parent separately are asked to indicate closeness and distance within the family by drawing the parents and child's position within a circle. Measurement of the relative distances between each parent and the child, and between the parents themselves, allowed classification into four family types, "cohesive", "detouring", "triangulated", and "separate". She also obtained a number of other measures, including a measure of marital adjustment, a parental self-report measure of marital conflict, a measure of the child's perception of parental marital conflict, and a measure, completed by each parent separately, of the child's internalising and externalising problems, the Child Behaviour Checklist (CBCL). Kerig also obtained information about family cohesion using a self-report measure. In this, in contrast to the other measures, the family was asked to work together and achieve a consensus.

The Family Cohesion Index showed that 60% of mothers, 59% of fathers, and 76% of children saw all three members of the family as close, cohesive in terms of the family classification. The remaining 40% of families were roughly equally distributed between the detouring, triangulated and separated categories, except that no child saw all three family members as distant from each other. Family members' perceptions of the family structure differed in many instances, with parents agreeing with each other 67% of the time, mothers and children achieving 58%, and father and child 55% agreement. On the measure of parental marital adjustment couples in the detouring families reported the happiest marriages, while parents in the triangulated families were the least satisfied with their marriages. Mothers and fathers who saw the family as triangulated or separate reported relatively more conflict in the parental marriage, while parents in the detouring families reported the least conflict. Children's perceptions of parental marital conflict followed a different pattern. In the cohesive families children reported moderate levels of conflict and low levels of self-blame, while children in the triangulated and separated families report relatively high levels of conflict, but intermediate levels of self-blame. By contrast children in the detouring families reported intermediate levels of parental conflict, higher than the cohesive families, but lower than the triangulated and separate families. However, these were the children who reported the highest levels of self-blame for the conflict. These were also the children who had the highest level of problems on the Child Behaviour Checklist. The interpretation of this data is complicated by the different pattern of responding by mothers and fathers. There was a marked tendency for fathers to report more externalising problems than internalising problems in their children, while mothers did the opposite. This might indicate that fathers are more concerned with "good behaviour" and disciplinary issues, while mothers give more priority to their children's emotional state. However, whether using mothers' or fathers' ratings, the children in the detouring families had roughly twice as many problems as those in the cohesive and triangulated families. Kerig argues that the study provides empirical support for Minuchin's (1974) proposition that marital cohesion can be bought at a high price by couples who focus on a child in a way that distracts from the need to recognise and resolve marital problems.

Attachment in infancy and childhood

Attachment theory sees a close link between the developing child's experience that the parent is available and provides security, the development over time of a working model of the relationship, and, subsequently, of a model of relationships in general. The child's sense of worth is closely tied to this experience. Attachment theory places the earliest beginnings of the sense of self in the interaction between parents and infants in which parents reflect back infants expression of emotional states in a modulated way, demonstrating that the parent is not him/ herself overwhelmed by the emotion. Attachment theory describes the relationship between children and caregivers, and the impact this has on the behaviour of the developing child that can be seen as continuing into adult life or beyond. Bowlby (1982) regarded the infant's early experience with its caretakers as establishing "internal working models" of caring relationships, models with the potential to last into adult life and to influence development in a wide range of ways. Hence in adult life the adult's style of relating in intimate relationships, their ability to regulate emotions, to relate in a reciprocal way and get their needs met would all be shaped by the early attachment to caregivers.

Attachment mechanisms and classification in infancy and early childhood

Ainsworth et al (1978) developed a classification system to describe differences in infants' attachment seeking behaviour. These were based on the systematic observation of infants in the "strange situation", a situation in which the child is left for a short time in the presence of a stranger while the parent leaves the room. The child's behaviour in that situation, and on being reunited with the parent, was observed. Some infants, on being reunited, seek proximity with the parent, are re-assured, and are able to turn their attention back to playing or exploring. In that case the child is classified as securely attached. Other children acted as if they did not notice the parent's absence and avoided proximity with the parent when reunited. This style of response was regarded as insecure/avoidant. Those infants who responded immediately to separation with displays of distress, and who were slow to accept reassurance were classified as insecure-resistant/ambivalent. The evidence is that in the absence of sensitive caregiving infants and young children develop coping strategies. The main insecure "styles" of attachment reflect two principle strategies in dealing with emotions: a "maximising" strategy in which the child turns their attention to their distress and behaves in ways which may engage the carer, giving rise to insecure-resistant/ambivalent behaviour, and a "minimising" strategy, in which the child turns their attention away from distress giving rise to insecure/avoidant behaviour. Insecure-resistant/ambivalent behaviours that engage the caregiver characterise those described as anxious/preoccupied or as ambivalent. By contrast insecure/avoidant behaviour minimises engagement of the carer. Subsequently, Main and Solomon (1986) added the category of disorganised attachment to describe infants who did not seem able to settle into any pattern of behaviour in relation to the separation. This is associated with more extreme experiences of abuse and neglect.

The attachment classifications ascribed to infants and small children describe the state of the relationship with a carer at a specific point in time. A child can display different qualities of attachment to different carers, feeling secure with one parent but not with the other for example. Bowlby (1982) regarded attachment security at this stage as depending on the child's experience of the availability of the carer. This in turn depends on their experience of communication with, and responsiveness from the carer. This would be true throughout life and not just during infancy and early childhood. The quality of attachment achieved in childhood sets the scene for the continuing development of attachment relationships, with family and peers, at adolescence.

Attachment theory sees the persons developing sense of self as being shaped by their early experience of care from parents or other caregivers. Responsive and available carers have children who can turn to parental figures for comfort and reassurance when distressed or anxious. The crucial issue here is parental attunement. From infancy onwards parents' responsiveness and communication with the child about his or her emotional state determines the outcome in terms of attachment. Parents who are available and attuned have children who develop a balanced capacity to explore the outside world and to seek support. The interaction with the carers is seen as the basis of an enormous amount of psychological development. The capacity to allow the self to experience, and then to process, emotion, is seen as arising from the internalisation of the interaction with the caregiver in infancy and early childhood. The capacity to understand that others have minds, and to begin to understand others' states of mind, is likewise seen as the internalisation of the process which occurs when the caregiver responds appropriately to the child's mental processes. The child's sense of her own value, her self-esteem, is seen as arising in the context of sensitive, attuned, attention from the caregiver. Some later developments of attachment theory, such as Fonagy et al (2004), concern the affect of attachment on the development of mentalisation. This is the capacity to understand one's own and other people's minds in terms of mental states, including ideas, feelings and intentions. This line of argument concerns the very early origins of the sense of self, and of the capacity to regulate emotions in the interaction between infants and carers. In particular, the parent's efforts to reflect back to the infant the infant's emotions and wishes, is seen as being crucial. This is done in a way that demonstrates to the infant that it is the infant's state of mind that is reflected back, not simply that of the carer.

Potential modifiers of attachment security in infancy

Attachment theory is focused on the relationship between the child and the carers. Other family factors are likely to modify the impact of this. The most significant are likely to be the child's awareness of the quality of the parental marital relationship, and the child's observation of their parents' relationships with other children in the family. There is not much evidence about the second of these issues. However, Fearon et al (2006) made a twin study that attempted to assess the extent of impact of genetic variation in children on their attachment to a parent at age one. They found that maternal sensitivity to the baby accounted for almost all the variance in attachment at age one, leaving little room for genetic explanations of the infant's attachment behaviour. However, one thing that did modify the attachment of the child towards the mother was her sensitivity to the twin. A baby who received sensitive care from the mother was less likely to be securely attached if his or her twin did not. So, even at this early age infants are able to sense something about the family over and above how the parent relates to them. No doubt there are many complex issues about parental relationships with siblings, and their effect on attachment security, that have yet to be elucidated by research.

Attachment styles developing during childhood

Crittenden (1997) provided additional elaboration to the attachment model of development. She noted that attachment behaviours became more complex during childhood, reflecting children's increasing cognitive and language abilities. In relationships with secure children it is possible for genuine feelings to be expressed and understood. Parents and children are able to negotiate differences and compromise. This mutual co-operation promotes an integrated experience of the self and the carer. It is a context in which there is little need for distortion of communication. It promotes the ability of the child to share responsibility for outcomes with her parents, rather than engaging in self-blame or blaming the other. By contrast, insecurely attached, anxious/avoidant and anxious ambivalent children, demonstrate strategies based on deception or coercion. For example she describes the way that most anxious/avoidant children, already before age five, have learned not to turn their backs and look away from parents as a way of maintaining distance, since this would be experienced as rude and elicit parental anger. Instead many by this stage present false displays of "over bright" positive feelings, doing as parents desire while maintaining psychological distance. However, in cases in which parents had demonstrated a more severe and consistent failure to protect the child, such young, anxious/avoidant, children demonstrate more extreme "compulsive caregiving" or "compulsive compliant" strategies. These behaviour patterns are strategies serving to disarm parents. Crittenden argues that these extreme patterns are associated with splitting of good and bad aspects so that the child experiences her "true" bad self as concealed by her "false" good self. She also argues that because such children know that their behaviour determines how the parent reacts, they experience themselves as fully responsible for negative parental responses when they have failed to conform to parental needs or expectations. This elicits a sense of shame. By contrast Crittenden sees direct and honest communication between children and their carers as the basis of positive self-esteem. Distorted and simulated communication has the opposite effect, leading to negative self-perception, and to inappropriate attributions of responsibility. Crittenden argues that children in compulsive caregiving or compulsive compliant groups experience high levels of anxiety, but do not display these to their parents. Presumably the reason for this is that their experience is that parents will not be supportive or comforting.

Children whose attachment style is anxious/ambivalent at the same age respond to parental inconsistency in caring by exaggerated displays of demands. These can be seen as a coercive strategy to get parental care. Crittenden argues that if the parent responds with anger, the child will respond with "coy" behaviour, to turn this parental behaviour into nurturance. When this pattern is demonstrated in a more extreme way, the child alternates between aggression and feigned helplessness. Such children she says "find themselves caught up in unresolvable struggles that, on the surface, look like endless fights, but function to maintain parental attention … . and hence safety." These patterns of behaviour persist into and beyond adolescence, with further elaborations of behaviour reflecting the increased intellectual ability of the adolescent and adult, but essentially reflecting the same underlying strategies in relationships.

Family attitudes to emotional expression

Another approach to the understanding of emotional expression in families sees it as a question of family attitudes. Katz et al (1999) argued that parents who hold a "meta-emotion philosophy" engage with young children in a helpful way. They do this because they value the expression of emotion. In interaction with their children they pay attention to the child's emotions, validate emotions and provide verbal labels for them. By "coaching" children through strong emotional events parents are helping them to calm down, to learn how to calm themselves down and self-sooth. Parents who are attending to their children's emotions in this way do not engage in critical or derogatory attacks on the child. In the research that Katz described, parents' meta-emotion philosophy was positively related to praise and negatively to criticism or derogatory attack on the child. In the study, children whose parents acted in this way had better academic achievement three years later. They also showed a lower level of physiological stress and reported fewer physical illnesses. While most of these effects could be seen as the direct effect of the parents on the children the parental attitude also had beneficial effects on the parents' marriage. Children whose parents had a meta-emotion philosophy were subjected to less stress arising from parental marital alienation and hostility. Katz and Hunter (2007) demonstrated that mothers whose behaviour demonstrated high "meta-emotion philosophy" in that they were both able to process their own feelings, and help their adolescent children to own their emotions, had adolescents with lower levels of depression, and better general adjustment, than the children of mothers who did not have these qualities.

Parental narrative support and the child's sense of self

An approach to the study of the child's developing sense of self sees its beginnings in the stories that children begin to be able to tell about themselves in the early years of life. One approach to the development of the child and adolescent is made through the study of narrative and particularly of the way in which families support the child in the development of a life narrative. Studies of the development of life narrative did not have their origin in attachment theory but in other areas of developmental psychology, for example in studies of how children develop and structure autobiographical memory. They show that parents may provide more, or less, support for the developing narrative capacity of the child. These studies also serve to illustrate the ways in which parents' interactions with children support the development of autonomy and self-esteem. Some of these studies are based on observations of parents and children in a situation in which they have been asked to discuss a recent significant issue in the child's life. This allows study both of the child's developing narrative, and of the way in which parents support and shape the narrative. This in turn can be seen as having a profound impact on the child's developing autobiographical memory, sense of self, and of self worth.

Pasupathi and McClean (2010), summarising previous work, propose that by age three children begin to coherently narrate past events through memory conversations with parents. They argue that this process of narration, with the parent, teaches children that remembering is valuable, and how to relate the past. Such memory narratives include reference to emotional states. The memory narratives of children have been shown to impact on their construction of a consistent and coherent self-concept, and on self-esteem. Pasupathi and McClean present evidence that children of parents who engaged with them in conversations including more elaborative remembering developed better coping strategies and had fewer internalising and externalising symptoms. During childhood the development of positive self-esteem, and of a coherent self-concept, can be seen as arising from these interactions with parents. These in turn lay a foundation for the development of a more elaborate sense of self in adolescence. For example, Habermas and de Silveira (2008) elicited life stories from children and young people aged eight to twenty in order to study the development of life stories over time. The length of the life story, and its overall coherence, increased with age. Eight-year-olds made few connections between past and subsequent events, but from age twelve onwards these connection were commonly made. The tendency to attribute behaviour in a situation to one's age or previous experiences increased rapidly between ages twelve and sixteen.

Fivush et al (2006) found that children whose mothers structured conversation with them in an elaborative and evaluative way had children who were able to tell richer and more evaluative accounts of the past. Haden et al (1997) found that three-year-old children whose mothers talked about emotional states and subjective judgements were children who went on to provide similar information to a researcher when they were five. Reese et al (2010) studied the impact of mothers' early style of reminiscing about life events with children at just forty months of age with the children's own style of narrative at age twelve to thirteen. Mothers who had referred to children's positive and negative emotions at forty months had early adolescent children who made more references to their emotions in accounts of their lives given at twelve to thirteen. In particular, references to negative emotions at forty months predicted references to emotions by young people at twelve to thirteen. Reese et al (2010) drew the conclusion from this and other research that the richness of child and parent reminiscing determined the development of the child's autobiographical memory, the memory of events and facts. However it was the in-depth discussion of negative events that particularly influenced the child's developing self-understanding. Mothers that emphasised positive aspects of the child's coping with events, whether the events themselves were positive or negative, had children who developed higher self-esteem. Cleveland and Reese (2005) and Cleveland et al (2007), in a study of young children reminiscing with their mothers, argued that support for autonomy takes the form of parental prioritising of the child's unique perspective. This certainly seems to be true too for adolescents, as we will see.

Narrative, autonomy support and adolescence

Weeks and Pasupathi (2010) discuss the inter-relationship between the development of a life narrative, identity formation, and achievement of autonomy. The concept of adolescent autonomy includes notions of separation, individuality and the child's ability to take responsibility for her own actions. However they comment that this is not at the expense of connectedness; autonomy involves being able to assert the self while remaining responsive to others. By contrast identity involves a sense of personal continuity and coherence, achieving role and value commitments and achieving self-understanding. They argue that both autonomy and identity are first achieved in a social, in fact in a family, context and require social validation both inside the family and outside it.

Weeks and Pasupathi argue that, for practical purposes, autonomy can be seen as the child's ability to speak and be heard, or, as they put it, to "voice" in Fivush's (2002) model of voice and silence. To Fivush the concept of voice implies power. The person who can speak has the power to be heard and to impose a version of events. This is interesting because, as we have seen, girls with anorexia "choose" self-silencing. Bohanek et al (2006) studied families' reminiscing about past events. The quality of family reminiscing in this setting was related to self-esteem. Families who constructed their story about a past event in a way that allowed all members to contribute had daughters with higher self-esteem. Grotevant and Cooper (1986) regarded individuation as reflecting both connectedness and individuality. They found that in family interaction tasks individuation in this sense was linked to identity exploration and role taking ability. Families whose interactions were characterised by the expression of difference and by mutual engagement had adolescents whose identities were more mature.

Narrative support interacts with attachment security

Newcombe and Reese (2004) argued that the capacity of the parent to support the child's narrative development reflected the child's attachment security. They found that only securely attached children internalised their mother's evaluative style by the end of early childhood. Equally, the mother's attachment security affects her capacity to support this development in her child. For example Reese (2008) found that mothers who were less elaborative and confirming in their reminiscing with their children were less secure on the adult attachment interview. Parents who were secure in relation to their own early experiences talked more openly and elaborately with their children.

Attachment in adolescence

Bowlby (1982) assumed that during adolescence parents remained crucial attachment figures providing a secure base for developing autonomy and exploration, including self-exploration. Attachment theory predicts that secure attachment promotes mastery of developmental tasks and that insecure attachment is a risk factor for problem outcomes. In adolescence security in attachment representation is likely to reflect the established capacity for self-regulation and emotional processing, on the one hand, and the current interaction with parents on the other. Secure attachment to parents in adolescence provides the framework for identity development, as well as providing the capacity to cope with challenges arising from life events within and outside the family.

The way the "internal working model" develops in late childhood, adolescence and adult life has been studied using the Adult Attachment Interview (AAI) (George et al, 1984, 1985, 1996). Hesse (2008) provides a useful description. For adolescents and adults the assumption is that the internal working model is the result of the participants' lifetime experience of processing attachment experiences with carers rather than reflecting one relationship at a particular point in time. The interview is used to allow a judgement to be made about the person's state of mind about attachment, their internal working model. The assumption is made that by this stage in development the different attachment experiences with each parent will be developed into an internalised representation of attachment experiences in general. This governs behaviour in ongoing relationships with parents, and shapes the adolescent's orientation to the formation of new relationships with close friends and romantic partners. The interview elicits a narrative about the experience of early relationships that is analysed in terms of its verbal and non-verbal content. The scoring of the interview draws on both the conscious constructs revealed in the response to the interview, the emotional content demonstrated overtly or covertly by such diffusing strategies as laughing when describing apparently upsetting events, and other non-verbal indicators such as the interviewees dysfluency, or unwillingness to give an account. In particular, analysis focuses on the relationship between episodic and semantic memory. Discrepancies between the persons overall report of their early experiences, and their ability to provide congruent examples or dysfluency in doing so, indicate insecure states of mind. Narratives elicited using the AAI can be classified as falling into one of three categories, corresponding to the attachment classification applied to infants. The classifications are: "secure" (sometimes called autonomous or balanced), corresponding to secure in infancy; "dismissive" (sometimes called avoidant), corresponding to insecure-avoidant in infancy, and "preoccupied" (sometimes called ambivalent) which corresponds to the insecure-resistant/ambivalent classification in infancy.

Attachment classification in adolescent and adult clinical populations

Research with clinical populations of adults, including those with anorexia and bulimia, requires further elaboration of this system with the addition of two further categories. Of these the "Unresolved" category is the one that seems to have most relevance to studies of severe eating disorders, especially to anorexia. Hesse (2008), describing these additional categories says that the first three categories are based on consistent strategies displayed by the interviewee in relation to the interview and interviewer. By contrast the unresolved category was added to take account of situations that arose when the interviewee displayed lapses in their reasoning or their discourse in relation to experiences of loss or abuse. These could suggest that the person enters into a compartmentalised or dissociated state of mind. The individual who is seen as unresolved in respect to loss or trauma has been unable to integrate specific memories with the result that those memories can be experienced as intrusive and overwhelming.

By contrast the "Cannot Classify" category is used for people whose interview accounts contain elements of both dismissing and preoccupied strategies to an extent that makes assignment to one or the other category impossible. Both these categories are additional insecure categories, and would usually be understood to reflect more severe difficulties with attachment than is indicated by the preoccupied and dismissive categories. They were introduced as a result of extending attachment studies to people with significant levels of personal disturbance.

In research with clinical populations the impact of the additional categories is substantial. Dozier et al (2008) reviewed a large number of studies of attachment classification in a range of mental illnesses, neurotic disturbance and personality disorders. Dozier noted that Fonagy et al (1996) conducted a study of attachment states of mind comparing a wide range of different disorders using the Adult Attachment Interview. Of forty-four patients with anxiety disorders, forty-one (93%) were classified as preoccupied using the three way classification (autonomous/preoccupied/dismissive) but when the four way classification was used, including the unresolved category, thirty-eight (86%) were classified as unresolved, and only one as preoccupied. Two other studies of patients with anxiety states, Manassis et al (1994) and Stovall-McClough and Cloitre (2006) produced similar results, but one, Zeijmans van

Emmichoven et al (2003) did not. The same effect is found in studies of severe eating disorders. Using the three-way classification Fonagy et al (1996) classified nine of fourteen patients as preoccupied, but using the four-way classification thirteen were seen as unresolved and none as preoccupied. Studies of community-based samples of patients with problems such as eating disorders have been undertaken using the three-way classification. However, in studies of more disturbed clinical samples with severe eating disorders and anxiety disorders the four-way classification including the "unresolved" category is needed.

Continuity and change in attachment in adolescence

Although many of Bowlby's (1982) propositions have been upheld by research, one has not. There is far less continuity of attachment from infancy, through childhood and adolescence into adult life than he had predicted. Attachment has been found to be relatively stable from infancy to childhood, and when the child's attachment classification changes that usually reflects changes in the family situation. However research on the stability of attachment from childhood to adolescence produces mixed results. A number of studies have failed to find high rates of concordance between early childhood attachment to mothers or fathers, as judged by response to the "strange situation" in childhood, and attachment states of mind in adolescence assessed with the AAI. For example, Becker-Stoll et al (2008) followed up forty-three sixteen-year-olds and their mothers. Their attachment had been assessed at ages one and six years using the "strange situation". At age sixteen attachment was assessed again using the AAI. No significant correlation between early attachment and current adolescent attachment representation was found. Changes in classification over time were related to the presence of a higher number of risk factors and so might be accounted for by real changes in the family structure and relationships that had occurred in the intervening years. However, adolescence is a time of change. The adolescents' need to achieve increased autonomy, and parental comfort or discomfort with that, may contribute to the greater fluidity of attachment relationships at this time.

Becker-Stoll (2008) was interested in the relationship between current and past attachment on the one hand, and adolescents' current pattern of behaviour in relation to their parents on the other. Mothers and adolescents were observed in two tasks. In the first the teenager and his or her mother was asked to discuss planning an imaginary holiday. The second task was to discuss a real ongoing area of disagreement between them. Both childhood attachment and adolescent attachment representation impacted significantly on the quality of behaviour during these tasks. Becker-Stoll noted that both early attachment and current attachment relationships independently contributed to the prediction of current problems and relationship styles. This being so it seems likely that even if attachment security breaks down for some adolescents, nevertheless security achieved during childhood continues to provide a degree of protection from unwanted outcomes. There may be various reasons for this. For example, the secure child's ability to process emotion, value the self, and balance attribution of blame, may persist in the adolescent, even if current relationships with parents no longer provide for his or her ongoing needs.

Security of attachment may change at any point in the life cycle for many reasons. One important factor with adolescents is that some parents who have been secure attachment figures for their children will have difficulty adjusting to the challenges presented by the needs of the adolescent. In particular a relatively rigid style of parenting seems to present less of an obstacle to secure attachment in childhood than it does in adolescence. Adolescents must negotiate increased autonomy while maintaining a co-operative relationship with parents. They are less likely to be able to do so in relationship to parents whose attitudes and behaviour are rigidly organised. Various factors can contribute to the reduction of attachment security during the teenage years. For example, Allen et al (2004) made a two-year prospective study of attachment in teenagers aged sixteen at the start of the study and eighteen at its end. Although there was a degree of stability in adolescents' internalised representation of attachment at the two time periods, there were also changes in attachment. Deterioration in security of attachment was predicted by the adolescents' behaviour towards their mothers. Those who displayed over-personalised disagreements with their mothers at the beginning of the research had lower levels of attachment security two years later. Adolescents who saw their mothers as more supportive at age sixteen had improved levels of attachment security at age eighteen. Other factors such as the presence of depressive symptoms in the adolescents at age sixteen, and family poverty, also predicted a reduced level of adolescent attachment security at eighteen.

* * *

Allen (2008) summarised the evidence on the adolescent attachment system, pointing out that the adolescent is able to enter into a kind of negotiation about the maintenance of the attachment relationship in a way that would not be possible for an infant. The adolescent relationship with parents is dominated by his or her struggle for autonomy. Adolescents invest increasingly in peer relationships, with friends and romantic partners. Yet, as Allen points out, evidence shows that adolescents, and even young adults, turn to parents as attachment figures under conditions of stress.

The adolescent's striving for autonomy is likely to put stress on their attachment to their parents. As Allen says "A secure goal-corrected partnership potentially allows both parent and teen to recognise the teens autonomy strivings and to support these while maintaining the relationship" Allen (2008, p. 424). For this to happen parents need to be willing to support adolescent autonomy seeking, and both parents and teens need a good ability to communicate about divergent perspectives and needs. Allen points out that communication is very important here. Studies have shown that mothers' accuracy in predicting adolescents' self-report is closely linked to adolescent attachment security. He argues that this is likely to be because secure adolescents communicate their emotional states to their parents accurately. Other studies have shown that insecure adolescents have parents who are less accurate in predicting their adolescents' responses to an inventory of psychological symptoms, but so are the adolescents' peers. This being so the difference is not likely to be accounted for simply by differences in parental attunement. Allen quotes a study by Berger et al (2005) who found that discrepancies between dismissing adolescents self-report and the report given about them by parents and peers could be in either direction. He argued that adolescents with a dismissing style simply did not give enough information to others to allow them to make accurate judgements. By contrast adolescents with a preoccupied style of attachment reported more symptoms in themselves than their parents and peers thought they had. On the face of it the preoccupied adolescents were reporting their distress but not being fully heard or believed by either parents or peers.

Studies of attachment and parental autonomy support at adolescence

Attachment states of mind affect the behaviour of adolescents in conflict situations with their parents. For example, Kobak et al (1993) observed the interaction of fourteen- to eighteen-year-old adolescents and their mothers in a problem-solving task. Teenagers who had been scored as securely attached on the AAI demonstrated balanced assertiveness. They persevered in putting forward their point of view to their mothers. They could both assert their own point of view and listen to their mother's point of view. By contrast, teenagers who were insecurely attached demonstrated more avoidance or dysfunctional anger in the problem-solving task. Boys responded with anger whether they had been assessed as having a dismissive or a preoccupied strategy. Kobak et al speculated that even boys who had a dismissive strategy could use expressions of anger. They could display this emotion when it served to distance them from their mothers. Girls were less likely to respond to their mothers with anger. Those girls who had a dismissive strategy allowed their mothers to dominate the discussions. They thought that girls had a higher expectation of maintaining relatedness to their mothers and so acted in this way to keep an emotional distance while avoiding an obvious break in the relationship. As Allen (2008, p. 425) says "teens with secure attachment states of mind tend to handle conflicts with parents by engaging in productive, problem-solving discussions that balance autonomy strivings with efforts to preserve relationships with parents … In particular the relationship maintaining behaviours in the midst of conflicts are most consistently linked to adolescent security …". By contrast adolescents with a dismissing style of attachment showed the least autonomy and relatedness in interactions with parents. Allen argued that their characteristic withdrawal stood in the way of renegotiating the relationship. Parents of these young people were also relatively unresponsive to them. Preoccupied adolescents, on the other hand, "overengaged" in arguments with parents in ways that ultimately undermined autonomy. He suggests the problem here is one of mental entanglement between the self of the adolescent and her parents. This can be seen to have deep roots. Allen and Hauser (1996) found it was predicted by the child's tendency to engage in overpersonalised conflict with their father ten years before. It also predicted difficulty in leaving home. Allen and Hauser commented that this kind of preoccupied relationship tended to reduce attachment security over time, and that it would be expected to produce enormous stress that could not be resolved in the ongoing relationship with the entangled parent.

Parental separation anxiety interacts with adolescent attachment security

Family therapists are bound to see attachment as a two-way process, meeting the needs of parents as well as those of children. Thinking along similar lines Hock et al (2001) studied parent's anxiety about separation from their adolescent children in early, middle and late adolescence, including those leaving home to go to college. As they expected they found evidence that some parents were anxious about separations and losses to them arising from their teenage children's developing autonomy. Adolescents who had secure attachment to their parents had parents who were less anxious. Parents who were anxious about separation from their teenager had teenagers who were less secure. This in turn led to conflict between the parents and their teenagers. Hock et al (2001) speculated, "… in families in which parents' anxiety about distancing is associated with over-protection or over-involvement, adolescents may increase the frequency and intensity of conflict to feel, and to be viewed as, independent", Hock et al (2001, p. 295). Hock and colleagues also demonstrated that parents varied in the extent to which they were comfortable continuing to offer support to their teenagers when this was needed. Here the issue was that some parents were more comfortable matching what they offered to their teenager's needs at the time. Parents who were comfortable with doing this had teenage children whose own attachment was more secure.

Attachment and the sense of self in adolescence

Secure attachment is important to the continuing development of the sense of self in adolescence. At this stage young people develop greater cognitive complexity and have the potential to develop a more complex, nuanced, sense of self. In the context of secure relationships this potential will be realised in the continuing development of a secure sense of self. Mikulincer (1995) described a series of studies that demonstrated this in groups of young people aged fifteen to eighteen. Young people who had secure attachment also had a positive, coherent self-structure. That is to say they saw themselves in positive terms, while being able to admit some negative attributes. They also had a more differentiated self-structure. They were able to see themselves differently in different aspects of their lives, for example as a student or as a friend. Yet this more differentiated structure was also more integrated, which is to say that the different aspects were not contradictory. By contrast young people with an ambivalent attachment style saw themselves in more negative terms, and described themselves in ways that were associated with more negative feelings, while there was some evidence that avoidant young people saw themselves in more positive terms. Young people with an avoidant style had a differentiated structure to the self, that is they saw themselves as different in different roles, but with a greater degree of discrepancy or contradiction between themselves in these roles. Ambivalent style was associated with less differentiation. Ambivalent young people saw themselves as much the same in different situations and roles. Lastly, in relation to the comparison between their views of themselves and the views they thought others had of them, secure young people thought their parents and friends had a more positive view of them than they had of themselves, while both avoidant and ambivalent young people thought the opposite, and the trend was for ambivalent young people to report this more strongly, as one would expect.

The sense of self, conflict about values and parental autonomy support

Another aspect of the development of self is identification of and with personal values. During the adolescent phase young people differentiate themselves from their families, in terms of attitudes and values, more than at any other stage. For example Moretti and Holland (2003) quote studies that showed that in mid-adolescence young people agreed with only 20% of the standards that they believed their parents held for them. By the time they reached their mid-twenties, young people accepted about 40% of their parents' attitudes and values for them. There was a marked difference between girls and boys as far as the emotional reaction to these differences were concerned. They found that both boys and girls were usually distressed if they felt they had been unable to live up to their own values. But boys were not distressed if they failed to come up to values expressed by parents, unless they had internalised these as values for themselves. The same applied to any discrepancy between boys' behaviour and their perception of their peers attitudes and values. By contrast girls in mid-adolescence were distressed by any discrepancy. Failing to live by their own values caused them distress, but so did any behaviour that did not fit with those parental values that the girls rejected, and the same applied to discrepancies with peer values. Hence, in mid-adolescence girls were trying to do the seemingly impossible, that is, to live in accordance with at least three discrepant sets of values so as to be "all right" with everyone. Here one is put in mind of Gilligan's (1982) observation that women typically place a high value on relationships and maintaining connectedness in relation to moral values. The findings described by Moretti and Holland indicate that in mid-adolescence girls typically have not yet achieved the ability to balance these different demands and perspectives in a comfortable way. Moretti and Holland suggest that this may explain the dramatic rise in rates of depression and eating disorder in girls in the early to mid-adolescent age group.

The situation is not as simple as this however, because although in general girls' self-esteem is compromised by disagreement with their mothers this is not always the case. Moretti and Holland (2003) describe another study that found that this did not hold true in the context of varying levels of maternal autonomy support. In this study they found that the girls who perceived themselves as at odds with their mother's standards for them, and whose mothers offered low levels of autonomy support, had the lowest self-esteem. The girls who perceived themselves to be at odds with maternal values, but whose mothers demonstrated high levels of autonomy support, had the highest self-esteem. Girls who simply did not feel themselves to be at odds with their mother's values had intermediate levels of self-esteem. Here we see that autonomy support allows a greater degree of challenge to parental values. The adolescent is free to engage in more exploration of values, in the context of high autonomy support, and this is likely to be particularly significant for girls in early and mid-adolescence, when they are most vulnerable to parental and peer judgements of their behaviour. It is a pity that this research has only been done with adolescents and mothers, as there are some indications that fathers are just as influential as mothers in regard to autonomy support, especially in relation to the development of eating disorder concerns and symptoms.

Attachment, internalising disorders and psychopathology

Attachment and depression

Kobak et al (1993) discussed the proposition that anxious attachment may be a risk factor for depression. They argued that the lack of availability of attachment figures through loss or parental depression leads to insecure attachment. This in turn perpetuates negative models of the self and others. Such models are "congruent" with aspects of depressive thinking such as negativity, feelings of worthlessness, self-reproach and excessive guilt. These experiences in turn make the individual vulnerable to depression. Kobak et al also noted studies that demonstrated that depressed mothers often had insecurely attached children, presumably because depression made the mother psychologically unavailable. They pointed out that the AAI assesses not only the adolescents' perception of their parents, but also their capacity to process the source of their perception. Anxious attachment restricts teenagers' ability to process their model of themselves and of their parents and so makes it difficult for them to re-evaluate or discount the validity of negative self-cognitions. In addition, failure to negotiate autonomy related issues might also cause the teenager to feel out of step with their peers and confirm a sense of isolation and low self-esteem. In these ways the power relationship, the way in which parental authority is worked out between the parents and the teenager, interacts with issues of attachment security.

Allen and Land (1999) argued that depression arises at the adolescent stage when parents fail to tolerate or support a degree of adolescent assertiveness that leads to conflict between the two. A manageable level of conflict is essential for the development of autonomy. Both extreme avoidance of conflict, and high levels of parental criticism in the event of conflict stand in the way of this. In this situation it is the adolescent's submissiveness and conflict avoidance that gives rise to adolescent depression. It is necessary for the adolescent to feel secure enough to express anger without fear of retribution. It is secure attachment to the parent that makes this possible.

Attachment and anxiety

Colonnesi et al (2011) conducted a meta-analysis of studies of the relationship between attachment and anxiety during childhood and adolescence. Just as the incidence of anxiety and anxiety disorders increases during adolescence, so too did the relationship between anxiety and attachment. The average correlations between measures of attachment and measures of anxiety were higher in studies of adolescents than it was in studies of children. Across all age groups the relationship with anxiety was stronger for preoccupied (Colonnesi uses the term "ambivalent") attachment than for insecure attachment in general.

Brumariu and Kerns (2010a, 2010b) reviewed fifty studies with varying methodology mostly concerning children in middle to late childhood through to adolescence. Results were mixed but they concluded that the evidence was of a consistent, but modest, relationship between attachment insecurity and both anxiety and depression. The associations were stronger for older children and adolescents than for younger children. The evidence was more consistent for the relationship between ambivalent (preoccupied) attachment than for avoidant (dismissive) attachment. However, avoidant/dismissive attachment was associated with internalising symptoms in "at risk samples". So perhaps the indication is that an avoidant/dismissive strategy does serve a protective function but it is brittle and breaks down when stresses become overwhelming.

Attachment and eating disorders

O'Shaughnessy and Dallos (2009) reviewed research studies of the relationship between attachment and eating disorders. They reached two main conclusions. These were, first, that women with eating disorders had suffered high levels of separation anxiety in childhood, and separation difficulties remained unresolved in adult life, leading to continuing extreme difficulties with feelings about separation. Second, a high frequency of unresolved traumas in the mothers of patients could be understood as creating a situation in which a mother's unresolved feelings would make it difficult for her to be attuned to her child's emotional needs. They suggested that anorexia resulted from two factors. First, parents own insecure attachment was a general risk factor for psychopathology in their children. Second, the deficiency in providing security at mealtimes in the parent's family of origin, and the parents' efforts to rectify this in their own families, created the specific risk for eating disorder.

Studies based on interviews

Cole-Detke and Kobak (1996) studied the attachment strategies of female students, comparing those with no symptomatic concerns with those with depressive, or eating disorder tendencies, or both combined. They used the Adult Attachment Interview (AAI) and the three-way (secure/preoccupied/dismissing) classification. They argued that depression reflected a state of preoccupation with neediness, while eating disorders reflected the opposite, since by controlling their world through controlling eating, students with eating concerns distracted their attention from their attachment needs. As they expected students with depressive tendencies used predominantly hyper-activating (preoccupied) strategies in the AAI, while students with eating disorder tendencies alone used predominantly deactivating (dismissing) strategies. Those who had both depressive and eating disorder symptoms were similar to those with depression alone. They commented that those who tended towards depression expressed anger towards parents in the AAI, demonstrated excessive processing of attachment information and presented themselves as feeling hurt. Those who tended towards eating disorder without depression denied or minimised expressions of anger towards parents and tended to restrict processing of attachment information. However, as we have seen, studies of more seriously affected populations found that patients often fell into hard to classify groups. Later clinical studies of attachment have tended to emphasise the patient's attempts to use attachment strategies, and issues highlighted in the AAI reflecting unresolved problems arising from loss or abuse, rather than attachment classification as such.

Barone and Guiducci (2009) analysed the AAIs of thirty patients with eating disorders, ten with anorexia, ten with bulimia and ten with binge eating disorder. There was also a comparison group of thirty women without a mental illness. Using the three category system, 60% of the non-clinical group was rated as in the secure category, but only three of the eating disorder patients were assigned to it. However these three all had anorexia, so 30% of them were seen as "secure". Of the remaining seven patients with anorexia, three were regarded as "dismissive" and four as "enmeshed/preoccupied". The eating disorder patients as a group reported more negative experiences than controls in all five domains rated and in relation to both parents. These differences became significant in relation to rejection by parents, neglect by parents, and role reversal by parents, and, in the case of the father but not mother, receiving less love. Although the eating disorder patients reported higher levels of demands for achievement this difference did not achieve statistical significance. The ratings of inferred states of mind were also on average more problematic for the eating disorder patients, but differences between them and controls only achieved significance in relation to two issues. The patients were seen as more idealising of the mother, but also as experiencing more anger in the relationship with the mother. The eating disorder patients were less productive in the interviews, offering fewer memories. Their accounts were markedly less coherent, and there were more instances of unresolved loss in their accounts, although not more instances of loss overall.

Inter-generational transmission of attachment difficulties and anorexia

There is some evidence of intergenerational transmission of insecure attachment in the relationships of girls with anorexia and their parents. Ward et al (2001) carried out AAIs with twenty patients with anorexia and with twelve of their mothers. This was a group of mostly adult patients (only three were younger than age eighteen) with a long history of eating disorder. Analysis of the interviews allowed allocation of the patients and their mothers to an attachment classification, and assessment of unresolved trauma or loss, as well as assessment of idealisation or derogation of attachment figures, and the capacity of the patients and mothers for "reflective functioning", which means the ability to think about their own and others states of mind. Only one patient and two mothers were assessed as secure. Fifteen of the twenty patients, and seven of the twelve mothers were assessed as dismissive. At least eight patients were seen as unresolved in relation to experiences of loss, as were eight of the twelve mothers. Both patients and mothers were more prone to idealising, less coherent, and poorer in reflective functioning, than comparison women.

A larger study, which also confirms this observation, is by Delogu et al (2008). In this study the AAI was completed with thirty-five girls with anorexia and their parents. They found that girls with anorexia showed a high rate of dismissive attachment style, that their mothers were characterised by unresolved states of mind about loss, and fathers also had a high rate of insecure attachment. Delogu et al thought that the girls' dismissing strategy might help them to cope with their parents' problems with emotion regulation.

Ringer and Crittenden (2007) analysed AAIs with sixty-two young women with eating disorders. Twenty of the women had restricting anorexia and sixteen had anorexia with bulimic symptoms, while the remainder had bulimia. None of the women had a secure attachment. There was considerable overlap between the diagnostic groups in terms of their attachment strategy. However women with anorexia were typically described as characterised by compulsive caregiving and compliance, and as idealising of parents, or as using styles that were cold and distant, or strategies exaggerating vulnerability and so exciting the need for rescue. They tended to use a number of strategies for managing their relationships. On the one hand were strategies that functioned to avoid emotional arousal, especially anger; on the other, strategies of compulsive caregiving and compulsive compliance. In addition, the patients engaged in idealising of parents, or one parent, and alternated between punitive and seductive behaviours towards caregivers. Idealisation of parents was sometimes a strategy that allowed distress about the family situation to be denied. On other occasions one parent was idealised in a way that served to derogate the other parent, suggesting an inappropriate cross-generational alliance.

Another important finding was that the patients had many unresolved problems about loss. Often these were not their own direct experiences of loss, but arose from over-involvement in parents' experiences of loss, or of the parents' unresolved conflict and disappointment in the parental marriage. All in all the description fits with clinical descriptions of girls in families who are poor at processing emotions while at the same time being intensely emotionally engaged with one another in ways that may be denied, and which cut across appropriate family boundaries. Sometimes these unresolved losses may reflect the large number of stillbirths demonstrated by Shoebridge and Gowers (2000) in the histories of patients' mothers. It is interesting to note that Hughes et al (2001) compared the attachment of infants born to mothers whose previous pregnancy had ended in stillbirth with that of babies whose mothers had not had a previous pregnancy. At age one babies whose mothers had experienced stillbirth in the previous pregnancy were three times as likely to have the relatively severe disorganised attachment pattern in the strange situation. Hughes also used the AAI with the mothers. Over half the mothers who had experienced stillbirth were in a state of unresolved attachment, reflecting the experience of the loss, compared to just 8% of the comparison mothers. It was the babies of mothers who had an unresolved loss after the stillbirth that demonstrated the disorganised attachment at age one.

Commenting on data drawn from an unpublished study, Ringer and Crittenden (2007) speculate that the attachment strategies used by women with anorexia reflect early experiences with mothers who themselves have high levels of unresolved trauma in their backgrounds. They thought that mothers wanted to be able to protect their daughters from threats and disappointments, but without explaining these to their daughters. They argue, "In their sadness, silence and fear, these mothers both sought a special closeness … with their daughters and also tried to shelter their daughters by walling off their own traumas …". The unresolved traumas and losses affected the mothers' behaviour in such a way that they became unavailable "just when the daughters thought they had been invited to approach", Ringer and Crittenden (2007, p. 127). A weakness of the study is that important conclusions are drawn about intergenerational transmission of attachment difficulties, but data from patients and parents were not drawn from the same families. A small study that corrects this is by Dallos and Densford (2008) and it confirmed Ringer and Crittenden's conclusions. Attachment interviews with four patients with anorexia, with their parents and a sibling provided the basic data for the study. Qualitative analysis confirmed the themes found by Ringer and Crittenden. Parents reported many difficulties in their own families of origin that they attempted to avoid reproducing in their own families. However, as the parents had been unable to resolve their emotional reaction to these issues they were to a considerable extent reproduced with their own children. Parents desire to achieve a different sort of relationship was often experienced by the younger generation as creating demands for unhealthy or inappropriate closeness. Dallos and Densford also found evidence in these interviews that parents' experience of mealtimes in their own families of origin had often been traumatic or neglectful, an experience that was often repeated for their children. They concluded that "Rather than emotions being simply restricted or suppressed, it appeared that these were a central concern to all of the family members. They shared concerns about being able to express themselves properly and about being confused and distrustful of what feelings were expressed …". These in turn lead family members to use "deceptive or masked communication, which in turn fueled a sense of insecurity …", Dallos and Densford (2008, p. 318).

Studies based on questionnaires

Questionnaire measures are intrinsically less satisfactory as an approach to understanding attachment. Dismissing strategies seem especially likely to be under-reported. However, a number of studies have used this approach. In reading these studies it is important to bear in mind that we are now dealing with what people say about themselves in questionnaires about relationships, rather than with what can be inferred by how they say it in an interview.

Ward et al (2000) studied the current attachment relationships of a large group of adult patients with eating disorders. More than half the group had anorexia. A questionnaire measure intended for the study of adult attachment relationships, the Reciprocal Attachment Questionnaire, was used to assess attachment style. Many patients reported on their relationship with a current partner but some regarded their mother as still their most, perhaps their only, significant relationship. They found that "our patients were most characterised by the apparently contradictory attachment styles of compulsive care seeking (anxious) and compulsive self-reliance (avoidance)" (Ward et al, 2000, p. 274). There was no difference between patients with anorexia and those with bulimia. Ward et al observed that patients who had partners seemed to be afraid to rely on them and alternated between compulsive care giving and angry withdrawal.

Troisi et al (2005) used the Attachment Style Questionnaire and the Separation Anxiety Symptom Inventory with seventy-eight women with eating disorders and a comparison group of women. Women with eating disorders reported higher rates of separation anxiety in childhood, lower levels of security in attachment, and overall higher levels of scores on scales measuring both preoccupied and dismissing approaches to attachment. However, the difference was not statistically significant on scales measuring dismissive attachment.

Community studies of eating disorder concerns and attachment security confirm these findings. Sharpe et al (1998) used questionnaire measures of attachment and eating concerns with a female student population. They confirmed the expected relationship. Insecurely attached students had more eating concerns. They speculated that the eating concerns reflected the lower levels of self-esteem and of confidence in social acceptability, experienced by students with less secure attachment. Likewise Back (2011) found that for female students higher scores on a measure of problem eating attitudes were associated with insecure attachment to the mother, and to the recollection of a higher level of food related family rules during childhood. Eggert et al (2007) found that the relationship between insecure attachment and disordered eating was mediated by neuroticism. This could be interpreted as meaning that insecure attachment led to increased disordered eating if it had first given rise to increased neuroticism, or that it only gave rise to eating disorders in people who were genetically predisposed. The latter interpretation is hard to reconcile with the genetic evidence, at least as far as anorexia is concerned.

Conclusion

Evidence supports clinicians' understanding that parental behaviour has a huge impact on the developing child. This is true both in respect of evidence on the impact of the parental marriage, and the child's involvement in it, and in respect of the direct relationship that the child and adolescent has with each parent. This holds true whether one looks at the relationships through the lens of attachment theory, or through that of narrative or meta-emotion philosophy approaches. In adolescence secure attachment to parents, and parental support for the developing autonomy of the teenager, becomes a crucial issue. This support primarily takes the form of prioritising the expression of the teenager's unique point of view. Research evidence supports the view that deficits in these areas contribute to the development of problems like anorexia, eating disorders in general, and related difficulties such as anxiety disorders and depression. It supports the model of anorexia proposed by Dallos (2006) that girls with anorexia are caught up in parental difficulties arising from unresolved trauma and loss experienced by their parents. It can also be argued that a range of factors bearing on attachment during childhood and infancy, and on the ability of parents to help their child develop self-esteem and the capacity for emotional processing, all contribute to the development of a personality vulnerable to the development of anorexia. This vulnerability usually does not arise because of experiences of abuse or what would conventionally be regarded as neglect. Instead it reflects a deficit in the parent's capacity to support secure and autonomous development in the maturing child.

The main weakness of this research is that some studies lacked comparison groups, and that in some studies the researchers who analysed adult attachment interviews were not blind to the patient's problem. Preconceptions about the relationship between the problem and attachment could have influenced the analysis in some studies. There is a need for substantial studies that would correct these faults. Nevertheless, the studies do provide an interpretation of the family experiences, and the vulnerabilities, of patients with anorexia and their parents, which clinicians should take seriously. Larger studies, with blind ratings and a non-clinical comparison group, would provide a more satisfactory test of the theory. Nevertheless, in the current state of our knowledge it is reasonable for clinicians to draw on these studies in thinking about how to direct their work.

The attachment difficulties thought to be characteristic of the families of patients with anorexia might give rise to a wide range of difficulties. O'Shaughnessy and Dallos (2009) proposed a second factor, that parents failed to provide security at mealtimes in the course of the patient's upbringing. It is hard to find research on patients with anorexia specifically on this point. Research evidence on the family transmission of problem attitudes to eating, weight and appearance will be discussed shortly. Attachment issues may not account for some other difficulties typical of patients with anorexia. For example, no link has been demonstrated between attachment and the development of perfectionism. It may be that that is better accounted for by another issue, the way in which parents control the behaviour of children and young people. That is the focus of the next chapter.

CHAPTER NINE

Parental authority

Studies of the way in which parents control children and adolescents have relevance for understanding the child's developing sense of self, the development of internalising disorders, and the development of vulnerable personality characteristics like maladaptive perfectionism and eating disorders. The research tradition on parenting style in relation to parental authority is rich and long established. It is another factor that has a major bearing on the development of autonomy in childhood and adolescence. Excessively controlling behaviour by parents, and submissiveness on the part of children and adolescents, has long been associated with the development of internalising disorders. In recent years, studies have extended our knowledge in this area to its influence on the development of maladaptive perfectionism, and to the development of depression and eating disorders including anorexia.

Styles of parental authority

A long-standing tradition in the study of family relationships concerns the way in which parental authority is exercised with the child.

Katz et al (1999) pointed out that factor analytic studies of parenting produced two major dimensions. The first of these was a permissive-restrictive dimension, which is about the amount of freedom of action that parents allow the child. The second was a warmth-cold/hostile dimension implying loving acceptance versus rejection. These dimensions can be used to describe parental styles. Authoritarian parents are those who make many demands, expect strict obedience and give little explanation. Their style is restrictive and cold. Authoritative parents set limits but are more flexible, give explanations, and are warm. Permissive parents allow far more freedom of action. Parents who are both cold and permissive have been described as indifferent. Baumrind (1966) drew the conclusion from her review of research that both authoritarian and permissive parenting might create "a climate in which the child is not desensitised to the anxiety associated with nonconformity". The child needed to learn how to dissent. She argued that "Spirited give and take within the home, if accompanied by respect and warmth, may teach the child how to express aggression in self-serving and prosocial causes … ." (Baumrind, 1966, p. 904). The danger was that over-controlling parents might express their needs in ways that intruded upon the child's ability to develop her autonomous self.

Barber and Harmon (2002) reviewed discussion and research on the topic of intrusive parenting, or, as they called it "parental psychological control". This consisted of parental behaviours that were manipulative or intrusive on children's thoughts, and their attachments to parents. Barber and Harmon regarded these parental behaviours as interfering with inter-personal boundaries, impairing the development of the sense of self and of individual identity. They commented that Steinberg (1990) had drawn attention to the distinction between psychological control, the attempt to control what a child or adolescent might think or feel, and behavioural control, which is the setting of limits to behaviour. Barber and Harmon argued that Baumrind's concept of authoritarian parenting overlapped with the concept of parental psychological control. Crucial to the definition of the construct is that it is defined in an interactive sense; the parental behaviours that are a problem are those which interfere with the development of autonomy. As Barber and Harmon say, the parent behaves in ways to manage the relationship to the parent's psychological advantage. These methods include inappropriate appeals to family loyalty, guilt induction, shaming, withdrawal of love, and instilling anxiety. They identified a number of other factors that related to the issue of parental psychological control. These included excessive parental expectations; achievement demands; avoiding tenderness; ignoring; affective punishment; rejection and hostile detachment; personal attack on the child; blaming the child for other family members problems; and erratic emotional behaviour, by which they meant alternating between caring for and attacking the child. They can also take infantilising forms. Barber and Harmon list numerous terms that have been used to describe this situation, or aspects of it. They include: babying the child; unduly emphasising affectional bonds between parent and child; fostering dependency, and placing the child in a subordinate position needing to conform completely to the wishes of the parent under penalty of extreme punishment. In addition, they highlighted the importance of parental constraining behaviours. These involve avoidance of communication and discouraging the verbalisation of ideas and emotions.

Parental authority and its impact on the developing child

Barber and Harmon (2002) argue that adolescents are adversely affected by psychological control, but benefit from behavioural control. Behavioural control can protect the adolescent from unhelpful influences and dangers. By contrast psychological control impedes the development of competence and self-direction. Parental behavioural contro*l*, which we often describe as limit setting, involves an emotionally neutral attempt by the parent to help the child fit behaviour to socially expected norms and to remain safe. By contrast the parent who uses strategies of parental psychologica*l* control can be seen as engaged in behaviour that prioritises parental emotional needs over those of the child.

To relate these concepts to those used by family therapy we could see parental behavioural control as roughly equivalent to the kind of directing, limit setting function of parents that keeps the child safe. It is the relationship quality expressed by the vertical axis in the traditional structural family map, at least as long as the parents are in the appropriate place in the map. By contrast parental psychological control is a very broad construct, encompassing a wide spectrum of parental behaviours which family therapists would see as unhelpful. Barber and Harmon proposed that enmeshment is the family system level equivalent of psychological control in the parent–child relationship. It is a construct which must map onto a wide range of family issues, such as inappropriate boundaries, inversions of parental relationship and so on.

The impact of parental psychological control

Parental psychological control is a factor that is seen as impacting in a very negative way on the child's sense of self. Barber and Harmon (2002) list numerous authors who have drawn attention to this, using such terms as self-will; self-regulation; self-reliance; self-discovery; ego development; self-expression; decision making; autonomy; individuality; independence; identity and emotional autonomy. Parental psychological control is also seen as leading to the development of internalising problems in children, particularly anxiety and depression. More recently it has been seen as implicated in the development of perfectionism, and of problems related to perfectionism, such as eating disorders, including anorexia.

Barber and Harmon reviewed a considerable body of research evidence that indicated that parental psychological control has a negative impact on the child. An important group of studies used the Child Reported Parental Behaviour Inventory (CRPBI) developed by Schaefer (1965). One of the scales of the inventory is a measure of parental psychological control. They reported on the results of thirty-nine studies using one or other form of this inventory, or the Psychological Control Scale, which has been derived from it. The studies are of groups of children and young people varying in age from age three to age twenty-five, but predominantly in the late childhood and adolescent age range. Each study correlated reports of psychological control with one or more measure of psychological adjustment. These included measures of self-esteem, and other measures of the sense of self, for example identity status, self-worth and self-confidence, and measures of internalising disorders such as anxiety and depression, of externalising disorders such as defiant behaviour, delinquency and gang membership, and of academic achievement. Some 21,251 children and young people participated in these studies. Barber and Harmon reported the relationship between parental psychological control and eighty-six outcome measures across the thirty-nine studies. These studies indicated that parental psychological control did indeed correlate with poorer outcomes whether viewed in terms of measures of the developing sense of self, or in terms of measures of internalising or externalising disorders. Within this group of studies, seven reported outcomes directly related to the sense of self. Six studies produced positive results. In the one exception, of four outcome measures three were positive, but one negative. With this single exception all the thirty-nine studies that tested the relationship between parental psychological control and internalising disorders, including measures of the sense of self, confirmed the expected relationship. The relationship with externalising disorders was less clearly confirmed. Not all studies confirmed the expected relationship between parental psychological control and externalising problems, and Barber and Harmon concluded that other influences, which may include other aspects of family relationships, peer and wider social influences had a greater influence on externalising than on internalising problems. Clearly this is likely to be so when factors such as drug use and gang membership are taken into account. In addition other studies indicate that lack of parental behavioural control, for example setting limits, and "monitoring", which means knowing where your children are and what they are doing, may be factors more predictive of the development of externalising disorders.

Barber and Harmon go on to review the results of nineteen studies of parenting in which psychological control was one aspect of the parenting dimensions studied, but could not be treated separately from other aspects. These studies were largely based on Baumrind's (1966) distinction between authoritative and authoritarian parenting. Barber and Harmon assumed that parental psychological control was one aspect of authoritarian parenting. Again these studies provided evidence of a relationship between authoritarian parenting and self-processes, internalising disorders and academic achievement, and, with some exceptions, with externalising disorders.

Taken overall the evidence Barber and Harmon presented impressively demonstrated the relationship between parental psychological control and the child's developing sense of self on the one hand, and disorders, especially internalising disorders, on the other.

Soenens et al (2010) found that additional studies confirm these findings. Parental psychological control was shown to be associated with depression in a study by Barber et al (2005), with anxiety in a study by Pettit and Laird (2002), and with low self-esteem in a study by Soenens (2005a). In addition he quotes studies that show that Parental Psychological Control can be seen as arising from parental marital conflict, in a study by Buehler et al (2006) and from parental perfectionism, in a study by Soenens et al (2005b).

Developmental origins of perfectionism and fear of failure

As we have seen, one aspect of internalising problems that is very highly related to anorexia is perfectionism. Perfectionism is seen as arising as a result of various parenting practices. Flett et al (2002) describe a range of theoretical positions about how it develops. The child's exposure to contingent parental approval has been seen as a very significant factor. It is seen as leading to a sense of helplessness. They comment that people who complain that they can never satisfy other's demands are likely to have been subjected to contingent love and approval. They go on to argue that this in turn promotes feelings of helplessness in response to negative feedback. Another proposed mechanism is drawn from social learning theory. It is simply that children imitate perfectionistic parents. Another possible route into perfectionism they term "social reaction". They argue that children who encounter adverse circumstances such as physical abuse, withdrawal of love, or parental behaviours that give rise to shame, may develop perfectionism as a coping mechanism. Perfect behaviour might serve to protect the child from further attack or it might serve to help the child to develop a sense of "control and predictability" in an alarming world. They also comment on what they call the "Anxious Rearing Model". Parents may experience anxiety about how their children will be treated or how they will be seen, and this may prompt them to remind their children to be on the look out for and prevent mistakes or faults. To this one might add that another possible factor here would be that parents are anxious about how they will be seen in the light of the way their children present themselves. Parental discomfort or anxiety about the social world could drive parents to act in this way.

Another issue raised by Flett et al (2002) is that praise can also be a potential source of difficulty for children. Praise focusing on children's attributes, such as intelligence, can be unhelpful, whereas praise focused on behaviour is helpful. They quote studies by Kamins and Dweck (1999) and Mueller and Dweck (1998) who demonstrated this effect. The argument presented by Flett et al is that children become reliant on this kind of positive feedback and are at risk of feeling helpless when it is no longer available. Hence, they argue that parental behaviour that is usually seen as positive (offering praise) can become a source of difficulty for the child. Another way of looking at this would be that the demand characteristics of feedback directed at attributes such as attractiveness or ability are unhelpful. Such feedback conveys the message that the child should live up to the parent's image of them, and that it is behaviour that does this, not the child's real self, that is valued. Here one might speculate that it is the parent's evaluative set about appearance, behaviour or achievement that is communicated by the praise that causes the difficulty. A further issue that Flett et al touch on concerns the development of what they call Narcissistic Perfectionism. This is the attitude of people who strive for perfection and feel confident that they can achieve it. They quote Millon (1998) who suggested such an attitude might be the result of overly positive evaluations by parents. This is likely to be a fragile adjustment that breaks down when achievement proves elusive.

A separate issue, but one which may also be a significant driver of perfectionism in some families, is competition among siblings. The extent to which competition is expressed, the ways in which parents respond by encouraging or moderating it, and the actual dynamics of the situation, for example the question whether one sibling usually wins or loses out in competition could all be significant factors in the development of both low self-esteem and perfectionism.

Flett et al (2002) assumed that perfectionism would be accounted for by a wide range of factors including the child's temperament and attachment style, the parents' goals, parenting and personality, and that the child's experience of other environmental pressures, such as those arising in school and from the peer group would also play a part. They proposed that self-oriented perfectionism would be particularly likely to result when the child perceived that there were domains in which they could achieve perfection, so that for example things like academic or musical ability might be risk factors. Research on the development of conscience indicates that some children are more open to socialisation. It is not clear what the precursors are for this. The psychological need for approval is likely to be an issue. This has often been attributed to child temperament. However, they observed that some children may respond to parental pressure in the opposite way, rebelliously rejecting parental demands and insisting that they are different. This would tend to prevent the development of perfectionism. The child's perception that they cannot achieve the standards demanded might be one reason for this.

Flett et al (2002) argue that perfectionists will want to be perfect parents who have perfect children. They review a number of studies that found that various aspects of perfectionism in parents led to parenting behaviours that were critical and over-controlling, and caused parents to demonstrate lower levels of sensitivity to children. Studies indicate that unrealistic attitudes and expectations about children, and towards the experience of becoming a parent, impact on the perfectionistic parent from the beginning. The perfectionistic parent may be driven from the beginning by fear of unwanted outcomes, and behave in overly controlling and intrusive ways as a result. Flett reviews further studies that found that in families with young children parental perfectionism was associated with parental stress, dissatisfaction and distress. One possible outcome is that the younger generation will develop perfectionistic behaviour to satisfy parental demands.

Craddock et al (2009) cite four studies that found evidence that authoritarian and non-nurturing parental styles were associated with dysfunctional perfectionism in the younger generation. He conducted a questionnaire study of psychology students, 70% female, to investigate the relationship between perfectionism and authoritarian parenting and psychologically controlling parenting and family enmeshment. Dysfunctional perfectionism was found to be associated with parental psychological control, authoritarian parenting and family enmeshment. By contrast functional perfectionism, which is to say having high standards and being highly organised, was associated with family enmeshment, authoritarian parenting and, negatively, with family chaos. The effects of family relationships were stronger for dysfunctional than for functional perfectionism. Fletcher et al (2012) in another study of psychology students found parental psychological control associated with two aspects of maladaptive perfectionism, doubts over actions and concern over mistakes.

As Soenens et al point out "Psychologically controlling parents have been described as critical, achievement-oriented, highly demanding, and strict …—characteristics that are closely related to perfectionism … as defined by the pursuit of personally demanding and self-imposed standards, rigid adherence to these standards, and high levels of critical self-evaluations", Soenens et al (2006, p. 540). It may be concluded that the development of maladaptive perfectionism is driven by the child, and adolescent, experience of relationship to a psychologically controlling parent. Drawing on the model developed by Hock et al (2001) they argued that parental psychological control demonstrated by mothers and fathers might arise either from parental discomfort with the developing autonomy of the adolescent, triggering anxiety about loss in the parent, or from the parents own maladaptive perfectionism. Hence "Whereas some parents may use psychological control because they feel anxious and insecure about the adolescents increasing autonomy. … others may resort to psychologically controlling parenting as a means to get their children to comply to their personal high standards (i.e., perfectionism)", Soenens et al (2006, p. 553).

Soenens et al (2008a) summarised research evidence that demonstrated that perfectionism in adolescent girls could be accounted for by parental psychological control, while fear of failure had been found to relate to mothers threats of withdrawal of love. They demonstrated that parental psychological control arose both from parental fears of separation from the adolescent, which they took to reflect the parents' own attachment history, and, separately, from parents' own maladaptive perfectionism. Parental psychological control, arising from either or both of these sources, predicted negative outcomes such as depression in the adolescent children. They speculated that parental psychological control might be expressed differently according to the source of parental anxiety. They thought that when it was driven by parental fears of separation it might give rise to anxious clingy behaviour by the parent. This pattern was more typical of mothers' expression of parental psychological control. When it was driven by parental maladaptive perfectionism it might give rise to excessively self critical and harsh evaluation of the self. They thought this would be more typical of the impact of fathers' relationships with adolescent children. Both these parental behaviour patterns might ultimately give rise to depression in the developing adolescent.

Submissive communication and depression in teenage girls

Powers and Welsh (1999) studied communication between mothers and daughters and the development of depression over time. They quoted research by Allen et al (1994) who had found that adolescent depression was predicted by family interactions that were less hostile, less autonomy promoting and more inhibiting of autonomy than interactions in other families. They reasoned that girls respond to puberty and adolescence with a challenge for greater independence. This would lead to a need for negotiation with parents. Where this negotiation was difficult conflict would follow. If girls responded to that conflict with submission, thus inhibiting their drive for independence, then depression would result. Powers and Welsh undertook a longitudinal study. Thirty-five teenage girls, ranging in age from fourteen to nineteen at the beginning of the study, took part. At the outset, and again a year later, they completed a questionnaire measure of internalising symptoms. Mothers and daughters took part in two discussion tasks and these were video-taped. In the first task mother and daughter discussed how they negotiated ways of being close. The second of the two tasks required them to talk about an area of conflict between them. After the interaction tasks had been recorded mothers and daughters came, separately, to view the recorded interaction and provided ratings of their understanding of what each person in the interaction was doing. The ratings were of the use of Support, Conflict, Submission, Humour and Sarcasm. The measure of internalising symptoms was repeated a year later.

The research question was the extent to which increased internalising symptoms reflected conflict and, more particularly submission, by the adolescent, as well as other aspects of the relationship. Analysis of the results indicated that the level of internalising symptoms at the one year follow-up could not be accounted for by the initial level, but were accounted for by the quality of the interaction. The results indicated that when girls who are already high on internalising symptoms negotiated interpersonal relationships with mothers that were characterised by high levels of conflict, humour, and sarcasm, then internalising symptoms increased. They did so much more if the girl responded in this situation with submissiveness. The girl's own ratings of her submissiveness were the crucial issue here, so that her awareness of giving in contributed significantly to her depressed affect. It is interesting that some girls were experiencing similar degrees of conflict with their mothers but not reporting internalising symptoms. Here the difference was that these girls were not experienced by themselves, or by their mothers, as submissive.

Another interesting finding was that in some cases if girls had high initial levels of internalising symptoms then mothers submissive behaviour in the interaction task predicted more severe symptoms at follow-up. Here Powers and Welsh (1999) drew a comparison with research on adult depression which shows that where depressed behaviour inhibits assertive or aggressive behaviour in significant others, depression gets worse. They drew the conclusion from this finding that the mother needs to be able to tolerate a degree of conflict if she is to be able to support her daughter's developing autonomy.

In the context of the mother–daughter conflict described here, humour was not a positive characteristic, at least not in the relationships of girls who reported internalising symptoms. For them humour and sarcasm were both aspects of a conflict situation that they were failing to manage. Another interesting finding was that the mothers of girls with internalising symptoms were not aware of their daughter's difficulties. They did not report high levels of conflict or submission in their daughter's behaviour, but instead saw humour. For them humour perhaps served to defuse conflict to such an extent that they were able to remain unaware of the significance the conflict had for their daughters.

It is also interesting that psychologically supportive behaviour was not found to be a helpful resource for the girls with internalising symptoms. Mothers' emotional support did not reduce the impact of problematic aspects of the relationship. In the context of intergenerational conflict that is being resolved by the younger generations' submissiveness, both "psychological support" and humour may be indicative of an unhelpful degree of evasiveness about the conflict. In other contexts, such as stresses arising outside family relationships, mothers' support may be more valuable.

We do not know whether or not maladaptive perfectionism and parental psychological control contributed to the girls' depression. If so it may have been driven by their experience of maternal dependency-oriented psychological control. The girls would have felt that they were failing if they upset their mothers by persisting in asserting their individual needs.

Parental psychological control and adolescent depression

Soenens et al (2008a, 2010) argued that parental psychological control could arise from different needs in parents. This in turn might create different effects in children. They commented that Blatt (2004), describing personality development, distinguished between a dependent and a perfectionistic style. These styles reflect preoccupations with either interpersonal relatedness, or with self-definition. Where difficulties arise in the sense of relatedness they give rise to problems in the management of separation and loss. By contrast difficulties with self-definition can be managed by the development of unrealistically high standards for the self, which creates a vulnerability to severe self-criticism. In theory both kinds of difficulty can lead to depression and other disorders.

Drawing on Blatt's account, Soenens et al (2010) comment that different childhood experiences are likely to lie behind these problems. Dependency would be expected to result when parents "manipulate the attachment bond with the child and use their love and care to control the child. Specifically, love and acceptance are made contingent on the child's dependence on the parents", Soenens et al (2010, p. 218). By contrast self-criticism could be seen as arising in a situation where parental love is seen as depending on meeting parental demands for achievement and good behaviour. Both developmental pathways create vulnerability to depression and internalising disorders in general. In addition gender would be a factor influencing this. Soenens et al (2010) thought that mothers would be expected to be more concerned with relatedness, and would be more likely to foster dependency, while fathers would be expected to be more concerned with achievement, and more likely to foster excessive concerns with achievement in their children.

Soenens et al (2010) reported a series of studies that set out to test these assumptions. They distinguished between two kinds of parental psychological control. Parental psychological control might be directed at keeping children dependent, which they called Dependency-oriented Psychological Control (DPC) or directed towards making children comply with parental standards of achievement, which they called Achievement-oriented Psychological Control (APC). Soenens predicted that children who experienced high levels of DPC from parents would be preoccupied with interpersonal closeness and dependency, while those who experienced high APC would be excessively self-critical about their achievements. In the first study they developed a questionnaire measure, the Dependency-oriented and Achievement-oriented Psychological Control Scale (DAPCS). Young people completed this scale and three other measures: a measure of parental autonomy support; a measure of perfectionistic family climate and a questionnaire measure of family enmeshment. Mothers were rated higher on

DPC, and fathers higher on APC. As expected DPC was correlated with enmeshment, APC with perfectionist family climate, and both were negatively related to autonomy support. In the second study a large group of parents of adolescent boys and girls completed the DAPCS, describing their own behaviour in terms of these variables, as well as measures of separation anxiety and maladaptive perfectionism. As was expected there was an association between parents' separation anxiety and parental dependency-oriented psychological control, and an association between parental maladaptive perfectionism and parental achievement-oriented psychological control. In the third study the participants were boys and girls aged fifteen to nineteen. They completed the DAPCS and measures of dependency, self-criticism and depression. The young people's ratings of maternal DPC were positively related to dependency in the younger generation, but fathers' DPC was not. Both fathers' and mothers' APC were positively related to young people's self-criticism. Measures of dependency in the young people, and measures of self-criticism, were both related to levels of depression. Further analysis of the data indicated that DPC was related to adolescent dependency, especially DPC perceived by young people as coming from their mothers. Hence it appears that maternal separation anxiety becomes internalised in the younger generation's dependency concerns. Likewise APC was related to adolescent self-criticism. Both forms of psychological control in turn led to depression. This supports the theoretical notion that young people internalise parental standards; when these are unusually demanding the outcome is excessive dependency and or self-criticism in the younger generation. Both adolescent dependency and adolescent self-criticism were found to predict levels of depression, and self-criticism was the stronger predictor.

Parental psychological control and maladaptive perfectionism

Soenens (2008a) tested a model that predicted that parental psychological control in adolescence would lead to maladaptive perfectionism in the adolescent, and that this in turn would lead to depression. They confirmed this for the relationship between both parents and adolescent boys' development, but for girls this was only true for the relationship between fathers and daughters. They speculated that while a father's intrusive parenting contributed to the development of maladaptive perfectionism in girls, and hence to depression, the mothers' contribution to depression in adolescent girls was more likely to result from behaviour that exacerbated concern about anxiety and loss. Hence "in mother–daughter dyads, dependency rather than perfectionism may be the intervening mechanism linking parenting to depressive symptoms", Soenens et al (2008a, p. 470).

Parental psychological control and adolescent eating disorders

Soenens et al (2008b) predicted that maladaptive perfectionism would play a mediating role between parental psychological control and eating disorder symptoms. To test this they used three measures of eating disorder symptoms derived from the Eating Disorders Inventory, measures of Drive for Thinness, Bulimia and Body dissatisfaction. Participants were thirty-seven patients with restricting anorexia and twenty-three with bulimia. All the patients took part during admission to a specialist eating disorder unit. They ranged in age from fifteen to twenty-five years. All were living with at least one parent prior to their admission. There was a comparison group of eighty-five female university students who were likewise still living with at least one parent. Both patient groups reported higher levels of psychologically controlling behaviour by both mothers and fathers than was reported by the comparison group. However, the difference only achieved significance in relation to father's psychological control in the group with bulimia. Both patient groups reported higher levels of maladaptive perfectionism than the comparison group, and these levels were highest for patients with anorexia. When the patient groups were combined and compared with the comparison group maladaptive perfectionism was positively correlated with Drive for Thinness and Body Dissatisfaction in both groups. As predicted, parental psychological control was predictive of maladaptive perfectionism, and this in turn mediated the effect of parental control on these eating disorder symptoms. The effect was stronger for paternal than for maternal psychological control.

Miller-Day and Marks (2006) studied related issues in a community sample of young adults. They compared scores on measures of disordered eating behaviour with scores on measures of self-prescribed and parentally prescribed perfectionism, personal control (the extent to which the young person felt in charge of their life), and measures of two aspects of each parents' communication pattern, a "conformity orientation" and a "conversation orientation". A conformity orientation would be one in which parents create a climate that enforces similar attitudes, values and beliefs among family members. By contrast a conversation orientation was one in which there is support for an open flow of communication. The study was entirely based on the young people's reports of their own behaviour and their perceptions of their parents. Young people who had maladaptive eating patterns also had a poorer sense of being in control of their lives, and higher levels of self-prescribed, and father-prescribed perfectionism, and fathers' conformity orientation. In general self-prescribed perfectionism was related to both parental prescribed perfectionism in mothers and fathers, and to both parents' conformity orientation in communication. However, analysis of the results indicated that it was *fathers'* prescribed perfectionism and conformity orientation that mainly predicted the development of maladaptive eating patterns, and that a father–offspring conformity communication pattern predicted maladaptive eating. Botta and Dumlao (2002) studied eating disorder concerns in another group of young women in the community. They found that when young women had a relationship with their father in which there was an established pattern of talking things over, and in which conflict was managed by collaboration and compromise the young women had a low level of eating disorder concerns. In yet another community study, this time of young people aged eleven to eighteen years, McEwen and Flouri (2009) found a positive relationship between eating disorder symptoms and fathers' parental psychological control.

The implication of these studies is that for young people with eating disorders it is usually fathers who are experienced as overtly dominating, to a greater extent than mothers. Soenens (2008a) suggested in relation to depression that it might be that mothers control daughters in a more subtle way, eliciting over-protective self-sacrificing behaviour in the daughter, who thus sacrificed her autonomy. A study by Bachar et al (2008) indicates that this is probably equally true of anorexia. They used the Selflessness Scale and a number of other measures with patients with anorexia, and their mothers and fathers, and with comparison individuals drawn from families free of eating disorder. They found that the mothers of patients with anorexia had lower levels of selflessness than comparison mothers, while daughters with anorexia had higher levels of selflessness than comparison daughters. Depression in the mothers of patients with anorexia was associated with still higher levels of selflessness in daughters.

Not all studies confirm the relationship between parental perfectionism and anorexia in a daughter. For example Woodside et al (2002) found that the mothers (but not fathers) of patients with anorexia had higher scores on the Maladaptive Perfectionism Scale than controls. However, in the case of patients with restricting anorexia neither parent scored high on maladaptive perfectionism.

Conclusions

Despite some negative findings, such as those by Woodside, the balance of the evidence suggests that parental behaviour relating to control has a significant effect on the development of depression and eating disorder symptoms in girls and young women. The effect seems to be a gendered effect. Typically, fathers' demands for achievement and conformity impact on girls and young women directly, and through their effect on promoting maladaptive perfectionism in the younger generation. Typically, mothers' dependency needs can lead to reduced autonomy in daughters who sacrifice expressions of autonomy in the interests of protecting their mothers from conflict and loss. Of course, in some families it may be the other way round. The research simply demonstrates what is most typical. Therapeutic interventions that support young people in naming and challenging controlling parental behaviour of all kinds, and helping parents to listen to their children's points of view, are indicated.

CHAPTER TEN

Family attitudes to eating and weight

Researchers have made important attempts to understand the relationship between parents (mostly mother's) attitudes to eating and weight, and the impact this has on the development of problematic eating attitudes and behaviours in the younger generation. Whereas very young children eat and stop eating, in relation to hunger and satiety cues, parental pressure to eat either more, or less, or both, or some foods rather than others, may disrupt this pattern. Children's natural ability to self-regulate food intake may be disrupted by feelings about what they think their parents want them to eat, and how they think their parents want them to look, in relation to fatness or thinness. This may set the scene for the development of more clearly disturbed eating behaviours and attitudes later. Additionally, children may internalise the idea that body weight is of importance to self-worth, a development that will make them more vulnerable to develop an eating disorder at a later stage of development. Studies have shown that the beginnings of such attitudes can already be detected in children as young as four or five.

Aspects of the way that parents communicate to children and adolescents may convey more complex relationships about parental expectations, and valuation of the child. Hence, communication about eating may include other aspects of communication that have impacts on security, self-esteem etc. Moreover, parents who themselves have eating disorders have high levels of relationship and emotional problems, and these factors impact on many aspects of parenting. In addition, there is an effect of age. Striegel-Moore and Kearney Cooke (1994) found that although parents are generally satisfied with their children's appearance, this is less so as children grow into adolescence. They found that 17% of parents of adolescent boys and girls had helped them to diet on at least one occasion.

* * *

Studies can be divided into four groups. The first group of clinic based studies concerns the impact of mothers with anorexia or bulimia on their children's eating attitudes, and on their general and psychological wellbeing. These include studies of the feeding behaviours of mothers with major eating disorders, for example, the classic study by Stein et al (1994), observed the interaction between a clinically identified group of women with bulimia and their babies and repeated observations of the children at a later date. The second group of studies is focused on mothers who seek help with young children with eating difficulties. The third group is focused on children, adolescents and young adults in the community and their parents eating attitudes and behaviours. A fourth group of studies starts with the patient with anorexia and her family, and is based on the patients' and families' reports. Some prospective studies measure some aspect of parental attitudes and behaviour, and then observe the development of eating behaviours in the younger generation over a number of years.

An important issue in these studies is the question of how the parent's eating attitudes are communicated to the younger generation. In some studies the younger generation are asked about pressure from parents in relation to eating and weight, and, in a few, parents behaviours in this respect are directly observed. However, some studies use parents' scores on eating disorder questionnaires, and there is no certainty that these attitudes are communicated to the younger generation. On the face of it there is no reason to assume that a mother's own experience of distress about food or weight need necessarily make her a "pressurising" mother as far as her daughter is concerned. In some cases the effect might be the opposite, she might be more alert to, and more sensitively aware of her daughters needs than a mother who had never experienced such concerns might be. On balance it seems likely that a mother who is still in the grip of a major eating disorder would be more likely than not to pressurise her daughter. By contrast mothers who have recovered from such disturbances are likely to be more variable in the extent to which they do this. Similarly, the relatively low levels of eating pathology in parents identified in community based studies are likely to be less problematic, and less consistently problematic, than the high levels of disturbance in mothers identified in clinic based studies.

The impact of mothers with anorexia and bulimia on developing children

Two studies of mothers with bulimia, Lacey and Smith (1987) and Stein and Fairburn (1989), found that the mothers were over-concerned about their babies weight, had difficulties feeding them, and might restrict their child's food to reduce their weight. Fahy and Treasure (1989) expressed the view, based on clinical impressions, that mothers with bulimia experienced difficulties feeding their children, but thought that mothers with anorexia were more likely to be trying to limit their baby's weights. Stein et al (1994) observed mother's who had suffered from bulimia, in play and mealtime situations with their child at age one, and a comparison group of mothers who had no eating disorder, and their infants. Mothers with a history of bulimia were more likely to direct critical comments at their babies at mealtimes, than were the comparison mothers, but no such difference existed when the mothers played with their babies. The mothers with bulimia were more "intrusive" in that they interrupted what the child was doing at mealtimes and were unresponsive to the infant's cues. There was also more conflict between the mothers with bulimia and their babies at mealtimes, and their babies weighed less. The babies' weights were correlated with the amount of this conflict, with high conflict associated with lower weight. Stein et al (2006) followed up thirty-four of these children at age ten, and compared them with a group of children whose mothers had not had an eating disorder. The children of mothers with eating disorders had higher scores on the Eating Disorders Examination (EDE), indicating higher levels of eating concern. These levels still fell short of levels reported in clinical cases of anorexia, but were comparable to clinical cases of food avoidance emotional disorder. Children of mothers with eating disorders reported more loneliness than controls did. Mealtime interaction was judged using a self-report questionnaire completed by the children. This reported no more conflict at mealtimes than was reported by the control group. Analysis of the data indicated that the children's eating disorder concerns reflected the number of years during their lives that their mothers' eating disorder had continued, and the level of conflict at mealtimes that had been recorded when they were five years old. Perhaps by age ten the children had internalised their mothers' attitudes to food, so that they no longer caused conflict in the relationship.

A small study by Waugh and Bulik (1999) observed mealtime interaction with ten mothers with a history of anorexia or bulimia and a comparison group of mothers and infants. The children were aged one to four years. Mothers with a history of eating disorder were less likely to eat with their children and made more negative comments during mealtimes. Another small study, Evans and Le Grange (1995) compared the behaviour and parenting concerns of ten women with, or with a history of, anorexia or bulimia, with ten comparison mothers. Mothers with a history of eating disorder reported more controlling behaviour in relation to food, and that they experienced more distress and upset themselves when feeding their children. There was a higher level of psychological symptoms among their children.

Hodes et al (1997) attempted to study all the children of women attending an adult eating disorder service. In this study, of the seventeen mothers among the patients twelve agreed to take part, and one mother with anorexia whose children were attending an eating disorder service also agreed to do so. In total, thirteen mothers (five with anorexia and eight with bulimia, and their twenty-six children) took part. Information was gathered by interview and questionnaire from the mothers and the children, and the children were weighed and measured. Of the twenty-six children, two had anorexia and nine others were considered to have other disorders. Children of mothers with anorexia were found to be lighter than the children of mothers with bulimia. Two boys, whose mothers had bulimia, were obese. Six children, (five female and one male) were sufficiently underweight to be regarded as wasted, but this included the two children recruited from the young people's eating disorder service. In all, one third of the children had abnormal weight or growth, and they were usually the children of mothers with anorexia. Van Wezel-Meijler and Wit (1989) also describe stunted growth in children of mothers with anorexia in a short pediatric case series.

Timimi and Robinson (1996) conducted a similar study of mothers attending an eating disorder service. They recruited eleven mothers to the study, six with anorexia and five with bulimia. The mothers had twenty-one children between them. Ten of the eleven mothers were divorced or currently living in conflicted marriages. Like Hodes et al (1997) they found evidence that mothers incorrectly viewed their children as overweight, and that children's access to food was sometimes restricted to the point where the children were severely underweight. They also noted that two of the children pretended to vomit in imitation of their mother's behaviour. One eight-year-old girl repeatedly stated that she wished to be as thin as her mother.

Woodside and Shektar-Wolfson (1990) described a series of case studies of the family relationships of patients who were also parents, who were attending a day hospital for treatment of eating disorders. In three instances children started to diet in response to a parent's weight loss. There was a high level of marital difficulty, and parenting problems. Of twelve parents, three had abandoned their children, or most parenting tasks, to others. There were many examples of distorted parent–child relationships, for example children becoming carers, with children becoming extremely involved in the parent's illness. It follows that parental eating attitudes are not the only adverse influence likely to be experienced by the children of parents with major eating disorders.

Mothers of young children presenting with eating problems

Stein et al (1995), found that mothers of young children referred for help with feeding disorders had disturbed eating attitudes and behaviours, compared to mothers of children with behavioural disorders or non-clinical comparisons. Likewise, Whelan and Cooper (2000) found that the mothers of four-year-olds with feeding problems were eleven times more likely than mothers of comparison groups to have a history of diagnosable eating disorder. Cooper et al (2004) reported the outcome of a study of the mealtime interaction of the families in the Whelan and Cooper study. Compared to both the comparison groups, the families of children with feeding problems demonstrated more "mealtime disorganisation" and more "maternal strong control and disharmony".

Community based studies of the effects of parents' eating attitudes

Effects on young children

There are numerous studies of the relationship between parental attitudes to eating and weight and the developing eating behaviour and attitudes of children. A number of studies demonstrate that the roots of problematic eating attitudes and behaviours are present at an early age, and that they reflect parental attitudes and behaviours. Stice et al (1999) followed up 216 newborn infants for five years. They demonstrated that some children had episodes of restrained eating (being shy about eating or preferring to eat alone), secretive eating (hiding favourite foods), overeating, or over-eating induced vomiting, according to parental report. By age five, 10% had exhibited inhibited eating, 18% secret eating, 33% over-eating, and 10% over-eating induced vomiting. Mothers had completed eating disorder questionnaires at the outset of the study, and mother's BMI six months after the birth of the baby was also measured. Secretive eating by children occurred most often in the children of mothers who had bulimic symptoms, while over-eating was more likely in children whose mothers reported eating restraint and drive for thinness. A history of overweight in the father predicted the onset of secretive eating.

In another study of five-year-olds, all girls, Carper et al (2000) found that parents who are concerned that their children should not over-eat, or eat junk foods, are often also parents who are concerned that their children should eat enough. They found that already at age five girls who felt parental pressure to eat more developed a full range of eating difficulties, sometimes restraining themselves from eating despite being hungry, but also sometimes eating more than they thought they should when tempting food was available, and sometimes eating in response to emotional cues. Girls who felt pressure to eat less were more likely to eat less when tempting food was available. Hence, all kinds of parental concerns about their daughter's eating appeared to interfere with appropriate self-regulation by age five.

Abramovitz (2000), in another study of five-year-old girls, demonstrated that ideas and beliefs about dieting were much more developed in the children of mothers who dieted, than in other children. Davison et al (2000), in a further study of five-year-old girls and their parents found that about 20% of five-year-olds were concerned about their weight. These concerns were associated with the mothers' (but not fathers') weight concerns, irrespective of the daughter's actual weight. Children's tendency to over-eat (disinhibited eating) has also been shown to reflect their mother's tendency to over-eat in response to emotional, social or environmental influences, Cutting et al (1999).

Effects on older children

Jacobi et al (2001) studied the relationship between eating concerns in eight-year-old boys and girls, and both mothers' and fathers' eating disorder symptoms. Parents completed questionnaires that yielded measures of "restraint", which is to say controlling eating according to what you think you should eat rather than by responding to hunger, and of "disinhibition" which is the tendency for eating behaviour to be prompted by situational or emotional cues. They also obtained information from the children about their perceptions that fathers and mothers thought it important that the child should be thin, and about critical comments about the child's weight or eating which made the child upset. They found that maternal eating disorder concerns were associated with more body dissatisfaction and dieting behaviour in girls, but not in boys. Higher maternal disinhibition scores were associated with girls' reports that their mothers wanted them to be thin. Fathers' eating disorder symptoms were not associated with eating concerns in either girls or boys. However, Jacobi commented that where one parent was overweight both boys and girls reported that it was important to the other parent that they, the child, should be thin. They speculated that, "if one parent was overweight, the other parent would express concerns .... affording a family milieu in which such concerns were frequently expressed", Jacobi et al (2001, p. 369) and this affected the children.

Hill and Pallin (1998), in another study of eight-year-olds, found that awareness of maternal dieting, BMI, and low self-worth predicted dieting in girls, but only awareness of maternal dieting predicted it in boys.

There is evidence that mother's modelling of weight concerns, as well as direct encouragement of thinness in their children, impacts on children's body dissatisfaction and restrained eating. Anschutz et al (2009), for example, obtained information by self-report from 501 children aged seven to ten years, after excluding any children who expressed a desire for a larger body size. The information reported was about maternal expressions of concern about the mother's own weight and appearance and about the mother's attitude to the child's weight, for example "Does your mother tell you to eat less because you are becoming fat?" In addition the children completed a measure of eating behaviour, which yielded a measure of eating restraint, and a measure of the child's body dissatisfaction. They also obtained height and weight data for the children. Children who reported that their mother's express concern about their own weight scored highest on the measure of restrained eating. Children whose mother's encouraged them to be thin had higher levels of body dissatisfaction and of restrained eating. Both effects were stronger in the older children.

Haines et al (2008) found similar results in a group of seventy-three primary school age children. They commented that children's reports of parent's comments about the children's weight, parental encouragement for the child to diet, and children's reports of parental dieting and parent's comments about their own weight were associated with greater body dissatisfaction, weight concern and dieting in the children themselves. They noted that parents reported lower levels of these parental comments and behaviours. They considered that this might reflect a social desirability effect, or that parents might regard such comments and behaviours as normative and so unworthy of comment.

Lowes and Tiggemann (2003) in a study that depended entirely on the reports of five to eight-year-old children found that girls' body dissatisfaction was associated with their perception of their mothers' body dissatisfaction, and that girls perceived more parental control over their eating than boys did.

Thelen and Cormier (1996) found that the nine- to ten-year-old children of mothers who encouraged them to lose weight dieted more frequently. However, although parental pressure for daughters to lose weight was associated with eating pathology in late childhood this did reflect the children's weight. When weight was controlled, only fathers' encouragement to control weight correlated with dieting. The parent's own desire to be thinner and diet had no impact.

Sands and Wardle (2003) in a questionnaire study of a large group of nine to twelve-year-old schoolgirls concluded that "… the interaction of girls with significant others (i.e., mother and friends) are likely to cause them to attach more personal importance to achieving the thin ideal …", Sands and Wardle (2003, p. 202). Media exposure alone did not have any effect.

Smolak et al (1999) attempted to differentiate between the effect on children of parents' discontent with their own (parents') weight, and weight loss attempts, and parents' negative comments to children about the child's appearance. Mothers' and fathers' behavior both independently affected their sons, but daughters were only affected by mothers' comments and behaviours. The overall effect of parents' behaviours and comments was substantial. For girls, the frequency of their mother's weight loss attempts, maternal comments on daughter's weight, father's belief in dieting and father's complaints about his own weight, taken together, accounted for 41% of the variance in daughters' eating and weight concerns.

Mothers' effects on adolescent daughters

Pike and Rodin (1991) studied eating attitudes, and reported family functioning, in seventy-seven pairs of mother–daughter pairs. The seventy-seven pairs were selected from a larger group of 350 pairs who had completed questionnaire measures of eating disorder symptoms. Two groups were selected. One group was selected because the daughters' questionnaires indicated a high level of eating disorder symptoms, comparable to a clinical diagnosis of bulimia. The comparison group was selected because they had low levels of eating concern. The mothers completed additional measures of eating disorder symptoms, a questionnaire about their own dieting and weight history, and questions about how they perceived their daughters weight (and how much weight they thought she should lose) and general attractiveness, as well as a research measure of family functioning. Pike and Rodin were concerned to answer the questions "To what extent do mothers and daughters share similar attitudes and behaviours about diet and weight", "How far do mothers serve as role models for daughters in these respects?" and "Do mothers serve as society's messengers, directly pressuring daughters to achieve the cultural ideal of thinness and attractiveness?" Mothers of girls who had high levels of eating disorder symptoms also had high levels of symptoms, and, on average had started dieting at an earlier age than the mothers in the comparison group. However, the most interesting differences concerned the mothers' perceptions of their daughters. Mothers of daughters with bulimic symptoms thought their daughters should lose weight, whereas in the comparison group mothers tended to think their daughters should gain some weight. The difference between the groups could not be accounted for by the girls' actual weights. The mothers of girls with bulimic symptoms also regarded their daughters as less attractive than the girls regarded themselves, to a greater extent than in the comparison group. Family variables did not significantly discriminate the groups, although there was a trend for both mothers and daughters in the bulimic group to be less satisfied with family cohesion.

Cooper and Burrows (2001) studied eating attitudes and beliefs in overweight and normal weight schoolgirls (aged eleven to twelve) and their mothers. In the normal weight group there was a close relationship between mothers' eating disorder beliefs and those of their daughters, but this did not hold true for the overweight girls and their mothers. This does suggest that in general there is such a relationship between mother's and daughter's beliefs, and that this is not accounted for by the fact of being overweight.

Yamazaki and Omori (2011) obtained questionnaire measures of young adolescents internalisation of a thin ideal (meaning acceptance that thinness is an important aspect of attractiveness) and of their mothers' internalisation of the same ideal. They found that mothers' internalisation of the thin ideal was associated with daughters' internalisation and to the daughters' drive for thinness and her dieting behaviour. They argued that mothers' influence came through two routes; one was the impact of mothers' acceptance of the thin ideal, while the other was the effect of the mothers' direct pressure about weight and dieting. Mothers could be seen to be the channel for social pressure on girls to be thin. This was not the case for mothers' impact on sons.

Benedikt et al (1998), in a study of mothers and teenage daughters (tenth and eleventh grade) found two effects of mothers' attitudes and behaviours on their daughters. Many mothers encouraged their daughters to lose weight, even though their daughters were not overweight. Daughters' body dissatisfaction and dieting were predicted by the mothers' encouragement of daughters to lose weight. The daughters more extreme efforts at weight control were associated with the use of similar extreme methods by the mother, and by the mothers own body dissatisfaction. These impacts on daughters were not accounted for by the daughters' actual weight.

Linville et al (2011) made a three-year longitudinal study of teenage girls aged fifteen to nineteen, and their mothers. They found that, at the outset, girls internalisation of a "thin ideal" for their body was associated with mothers' and peers' thin ideal, and with peers' use of abnormal weight control methods, and, marginally, with mothers' level of body dissatisfaction. Mothers' thin ideal predicted increased use of abnormal weight control methods by daughters over the four years of the study.

Steiger et al (1996) found direct correspondence between mothers' and daughters' levels of weight concern. Elfhag and Linne (2005) found a positive association between most measures of eating disorder between mothers and adolescent daughters, aged sixteen and seventeen, after controlling for the effects of high weight. No such association was found in relation to mothers and sons.

Hill et al (1990) found a link between mothers' and daughters' levels of dietary restraint. Snoek et al (2009) found that adolescents' and parents' eating behaviour, but more particularly mothers' and daughters' behaviour, was similar: however there was no evidence that mothers' attitudes led to an escalation of daughters' restraint over time during adolescence.

Studies of both mothers and fathers

Brown and Ogden (2004) found an association between parents' body dissatisfaction and that of their children in the age range nine to thirteen, as well as evidence that the children of parents who tried to restrict the child's eating often responded to this by eating more.

Levine et al (1994), in a study based entirely on self-report questionnaires completed by adolescent girls, found that reported parental investment in girls' slimness was one of several factors that predicted the onset of pathological dieting in a group of 382 American Middle School age girls (sixth to eighth grade). They commented that it was not possible to determine from this data whether the girls' perception that parents put a high value on slimness was justified by parents' behaviour, or whether it reflected increased sensitivity to the issue on the part of the girls.

Dixon et al (1996) in a study of girls attending secondary schools found that parental encouragement to diet was associated with the use of smoking as a weight control method and the use of more extreme methods of weight control, including fasting, self-induced vomiting, and the use of diet pills, laxatives and diuretics.

In another study based on adolescents' self-reports, Vincent and McCabe (2000) obtained information about both mothers and fathers, as seen by their children. Three hundred and six girls and 297 boys took part, and all were in the age range eleven to eighteen. Using self-report measures they obtained a wide range of information from these young people. This included information about family relationships, using the Family Cohesion and the Family Adaptability subscales of FACES II, as well as the Parental Bonding Instrument. In addition they devised questions to measure modelling, encouragement to lose weight, criticism, and discussion of weight loss with peers and with both mother and father. The young people completed measures of body dissatisfaction and disordered eating. Eating disordered behaviours and attitudes were found to be related to high BMI and to encouragement of weight loss by peers and by both parents, but not to other aspects of family relationships.

McCabe and Ricciardelli (2005) in a study of young adolescents aged twelve and thirteen found that girls' increased use of extreme weight loss strategies was associated with pressure from mothers and friends.

Information gathered in a very large scale longitudinal health survey of nine to fourteen-year-olds in the United States by Field et al (2001) found that girls who reported that they thought it was important to either parent that they (the child) should be thin, were twice as likely as others to become highly concerned about their weight in the following year. Peer influences were not found to influence this, but the child's expressed desire to look like people in the media did predict future weight concern and dieting.

Striegel-Moore and Kearney Cooke (1994), in a very large survey of parents' attitudes and behaviours towards their children found that parents who had dieted during the year of the survey were more likely to have helped their child to diet.

Leung et al (1996), in a large study of adolescent girls found that family attitudes to weight and appearance contributed to the development of both body dissatisfaction and eating disorder symptoms. They argued that problems in family functioning had an effect on reducing girls' self esteem, and hence, indirectly, to the development of eating disorder, and other psychiatric symptoms, while family attitudes to weight and appearance had a direct effect.

Fathers' impact on daughters and sons

Lam and McHale (2012) followed adolescent boys and girls, aged ten to twelve at the outset, and their parents over a ten year period taking repeated questionnaire measures. Fathers', but not mothers', weight concerns, predicted the development of weight concerns in adolescent girls over the period of the study. In the study by Dixon et al (1996) fathers' dieting was associated with more extreme dieting by their children, but fathers' influence was not distinguishable from that of mothers' in other respects. However, Dixon considered it possible that for girls in their early to mid-teens fathers' attitudes to daughters' weights could be a significant influence at a time when girls were beginning to have to think about themselves in terms of their attractiveness to the opposite sex. In the study by Field et al (2001) it was those girls and boys who had said it was important to their fathers that they should be thin who were more likely than their peers to become "constant dieters" in the following year. McCabe and Ricciardelli (2005) found that boys' increased use of extreme weight loss strategies was associated with pressure from their fathers and from media images.

Studies of parental influences on young adults

Studies of students report similar findings. Moreno and Thelen (1993) found that students whose mothers encouraged them to lose weight had higher levels of weight concern. Another study of students, Mukai et al (1994) obtained similar results with a group of Japanese schoolgirls aged sixteen plus. Rieves and Cash (1996) found an association between young women's retrospective reports of their mother's satisfaction with their (mothers) body image, when they were growing up, and the young women's satisfaction with their own body image at age seventeen to thirty-four. Krcmar et al (2008) found that female students who achieved low scores on a body esteem scale were more likely than others to describe their parents as people who valued thinness and made negative comments about their daughter's weight and shape. Stice et al (1998) found that female students who perceived pressure from their families and peers to lose weight were more likely to engage in dieting,

Puhl and Schwartz (2003) found that both binge eating and dietary restraint were more common in men and women who remembered their parents using food rules as reward for good behaviour, and withholding food as punishment for bad behaviour. Memories of other food rules, such as rules that you should eat everything on your plate, or that you should not eat unhealthy foods, were not associated with these eating problems in adult life.

* * *

The pattern is clear, and yet there is some variability in these findings. For example Keery et al (2006) found that adolescents reports of mothers' dieting was associated with the adolescents' weight concerns and unhealthy weight control behaviours, but mothers' own reports of their dieting did not. However, when the measures of eating disorder concerns were repeated with the adolescents after five years, van den Berg et al (2010), the original judgements given by both the mothers, and the adolescents, about the mothers' dieting behaviour, were found to predict the eating disorder symptom outcomes in girls at that time. Hill and Franklin (1998) found only very slight differences between the mothers of eleven-year-old girls who had high levels of weight and dieting concern and those who had low levels. However, high levels were associated with mothers who rated daughters as less attractive and with lower levels of satisfaction with family life reported by both mother and daughter.

Baker et al (2000) in a study of young adults and their parents found that young people's perception of mothers' criticism of their weight and shape was associated with their scores on a measure of eating disorder symptoms, and to a measure of weight and shape concerns. By contrast the parents' reports of their criticism, or of their own weight control behaviours, were not associated with their sons' and daughters' concerns, except that mothers' reports of their criticism of their daughters' weight and shape was related to their daughters' frequency of weight loss attempts in the past.

Effects of early intervention

Overall, there is quite a lot of evidence that mothers' attitudes about their own and about their daughters' weight and eating have an impact on daughters' attitudes to those issues. Moreover, a programme designed to modify mothers' attitudes has been shown to improve the outcomes for their daughters. Corning et al (2010) worked with girls aged twelve to fourteen, and their mothers. They provided an experimental intervention aimed at mothers' behaviours, which included psycho-education, skills training and group discussion, aimed at preventing negative, and fostering positive interactions between mothers and daughters about issues of weight and appearance. The intervention included homework tasks to be completed by mothers and daughters together between sessions. After this intervention, and at three month follow up, girls reported reduced "maternal pressure to be thin" and lower scores on the "drive for thinness" subscale of the Eating Disorders Inventory, compared to their levels before the intervention and to levels reported by a comparison group.

Effect of "family preoccupation with appearance"

Attitudes to weight can also be considered as part of a more general attitude to the appearance of the family, that is that the family should appear in a favourable light. Lieberman (1995) proposed, on the basis of clinical experience that "keeping up appearances", both with other family members, and with the outside world, might be critically important in the families of patients with anorexia. He thought this might stand in the way of sharing experiences and feelings in the families and might account for the families' low levels of expressiveness.

Davis et al (2004), in a retrospective study of young women's weight preoccupation, demonstrated that, after controlling for BMI, weight preoccupation reflected a combination of anxiety and awareness of family preoccupation with appearance. Laliberte et al (1999) investigated a range of family attitudes in young women and their mothers, and the relationship of these attitudes to eating disorders. They found that general measures of family functioning, such as measures of family conflict, cohesion and expressiveness, contributed to the development of low self-esteem and to general psychopathology in the young women. However, a particular group of family values was associated with the development of eating disorders. Families who valued slimness also valued appearance, in terms of being well dressed and presenting a favourable image to the world. They also valued achievement. They described this complex of values as the "family climate for eating disorders". It was associated with eating disorder symptoms in the young women, and discriminated between eating disordered and depressed patients in a clinical population.

Negative findings

There are also some negative results. For example, Ogden and Steward (2000) obtained contrary results in a study of thirty mothers and their daughters aged sixteen to nineteen, using different measures of family relationships, this time focusing just on the mother–daughter relationship. They found no relationship between mothers' and daughters' weight concerns as expressed through questionnaire measures of restrained eating and body dissatisfaction, despite the fact that mothers and daughters were quite closely matched on BMI. They considered that other aspects of the mother–daughter relationship predicted eating pathology. Byely et al (2000) found no relationship between measures of mothers' and daughters' dieting and difficulties with body image, either concurrently or prospectively over one year. Like Ogden and Steward (2000) they reported that aspects of family relationships, as reported by the daughters, were more predictive of the development of eating disorder symptoms. Similarly, Ogden and Elder (1998) did not find concordance between mothers and their young adult daughters in regard to body image or eating behaviour in British Asian or White families. Leon et al (1994) found no difference in eating restraint scores between parents of adolescents who reported eating disorder symptoms and concerns, and the parents of young people who did not. However, Leon et al (1994, pp. 511–512) observed that "The lack of congruence between risk group female adolescent perceptions of communication with the adolescent, and overall family satisfaction suggests a lack of sensitivity .... to the feelings of the adolescent, or the minimization of problems". Fulkerson et al (2002) found no relationship between mothers' self-reported dieting, and encouraging daughters to diet, and daughters' weight related concerns or unhealthy weight control behaviours, once the daughters' BMI was controlled for. By contrast they did find such relationships for adolescent boys and their mothers. However, positive findings of family influence seem to greatly outnumber negative ones like these.

Patients with anorexia and their parents

Here we encounter a major difference in findings between information gained from clinical and research interviews and information obtained by self-report by the patient's family. Studies based on clinical and research interviews with patients with anorexia and their families, such as Kalucy et al (1977) and Haworth-Hoeppner (2000), confirm the existence of high levels of eating pathology in the families of patients with anorexia. Kalucy et al were able to draw on clinical assessments and notes of family and individual sessions accumulated over eighteen months of work with the patients and their families. Kalucy et al found that 16% of the mothers and 23% of the fathers had experienced an anorexia-like episode during their own adolescence, that 27% of mothers and 16% of fathers engaged in dieting, often despite not being overweight, and that 11% of mothers and 21% of fathers had abnormally high physical activity levels. Haworth-Hoeppner (2000) conducted two-hour interviews with twenty-one adult women with major eating disorders and eleven women without an eating disorder as a comparison group. She argued that a "main discourse on weight" was considered to be the sole family pattern contributing to the eating disorder in only two of twenty-one cases of anorexia, but it was also entirely absent in only two cases. She argued that almost certainly other difficulties in the family usually combine with this factor in the development of major eating disorders.

Self-report studies based on questionnaire responses by patients with anorexia provide limited confirmation. Krug et al (2009) in a large study of clinical cases of eating disorder in five European countries obtained patients' retrospective accounts of family eating patterns and rules that they had encountered as children. The study confirmed some differences between patients and comparison women in relation to family rules about food and to "food used as individualisation", which referred to the preparation of different food for the patient, perhaps a response to "picky eating". There was no marked difference between the patients with anorexia and the patients with bulimia in these respects. Wade et al (2007), drawing data from a very large community sample of twins found that those who had a history of anorexia or bulimia reported that they heard more comments from their families about weight and shape when they were growing up. Woodside et al (2002) found that mothers of patients with anorexia had higher scores than a control group of mothers on the Eating Disorders Inventory. By contrast Garfinkel et al (1983) found no evidence that parents of patients with anorexia themselves had eating disorder concerns, based on parents' self-reports. Garfinkel et al observed that the mothers of patients with anorexia were themselves rather underweight, since on average mothers were 88% of their expected weight. They dismissed this fact, on the grounds that it was not significantly less than the mothers of the comparison group who averaged 93% of their expected weight. Here it might have been more sensible to rely on published norms. The average weight of the mothers was only just above the anorexic weight range. A significant proportion of the mothers' weights presumably were within that range. This is not a normal state of affairs, notwithstanding the weight of the comparison mothers. Hall et al (1986) found that mothers of patients with anorexia reported significantly less past dieting behaviour, and equivalent low levels of concern about weight, appearance and looks, when compared to the mothers of a comparison group.

Another, largely negative finding is that of Steiger et al (1995). The study compared scores on questionnaire measures of eating disorder attitudes and behaviour reported by patients with those reported by their parents and siblings. They found no increased eating concerns in the first degree relatives of a group of patients with major eating disorders, including twenty-five with anorexia. They did find moderately increased levels in a comparison group of "normal dieters". These were women who had relatively low levels of weight concerns, not amounting to a diagnosable eating disorder. A further analysis of data from the same study confirmed the relationship between mothers' and daughters' eating restraint, except in the case of the families of women with major eating disorders. The findings of the Hall et al (1986) and Steiger et al (1995) studies would be consistent with a high level of denial in the parents of patients with major eating disorders.

Conclusion

Overall the evidence suggests that mothers who are in the grip of severe eating disorders pass on eating difficulties to some of their children at an early age. More generally mothers who have less severe concerns about weight and eating, pass on similar problematic attitudes to their daughters, and some studies suggest fathers' attitudes are also important in this respect. Some studies indicate that boys are less responsive to such parental concerns. The research indicates that children can internalise problem attitudes to eating and weight at an early age. Parents are a major source of influence, and this seems to be especially clear for the influence of mothers on daughters.

Clinical and interview based studies suggest that high levels of parental eating disorder are common in the families of patients with anorexia, while questionnaire studies of this question have produced inconsistent results. Probably many parents of patients with anorexia have high levels of eating disorder concerns and behaviours, but this is denied at least in fairly superficial enquiries such as self-report questionnaires. In our clinical work we might expect that these difficulties will come to light with the passage of time, and often will not have been reported at the outset. It would be hard to disagree with the conclusion of Haworth-Hoeppner (2000) that such parental attitudes and difficulties are seldom sufficient on their own to cause a major eating disorder in a daughter, but that they are nevertheless a significant contributory factor in many cases. In general other factors such as insecure attachment, intrusive parenting and more general family attitudes are likely to combine with parents' difficulties about weight and eating in the aetiology of severe eating disorders like anorexia and bulimia. The implication of the research is that many patients have internalised problem attitudes about food and weight that have been expressed by their parents, often at a very young age. Family therapists should be ready to address these issues in treatment.

CHAPTER ELEVEN

Beyond the Maudsley Model

The research outlined in the previous chapters implicates family relationships as the principle source of the developmental difficulties that culminate in the development of anorexia. The implication is that certain family factors, in various combinations, lead to this result. What use is such a family model? Alan Cooklin used to say that the family therapists ask themselves the question "What is the avoided interaction?" The value of a family model is simply that it leads us towards asking the question. The implication of the research is that the family therapist should approach the family of the patients with anorexia with certain things in mind. These are:

1. Parents and patients are likely to be vulnerable in similar ways. Ultimately this shared vulnerability usually has its origin in the parent's own unresolved emotional difficulties, reflecting unresolved trauma and loss in their own life experience.
2. Parents are likely to be experienced by patients as more controlling.
3. Parents are likely to have difficulty managing conflict in the marriage. Sometimes the patient will be involved in parental conflict in the ways described in the Psychosomatic Family Model, and in other ways.

4. In many cases the patient will not have had the opportunity to internalise conflict resolution skills modelled by her parents.
5. Parents and other family members are likely to share dysfunctional attitudes to food, exercise, appearance and achievement. This is likely to be something they will find it difficult to acknowledge or discuss.
6. Not all the factors described above will be present in every case.
7. There may well be other family factors contributing to the development of anorexia that have not been identified here.
8. In addition to addressing the issue of patient's safety and nutrition, the therapist's role is to engage the family and increase the range of emotional expression and of communication about relationships in the family.
9. Families vary in regard to the extent of difficulty they present and therapy needs to be calibrated to match the level of difficulty presented.
10. The psychological difficulties of the patient reflect her experiences in her family. They can change when they can be named and acknowledged in the family context.
11. Ultimately the patient is likely to recover most completely when she is helped to communicate directly with her parents about difficulty and distress, including distress arising in her relationship with them, and they are helped to acknowledge this.

The families of girls with anorexia are not all the same. There is a spectrum of background problems and a range of levels of difficulty. Family therapists need to be able to calibrate their input to meet different kinds and degrees of difficulty. The level of difficulty is not always obvious at the outset but quite often it is. First and foremost the family therapist must draw on their experience of the family in interaction. The therapist will experience the family's reaction at an early stage, and adjust plans accordingly. In addition known indicators of treatment resistance are of some value. Known indicators of treatment resistance include previous unsuccessful treatment and extreme emaciation in the patient at the outset of treatment. However, neither of these signs indicates treatment resistance in every instance. Other factors which seem very likely to be negative predictors are severe parental marital conflict, and parental mental illness, including acknowledged or, more often unacknowledged, parental eating disorder. In addition, as we have seen, greater obsessionality in the patient, and a single parent family, are both factors that at least predict the need for a longer course of treatment. Faced with different levels of difficulty in the family, or different levels of treatment resistance, we as therapists need a choice of strategies. More vulnerable parents need more input, although they may be reluctant to accept it. Attachment theory approaches, because they are oriented towards vulnerability in both the older and the younger generations, offer a variety of ways of approaching such issues.

Three approaches to the attachment focus in family therapy

The therapeutic operations described in the FBT treatment manual are not sufficient to maximise outcomes. In order to improve the approach we can draw on the techniques of structural and strategic techniques used in early studies but now largely set aside. We can also consider new ideas brought into family therapy from Attachment Theory. The advantage of doing so is that attachment approaches address concern about guilt and blame in a dynamic way. Therapists using an attachment approach in family therapy all think in terms of the family therapy situation itself as providing a secure base for the family. Three authors, Diamond and Stern (2003), Dallos (2006) and Dallos and Vetere (2009), and Hughes (2007), give accounts of the use of attachment perspectives in family therapy. Of these, only Dallos (2006) and Dallos and Vetere (2009) specifically discuss the approach as a treatment for anorexia. They vary in the extent to which they work with a specific focus on the creation of a secure base at the beginning. One might argue that they vary as to how much they assume that families will be trusting at the outset. Some assume that there is a need for an intense focus on building the secure base before attention can be switched to the family relationships. Diamond and Stern give the least emphasis to this need, while Hughes gives the most. We should welcome this difference of emphasis, since it presents alternatives that we can use in thinking about work with more and with less difficult families. In this context a more difficult family would be one whose members are more wary of trusting to the therapeutic situation. This may reflect a wide range of negative experiences, sometimes with therapists and mental illness services, sometimes with one another, and often with the previous generation in their families.

Diamond and Stern (2003) present an attachment-based approach to family therapy with depressed adolescents. Their short account presents the treatment as an attachment repair process. They argue that depressed adolescents present, at the outset, with apparent indifference to, and rejection of, parental concern. However, patients are concealing a preoccupation with their parent's welfare and ability to cope. This, of course, is very much the pattern that we would expect to encounter in the patient with anorexia, a pattern that seems to have been demonstrated by the research summarised in Chapter Eight. If anything we might expect this pattern to be more extreme in the young patient with anorexia than it is in depressed adolescents that Diamond and Stern describe.

Diamond and Stern (2003) comment that the therapy is based on the assumption that therapeutic conversations between adolescents and parents can serve a reparative function. The attachment bond can be repaired when adolescents achieve an "earned security" in the context of conversations about negative life experiences, with parents who are partially responsible for those experiences. These conversations allow the adolescent to verbalise feelings that have been concealed, feelings about parental failure to protect, acknowledge, and value the child. They see a close parallel with the process through which people achieve a sense of forgiveness. The therapist's role is to prepare the ground for, and to facilitate, this conversation.

Diamond and Stern present three phases of the treatment. In the first phase there are three tasks. At an early stage the therapist asks the adolescent, in the presence of the family, "When you feel so depressed and think about hurting yourself, why don't you turn to your mother for help and comfort?" Diamond and Stern (2003, p. 196). This sets up a conversation in which the therapist will present the family with a relational reframe in which reestablishing trust between adolescent and parent(s) is presented as the solution to the problem of the adolescent's depression. Next, in an individual session, the therapist explores the adolescent's feelings about family events, listening and empathising with what she has to say, and preparing her to discuss this matter with her parents. Then the therapist meets the parents, and explores the attachment issues in their current situation, as well as issues arising from their attachment experiences in their own families of origin. The therapist works to encourage the parents' abilities to listen to and accept the adolescent's feelings about family relationships and circumstances. The therapist now brings the adolescent and her parents together and promotes direct conversation between them. Here they argue that it is very important that the adolescent can express her emotions, especially angry emotions, about what has happened to her in the family. The therapist's role at this point is to support the parents in listening to what the adolescent has to say. The therapist intervenes to prevent parents from offering defensive comments or too much explanation at this stage. The therapist also seeks to support the adolescent in expressing herself in language that conveys her feelings without becoming so extreme or hostile as to make it too difficult for the parents to listen. The therapist prompts active listening from the parents. They may also ask the adolescent about her thoughts about why things happened the way they did, encouraging her to address parental motivations or states of mind.

In the second phase of treatment, which follows when the adolescent has been able to express her experience of the relationship with her parents, parents are encouraged to respond with more self-disclosure, and with explanation of the parents' states of mind. In this conversation the adolescent may gain a new perspective on her parents. At this stage as they put it, "Parents are momentarily viewed as mortal, independent human beings with their own vulnerabilities and challenges. This is particularly important for the older adolescents who have to begin demythologising their parents and start accepting them for who they are. Simultaneously, by learning that they experience similar experiences of victimisation, many adolescents feel a new affiliation with their parents", Diamond and Stern (2003, p. 205).

In the third phase of treatment the parents' disclosure is seen as laying the foundations for a more equal dialogue. The parents' attention needs to be balanced equally between listening to the adolescent, and disclosing their own experiences and views, in order that the adolescent is not made to feel burdened by parental vulnerability.

Overall, the process is one in which the adolescent can express her anger and hurt, and the parents can empathise with that and, subsequently, offer their own experience and explanation. It is expected that the outcome will be one in which the parents come to understand the adolescents feelings and the adolescent forgives her parents for their inadequacies. Diamond and Stern conclude their description with the suggestion that therapists should avoid intellectualising explanations and should conclude the therapy by complimenting the family on their direct and honest communication.

It may often be difficult for the family therapist working with the patient with anorexia and her family to go straight to the question

"Why don't you use your parents to help you, rather than using symptomatic behaviours?" in the way that Diamond and Stern (2003) propose in their work with depressed young people. Yet the therapist who holds this question in mind may find it helpful when asking himself or herself "What is the avoided interaction?"

* * *

Hughes (2007), Dallos (2006), and Dallos and Vetere (2009) would probably accept the description of therapy and therapeutic change that Diamond and Stern (2003) have given. Their accounts give more emphasis to the requirement that therapists need to set up the therapy situation as a secure base.

* * *

Accounts of Attachment Narrative Family Therapy, in Dallos (2006) and Dallos and Vetere (2009), include case studies of the use of the attachment-narrative approach with two families whose daughters had anorexia. Therapists who intend to use this kind of approach will read those accounts. For the purpose of this discussion a brief description is given here.

Dallos (2006) sees the family therapy as having four stages. The first stage addresses the therapy situation as a secure base; the second, the problem as it is experienced by the family; the third, trans-generational issues and the way the parents' approach to parenting has been shaped by their own experiences, while the last phase is focused on ending and how needs will be met in future. In each both the parents and the patient are present.

In the first stage the therapists seek to make the therapy situation a "secure base" for all the family members. The core task is to make family members feel safe, to adopt a non-blaming stance and to go at a slow pace. This starts with negotiation about the method of working, introducing team members and technology. The therapists present the idea that the work would be aimed at eliciting everybody's ideas, in order to find ways to help them with the problems they face. In this context the therapists say they do not want to make anyone feel blamed. One goal is to slow down the process if emotions seemed to be running away with the session, and to achieve a balance between structured content and emotional expression. In the early stages of the session the therapist presents the idea that discussions of problems are often difficult and painful, and that the family members should say when something was too much for them and they needed to stop. Hence the therapist presents the need to "talk about talking" and find a way to set rules for emotional safety. If the issue of blame arises the therapists would acknowledge that people might have uncomfortable feelings about this, but that it was not the therapist's intention to make anyone feel blamed. The therapist's style is one that involves a lot of education about vulnerability in relationships.

The second phase begins with the problem, and how it makes family members feel. This leads in turn to discussion about comforting, a central issue for this approach. A trans-generational genogram is used to focus attention on links between current patterns of comforting, and those experienced by the parents in their families of origin. The use of food in giving comfort or responding to emotional upset is also explored in this context. This in turn leads to a focus on the parents corrective and replicative scripts, ways in which they have tried to make things in their family different from their family of origin.

It also includes the younger generation's ideas about the future, and how they would like things to be, for example issues relating to comforting when they have their own children, can be explored here.

The third phase is intended to improve the attachment security in the family by developing the idea that links exist between the attachment experiences of the parents, and the way they relate to their children. Often parents try to relate in a way that will protect their own children from the hurt they themselves suffered as children. In particular, Dallos proposes that links between comforting and food would be explored further at this stage. The parental marriage might also become the focus of work at this stage, in conjoint sessions for the parents alone. Improvements in the relationship could free the patient from demands to keep the peace or look after a parent who was distressed by the marital relationship. Subsequently, this issue could become a focus of the work with the patient and her parents.

The last phase is preparation for the end of the work. This involves planning how family members' future needs will be met, and predicting that there will be future difficulties and discussing how these might be managed. The therapists make themselves available to be contacted for further support after the end of treatment. Dallos argues for the maintenance of the secure base even after the therapy work has finished.

For this reason the model does not fit easily into a rigidly defined time limited format.

Two issues are not addressed in the descriptions by Dallos. They do not specifically address the issue, crucial to our work in the community, of how to safeguard the patient, and the therapy work, by getting the patient eating again. In addition, no concrete information is provided about outcome in terms of the severity of symptoms or of weight loss, before and after treatment, in either of the case descriptions.

* * *

Hughes (2007) describes an approach to family therapy based on attachment theory that is oriented towards especially severe attachment difficulties. This approach might be useful in cases in which parents have especially severe difficulties and need more separate attention. His work is oriented towards work with families and carers of children who have suffered neglect and abuse. It has not been related to anorexia. Here there is an even stronger emphasis on the therapist building a relationship with the parents in order to provide a secure environment for the work with the parents and children. Hughes gives prominence to the idea that work may be needed to help parents address their own attachment difficulties, before they will be able to change in their relationship with the children. This reflects the origins of the work. However, the approach might also be appropriate for parents with severe unresolved attachment difficulties of their own and so may be appropriate for many families whose daughters have anorexia. Hughes sees initial meetings with parents without the child as a crucial stage in setting up therapy as a secure base.

Hughes emphasises the need to develop a sense of safety in the relationship. He observes that parents are in a state of enhanced vulnerability at this time, and that "If they feel judged and criticised as parents they are likely to react with shame, defensiveness, and resentment. They may respond with increased efforts to convince the therapist of the severity of the child's problems", Hughes (2007, p. 123). This is a point of view with which no family therapist is likely to disagree. Here Hughes expresses the same concerns expressed by the Maudsley therapists and the FBT manual, but Hughes has a more sophisticated approach to it. In alliance building meetings with the parents the children are not present. The therapist responds with understanding in a way that makes the parents feel safe. This is the same quality of relationship that the therapist hopes the parents will then be able to offer to the children. Hughes expresses the expectation that if the therapist succeeds in creating this safe relationship for the parents, then parents will experience "realistic guilt", rather than shame, about their parenting mistakes. Hughes argues that the therapist should raise the issue of blame with parents at the outset. The therapist's message is that he or she does not wish parents to feel blamed and hopes that parents will feel able say if he does so. At the same time the therapist insists that he will need to tell the parents if he thinks they are doing something that is unhelpful for the child. Hence Hughes gives the message that parents may feel blamed by the therapist even though this is not the therapist's intention, and that the most helpful thing the parents can do is to say if they feel blamed. At the same time he insists on the need to give feedback, when it serves the interests of the younger generation and of the parents' relationship with them.

Hughes describes the therapeutic relationship as one in which the therapist offers "playfulness, acceptance, curiosity and empathy". Hughes regards these qualities as the qualities that parents of securely attached children provide. He is explicitly saying that the therapist is offering a kind of secure attachment relationship to the parents in order that the parents can in turn offer this to the children. However, Hughes seems to be going rather further than other family therapists in proposing that these early sessions with the therapist, from which the younger generation are absent, constitutes a kind of attachment therapy for the parents, as a necessary precursor to the work with both generations. This might be a fairly protracted process. Hughes talks of this phase requiring "between a few and several sessions" with the parents.

When the initial goals have been addressed, and still in the very early stages of engagement, Hughes proposes that the therapist should talk to the parents about how their feelings about the child have developed over time. He suggests the therapist start by enquiring about each parent's hopes and dreams before the child was born, and how these developed at the time of the birth and the early years of the child's life. Then the therapist should discuss how concerns developed in the parents minds about how the child was developing. At this stage parents may be able to allow themselves to be vulnerable, which allows the therapist to demonstrate an empathic response. After this, the parent's sense of loss or grief about the child's developing problems is discussed, as is any sense of shame about the parent's failure to rectify the situation, or resentment towards the child. The intention is that the parents' experience of the therapist's acceptance of their experience will make them more comfortable and less defensive in further discussion and will facilitate commitment to the therapy process.

The intense interest that the therapist displays at this point, focusing on the parents' internal working models of the child, seems more intense than that to be found in more traditional structural or Milan-Systemic approaches to family therapy. Nevertheless, much of the therapy process, as described and illustrated by Hughes, is reminiscent of post Milan-Systemic Therapy in that the focus of the therapist's work is on encouraging each family member, but especially parents, to think about what is going on in the mind of the other. In addition, the therapist working with this approach often verbalises for family members the feelings that he thinks may have been elicited by what has been expressed in sessions. Hence, he seeks to help them develop the ability to articulate feelings which may have been too painful for them to recognise or articulate for themselves.

Hughes highlights the emotion of shame as being one that is highly problematic for therapy. Since shame is an emotion that causes people to withdraw from engagement with others, including attachment figures, it stands in the way of the development of the self, and in the way of therapeutic engagement. Hughes sees transient experiences of shame as an inevitable aspect of early life, occurring at moments when parental figures lack attunement to their child's needs. However, in the relationship to a responsive parent such moments are relatively brief. Shame might be aroused in relation to discipline or parental disapproval of behaviour, but the responsive parent's attunement to the experience of shame allows the child to develop the capacity to regulate this emotion. In that case the emotion that will be elicited by the experience of doing something wrong will be guilt. Unlike shame, guilt is an emotion that creates engagement, since it motivates the person to say sorry or to seek to make amends. Hughes is particularly concerned that the therapist should be watchful for signs that they elicit a sense of shame in members of the family, especially parents. Having sensed that this is the case the therapist seeks to repair the "break" in the therapeutic attachment relationship by enquiring about the parent's feelings, apologising for causing them, and explaining her intentions.

Hughes comments that moments will occur in all relationships when one person feels misunderstood, ignored, devalued or criticised by their partner or another family member, and that the same is true for the relationship between the therapist and family members. He argues that the therapist must constantly monitor the existence of such "breaks" in the intersubjective relationship between therapist and family members. The therapist's role is to actively address those "breaks", enquiring about them, expressing concern and seeking to repair breaks, and discussing them with the family when they have not been repaired. In this way Hughes goes further than Dallos (2006) and many other therapists who simply propose that family members should be encouraged to indicate that they feel they have been blamed by the therapist in some way. This kind of activity by the therapist may be especially significant in work with the most vulnerable families. Probably the more vulnerable the family the more the therapist would need to display this kind of active, sensitive engagement with family members, in order to create the secure base in therapy which would allow parents to offer the same quality of relationship with their children, and with each other. Therapists who are better at doing this should be more successful in general, and particularly when working with more treatment resistant cases.

Calibrating the therapists approach

The families of people with anorexia present varying levels of difficulty for the therapist. The attachment frame of reference provides a way of thinking about this in terms of parental vulnerabilities. This may be more helpful than Minuchin's (1978) assumption that the patient was always hampered by her over-involvement in her parents' marital difficulties, although that may sometimes be the case. From the attachment point of view marital problems, which certainly exist in some instances, are nevertheless perhaps best seen as reflecting each parent's individual vulnerabilities. The attachment framework may be more useful as an approach to thinking about calibrating the approach to different levels of treatment resistance. It would be possible for a therapist to proceed along the lines proposed by Diamond and Stern (2003) in cases that seemed to present the lowest level of difficulty, for example in cases where parents seemed emotionally available and alert to their daughter's emotional needs. Clinical experience suggests that that situation is relatively uncommon in families whose daughters have anorexia. More often therapists might choose to proceed along the lines proposed by Dallos (2006), Dallos and Vetere (2009). In the most difficult cases, which would probably include cases in which parents themselves were suffering from eating disorders, or other mental illnesses, or were traumatised by previous experiences with mental health services, the approach described by Hughes (2007) might be more appropriate. Cases in which parents are critical or rejecting of the patient would probably fall into this latter group.

A new approach to family therapy for anorexia

An implication of the attachment approach is that therapists need to talk to families about the secure base issues at the outset. This means having talks about talks, along the lines suggested by Dallos (2003), and raising the issue of sensitivities to feelings of blame, along the lines described by Hughes (2007). The difficulty is that the therapist has a great deal to do in the initial phases of therapy, when therapist and parents are likely to be driven in the direction of finding practical solutions because of their concern about the patient's starvation. This need not prevent the therapist raising those issues, and by returning to them from time to time, demonstrating an active concern with the family's experience of safety in the situation.

Managing the anorexic crisis while engaging the family

The first move in family therapy with anorexia has to be to make sure that parents can keep the patient safe by insisting on refeeding. The therapist is forced into a crisis intervention approach before he or she has time to get to know the family well or intervene at length to build a more secure relationship with the parents. Effective family therapy treatments of anorexia usually have to start by putting parents in charge of their daughter's eating and of their other pathological weight control strategies. From the point of view presented here this starting point is a way of communicating to the patient that the parents will take action to keep her safe; the first thing that needs to be established in order to re-create a secure attachment. In the course of doing so the therapist provides a containing environment for the parents and this can be seen as the first move in building the therapy as a secure base for them.

Ensuring the patient's safety

Every team will have a protocol specifying the issues that have to be addressed to ensure that the patient is adequately assessed and monitored to ensure her safety as far as her physical health is concerned. The family therapist keeps this in mind during their work with the patient and family. Sometimes the patient will already be too much at risk as a result of their physical deterioration. In those instances a short admission to the children's ward of a hospital will often address their immediate medical needs. If so the therapist must take this opportunity to engage the family during the admission and start to build a secure base with the parents and family.

First contact with the family

The FBT treatment manual emphasises the importance of making first contact by phone, in order to initiate communication with the family. This is something family therapists will be used to doing. A great deal is lost if this is not done. The phone call will be made to one of the patient's parents. It is an opportunity to start the process of joining with them along the lines suggested by Minuchin et al (1978). In most instances referral will have been made because of parental anxiety about their daughter. It is surprising how often parents have found it difficult to get the health system to agree with their concerns and take action. The phone call is an opportunity to support them by congratulating them on seeking help and sharing their concerns, and by discussing practical questions about their daughter's safety, such as whether she is drinking enough, whether necessary blood tests have been done etc. In this way they are treated as responsible parents, and given a sense of being held by a therapy system that understands their situation. This provides containment for parental anxiety. Further joining can be achieved by discussing any practical difficulties about meeting the whole family, such as difficulties with getting away from work.

This kind of approach to convening will often be sufficient when parents are fairly well functioning people, and able to co-operate with each other in the interests of their children. Different considerations apply in families in which parents themselves are very vulnerable, or in which the parental relationship itself is under great stress. If information about issues of this sort is contained in the referral then the therapist should sympathetically refer to the difficulties in the course of the call. If not, the therapist might well ask a general screening question along the lines of "… and apart from that, how have things been going for you as a family just now?" providing an opportunity for discussion of other difficulties which may be relevant. In either case it is important to know what the children understand about any parental difficulties. Sometimes it may become clear that one or both parents are unhappy about the referral. For example, a parent who has been traumatised in the context of a family history of severe eating disorder, and witnessed repeated admissions of a relative to an institution, may be very fearful of the consequences of contact with mental health services. In situations of this sort it may be helpful to meet the parents initially without the children to talk about expectations and anxieties and to offer some reassurance about the potential course of treatment. Sometimes such an approach may need to be developed along the lines suggested by Hughes (2007). In such instances there may well be a need to maintain parallel separated sessions for parents and patient, with a view to returning to conjoint sessions at a later stage. Similarly, if the circumstances are such that parents feel blamed, by the referrer for example, an initial meeting with parents alone may be indicated. In other circumstances, for example when a parent is mentally ill, or the marital relationship is under great stress, therapists may prefer to integrate other techniques into the process of convening and engaging the family. For example techniques taken from attachment-based approaches to family therapy, such as those described by Dallos (2006) and by Hughes (2007), might be added to the first session or to subsequent sessions.

The first meeting with the family

The family should be greeted warmly. At the beginning of the first meeting the therapist will have to say something about the reason for the meeting. The FBT treatment manual assumes that somebody else has already undertaken a process of diagnosis, assessment and engagement. In the Child and Adolescent Mental Health Service the meeting with the family therapist may be the first meeting the family has after referral to the service by the General Practitioner (GP). It is possible that some family members may be unclear about the reason for the meeting. All of them are likely to be unclear what to expect. The therapist might explain this by saying something like "Mary, Dr. X wrote a letter expressing concerns about you. I spoke to your Dad/Mum on the phone and I know your parents are very concerned about you too. That is why we are meeting today. What I want to do today is to get to know you all a bit as a family first, without talking about the problem, then to hear from you all about that. Then I want to talk to you, Mary, on your own for a little while, and after that to talk with your parents on their own. Then we will get together and talk about what we can all do to help, and think about meeting again." Then the therapist might introduce the social phase, saying "But before I hear about the problem I would like to get to know each of you a little as a family".

The social phase

The tradition is to ask an open question "Who will start?" as a way of beginning to join with the family and assess the family structure. However, another way is to begin with the patient, addressing her by name, saying "Will you begin by telling me something about yourself?" and drawing her into a brief discussion of herself, her friends and her family, and her future plans. There are a number of reasons for starting this way. In the first place it is surprising how often the patient herself is marginalised or ignored in the early stages of therapy. This happens for a number of reasons. Parents are likely to be the ones who have the anxiety and concern, while the patient usually presents a state of denial that allows her to keep her fears for herself beneath the surface. Parents therefore urgently wish to speak about the patient and her problem. Equally, the therapist may be preoccupied with the need to engage with the parents and start building an alliance so that they will begin to tackle the task of refeeding. Another issue is that the patient, being in a state of denial, may be dismissive or even rude to the therapist. The therapist could be uncomfortable with this possibility, and parents may be very uncomfortable with it, if they feel that it reflects badly on them. Starting with the patient has a number of advantages. If she wishes to be rude and dismissive about the problem it is nevertheless difficult for her to decline a more general discussion about herself and her family. Putting the focus on her begins to signal that the therapist thinks that what she has to say is important. Should she actually be rude or dismissive it is an opportunity for the therapist to demonstrate his or her ability to maintain a therapeutic stance. Having engaged the patient it makes sense then to draw out the other children, and then move on to the parents. Often the children do not have much to say, and in that case the therapist might turn to one or both parents and say, "The children (naming each child) haven't had much to say, I guess they may be quite shy in this situation" and then draw out the parents' views. Talking about the children first, and having the parents talk about the children before they speak about themselves, is a way of framing them as parents, which is the therapist's immediate interest in them. The therapist can then talk to the parents about themselves.

As therapists are often anxious about managing the presenting problem they may be tempted to end the social phase too soon. The therapist should remember that this is a rare opportunity that will not come again. It is an opportunity for a discussion of the family that is underfocused in that it is not contextualised by the discussion of the problem. It is an opportunity for the family to experience the therapist's benign interest in them at a point when they do not experience themselves as being judged in relation to the problem. The point can be illustrated by returning yet again to the first session with the family of "Susan" illustrated in the treatment manual, Lock et al (2001), Lock and Le Grange (2013). One interesting thing that emerges in this social phase is the step-father, Tom's, declaration that "I'm the newest kid on the block here" (Lock & Le Grange, 2013, p. 69). As I have already suggested this is an opportunity to talk about the family transition without connecting it to the fact that two years later the oldest child has a serious mental illness. Should the parents make that connection the therapist might acknowledge this, saying something like "Well you are thoughtful people and I am sure you have thought of lots of things that might have troubled Susan but there are also lots of positive things about this sort of transition, so let's think some more about how it has been in your family". The therapist could comment that the arrival of Tom, the step-father, in the family provided a new resource for mother as a parent, and a new male figure, or an additional male figure, for the children to relate to, and to illustrate this with observations about how the parents work together, how Tom relates to each child etc. In the social phase the therapist takes the opportunity to make positive observations about all the family members and their relationships. Such observations serve to set up an expectation that they will not be critical when they hear about the problem. That does not mean that the therapist cannot take note of relationship issues that the family raise. It is the therapist's role to facilitate, not prevent, discussion or emotional expression.

Goals for the social phase

Minimal goals for the social phase will be achieved if something positive has been said about each individual and family sub-system. A more ambitious target would be that something new and unexpected was said that presented one or more family members in a positive light. The most obvious example of this would be the reframing of critical comments in a way that presents behaviours that are criticised in a positive light. Since, as we have seen, the families are quite reticent about making critical comments, opportunities to do this may not always occur.

The problem phase

Turning to the problem, the therapist could ask an open question, or start with the parents. Again it may be better to start with the patient. The reasons for this are much the same as with the social phase. The patient can easily be sidelined in this conversation, and now may also feel criticised. To begin with the therapist should track the process that has led to the referral and the assessment meeting. The therapist might say to the patient something like "Now we need to talk about what you have come about. I arranged this meeting because of the referral from Dr. Smith. How did it come about that you went to see her? Was it your idea? Your Mum's idea? Your Dad's idea?" The therapist can begin a conversation tracking the patient's knowledge of each person's concerns. Since it is likely that the patient is unconcerned about her symptoms and may wish to reject help, the therapist has the opportunity to model how to listen to and hear from somebody without necessarily agreeing. At the same time the process can be one that focuses the patient's attention on what her parents' concerns are. This is an important prelude to the account which the parents will give next about how their concerns have developed, and what they see about their daughter which drives these concerns. The therapist would then track, with all members of the family, what has been tried so far to tackle the self-starvation or other pathological weight control strategies presented by the patient.

The FBT treatment manual proposes that the therapist track the problem at this stage by asking each family member what effect the problem is having on them, and to deepen emotional expressiveness about this. The authors are not explicit about why questions should take this form. Perhaps it is intended as a way of communicating their view that family difficulties do not cause anorexia, but anorexia does cause family difficulties. There are some dangers in doing it this way, particularly given the personality of many of these patients. The family's comments on negative effects on them are likely to be experienced as critical of the patient, even if this is not the speaker's intention. Therefore, especially with parents, the therapist might do better to focus on what the family members see and know about the problem, and what they have tried to do to help. It is important to understand what the families attempted solutions have been, and the roles played in these by each parent and sibling.

An important goal for the first meeting is that family members should experience the session as a place in which it has been possible to speak to each other, not just to the therapist. Ultimately it is the family members' ability to communicate with each other that will determine the outcome, as far as psychological recovery is concerned. The therapist can achieve this by asking the parents to talk to each other and the children about the ways they have tried to tackle the patient's reluctance to eat, and other weight control behaviours such as over-exercising. He or she could set the family this task and say that she will sit out of the circle and take note of what they all have to say about this. If this proves difficult for them, the therapist can intervene to make suggestions to the parents about how to go about it, but should resist getting drawn in to the discussion as the "interviewer". It may be helpful for the therapist to make some normalising comments, for example along the lines of saying that often parents have sometimes tried to be permissive to avoid conflict, and have sometimes tried to be firm, but feel defeated. The therapist might also say that the process is often upsetting for everyone in the family. That is only to be expected. At the end of this task the therapist summarises what they have heard about the parents' efforts, the siblings' involvement, and the patient's reaction. Positive statements about the family's efforts and their ability to communicate with each other will be made at this stage. The therapist may suggest to the patient that while it is probably uncomfortable for her to hear about her family's concerns for her, yet her family are right to be concerned, and that their concern for her shows their love for her.

The therapist may feel concern for the welfare of the other children in the family, and for the parents themselves, but that is a concern to share with the parents, and the therapist might decide to discuss that with them separately at this point. This phase of the meeting might be drawn to a close by thanking the family for explaining their concern for their daughter or sister with some general comment along the lines of the family being one in which people are able to express concern for each other's welfare. The therapist might now move on to seeing the patient separately, and the parents separately after that. This order of events fits with most families' expectations, and gives the therapist the opportunity to report back to the parents to some extent on the discussion with their daughter.

Goals for the problem phase

Goals for this phase are that the therapists, and all the family members, hear about each person's perception of the problem, and their thoughts about it. This should be communicated in a way that is respectful of different views, but prioritise the parents' and therapist's concerns for the patient's welfare.

Meeting the patient alone

The purpose of this initial meeting with the patient on her own, which is likely to be quite short, is to continue to build a therapeutic alliance with her. A starting point is to talk about how difficult this situation is for her and to foster any expression of concern she might have for herself. The therapist can introduce the idea that anorexia functions to protect her from very negative feelings about herself, and see if she can engage with that idea. He or she can also express to the patient some understanding of the psychological processes that are likely to be dominating the patient's mind, such as the intrusiveness of thoughts about weight and eating in many situations. Although many patients with anorexia are very well behaved and want to be liked, others will be rude and angry, and the therapist needs to approach the session ready to continue to model behaviour that expresses acceptance and warmth towards the patient, while insisting on the need to intervene to ensure her wellbeing. There needs to be a psycho-educational element to this; an explanation of the extreme dangers of anorexia, both to future physical and to mental health. The therapist will need to discuss the limits of confidentiality, which in this sort of case includes the fact that the therapist will not keep secret from her parents any issues to do with weight, eating, or weight control methods. They should also express a preference for sharing the content of individual discussions with parents, but that the way this is done should be agreed between them at the end of each meeting. This is also the point at which to weigh the patient and to explain that information about her weight will always be shared with her parents.

Meeting the parents alone

This is an opportunity to hear from the parents about their own vulnerability and distress. At this point the therapist might want to introduce the issue of blame, at least to the extent of saying that parents sometimes feel that they are to blame or that they are blamed, and that this is not the therapist's intention, and so on, along the lines proposed by Dallos (2006) or Hughes (2007). Parents should be given the opportunity to say anything, or raise any questions, that they chose not to discuss in front of the patient and other children. Parents need to hear some positive feedback about their daughter as a person, as well as a brief assessment of her mental difficulty, in terms of the intensity of her preoccupation with food and weight issues for example. Insofar as the patient is dismissive of her own needs, or even nasty and attacking of the therapist's and parents' concerns, the therapist should convey "This is what the three of us will work together to manage" but only in the context of also conveying something positive about the patient. Quite often one or both parents hope or expect that their daughter will be admitted to hospital, and that this will provide a solution. The therapist needs to be able to provide some education about treatment options, giving realistic information about the low level of recovery achieved by in-patient treatment, on the one hand, and the high level of success achieved by parents, working with a therapist, when they help the patient to improve her food intake, and to express her own views and feelings in the family. In addition, the opportunity should be taken here to discuss any differences between the parents in handling the mealtime situation, and weight loss strategies, and to set up the therapeutic task of insisting their daughter eat more in the time before the next meeting. At the end there should be a brief discussion of what will be fed back to the family about the discussion.

Sharing an understanding about the problem and treatment goals

At this point the therapist can make positive observations about the family and talk about the task that has been set for the parents, as well as an outline of the agreement reached about future sessions. This is an opportunity to reiterate the therapist's general goals with the family, in relation to finding ways to help them support the patient in eating, but also in helping her to improve her ability to assert her personality and individual needs in the family context. It would also be a good point to make some reference to the need for talks about talks, to the fact that people do not always find it easy to talk together as a family, and do not always find it easy to agree what to share about what has been said in separate time with the therapist.

The second session

This session corresponds to the family meal session in the FBT treatment manual. However, if the therapist has taken on the case without the benefit of a previous assessment having been made, it may be too soon to do this. The second session could be used to hear about the family's experience of the therapeutic task, and to prepare the ground for a family lunch session in the next session. Although therapists in the UK generally do not use the family lunch session, the arguments against doing so are not well founded. Therapists in many countries continue to use the approach apparently with considerable success. The evidence from the FBT outcome studies shows that the approach often leads to rapid weight recovery in treatments as short as ten sessions, and this observation is consistent with the much older observations about these sessions, such as Rosman et al (1975). It is hard to see why we would not usually use the supportive approach to the family meal enactment described by Lock et al (2001) and Lock and Le Grange (2013). They make a convincing case for doing so in that the therapist must help the parents form an alliance to be effective in refeeding their daughter. However, exceptions probably could be made in cases where parental attitudes make it difficult to achieve a sufficiently strong therapeutic alliance at such an early stage.

Clinical experience shows us that families often present the difficulties around the patient's eating at home in a way that is greatly understated.

Often a good deal of behaviour by the patient, and sometimes by her parents and siblings too, is not reported to the therapist. When this is the case, the family must feel that the therapist does not really understand, since she has never been told, or seen, what really goes on. The family lunch session brings these difficulties vividly to life in the therapy room. Even if the patient, or for that matter the parents, remain on their best behaviour during the enactment, it presents an opportunity for the therapist to ask, "So how would this be different at home?" The challenge is to the therapist's ability to join with each member of the family, since the session must be managed in a way that allows each individual to feel understood and supported. With the parents the therapist needs to approach this as a shared task, to which parents and therapist will bring their own ideas. Equally, the therapist can join by sympathising with the patient, saying "I know this is awful for you but it has to happen". Despite the tension in these sessions the therapist should not rule out the possibility that the patient will offer some constructive engagement, for example by saying to her parents what she finds more, and what she finds less, helpful about their approach. Two other important issues arise here. One is that the patient may respond to her parents by eating, and then burst out with an attack on them, verbalising some resentment she feels towards them. She might express resentment about the way they control her, or about feeling that a sibling is treated better than her, or about the way somebody else in the family does or does not eat etc. The therapist needs to be ready for that and to be ready to be supportive to both the patient and her parents in such an eventuality. Another thing to bear in mind is that sessions of this sort sometimes lead to a breakthrough in which the patient starts eating again. This can become a reason for the family to finish therapy. There is no objective information about how stable such changes are or about the quality of psychological recovery that is to be expected. So again the therapist needs to be ready to respond to this eventuality. Whatever the outcome, at the end the family need to leave the session with something new and different to do in relation to the symptomatic behaviour.

The therapist will need to feel comfortable about the possibility of failure. Even Minuchin's (1978) high intensity meal enactments did not always end with the patient eating. The FBT manual usefully frames the meal situation as one in which every mouthful that the patient eats, over and above what she was willing to eat at the outset, is a sign of progress. The therapist may be daunted by the fear that even this will not be achieved and that he or she will be shown up as a failure. In that case the therapist needs to be able to say, as Minuchin said in the same situation, "We will help you" taking responsibility for continuing to lead the family towards resolution of the conflict around eating.

* * *

From this point on, one of the tasks of the therapist must be to monitor progress and help the family overcome setbacks. However, there is also a need to foster the ability to communicate at a time when levels of anxiety and tension are still likely to be high. Parents will need continuing support in undertaking a challenging, often conflict-laden task. Supporting the patient in talking about what the refeeding situation is like for her can also be a useful starting point here. Often patients are acutely aware of nuances of communication, of what is said and not said, and the way things are said, tones of voice that are more or less helpful. Communication about this can serve to improve the relationship between the patient and her parents at a point where discussion of "adolescent issues" might be premature. The issue here is that refeeding supervised by parents' addresses a biological need—nutrition, and a psychological need—attachment. If the patient can be helped to communicate to her parents something about how she experiences them in this situation then it can come to serve a developmental purpose as well. It will be an initial step in the direction of finding her voice. Such communication represents an initial move towards greater autonomy.

Presentation and timing of a relational reframe

The therapist needs to draw on his or her knowledge of the psychology of anorexia, and their knowledge of the process of change, in order to set the scene for the family. In essence the first message is "starving yourself and focusing your attention on control of your weight gives you a sense of accomplishment, and this is the only thing that makes you feel good about yourself. To recover you have to eat and find another way to deal with the distress that will cause you. Putting your feelings into words will help you. I am here, and your parents are here, to help you to do that." The second message is "your daughter is someone who has got into the habit of keeping her anger and distress to herself. She needs to be able to talk to you about the things that upset her, and it will be important that you can listen to what she has to say, even if you do not always agree". These statements set the scene for therapeutic change. They provide a context for the tasks that the therapist will ask the family to undertake in subsequent sessions. Some therapists may choose to begin to introduce these ideas at the very beginning of treatment, even mentioning them in the initial phone call to the family. Others may feel that there is too much to do in the initial contacts with the family. In that case a choice might be made to introduce them in the context of a review of the first two or three sessions. They could be introduced at the same time as discussing other decisions, such as how much to work conjointly or separately in the immediate future.

The next session

The next session could be thought of as a choice point, and a moment at which to review progress with the family and discuss family members' feelings about therapy. At this point it would make sense to address issues about the family therapy as a secure base, if these have not been addressed already. It is an opportunity to return to address the secure base issues along the lines presented by Dallos (2006) and by Hughes (2007), now that the family has had some experience of the family sessions.

* * *

So far what has been proposed follows the general line of the FBT treatment manual in assuming that time will be spent mainly in conjoint sessions. The advantage of that is that we can expect to see a fuller recovery in patients successfully treated this way. Evidence suggests that in more difficult family situations (strictly speaking, in families in which mothers are a bit critical) separated sessions may be better at this point. We can argue, although we cannot currently demonstrate, that some separated time would be useful whenever family relationship difficulties feel acute. Time spent in this way may help the therapist maintain the alliance with family members who are at times uncomfortable in one another's presence. In cases of more extreme difficulty arising from family relationships, or parental disturbance, even mental illness, more time may need to be given to separated sessions. In such cases the therapist might need to draw on the attachment approach more completely to make the therapy situation a "secure base". Sometimes, especially in situations where the therapeutic alliance seems weak, or where the therapist sees that the parents are especially vulnerable, this may be best addressed with parents and patient separately. In the most extreme instances, a family therapy in which the parents are put in charge of their daughter's eating, might be unlikely to succeed. In some cases the daughter may be too ill, physically and mentally, for further out-patient treatment, and an admission with a focus on engaging the parents might be a better option. The goal would be to allow family therapy time to empower the parents to take charge when their daughter is discharged. The dynamics of such admissions are discussed in the next chapter.

Holding separated therapies together

A difficulty that can easily arise is that separated family therapy can turn into two, unrelated, attempts at individual therapy. The danger is probably greatest in situations where one or both parents present themselves as exceptionally vulnerable or needy. Another factor that can give rise to this result is that parents and patient see different therapists. Therapists may begin to develop a special relationship with "their" family members, a relationship they are reluctant to put at risk by tackling difficult issues. A common problem in this arrangement is that the therapist may become the keeper of secrets that one side of the family or the other does not want to share. One way to try to prevent this problem developing is to make the last part of any session a conjoint review in which something of what has been discussed in each separate session will be shared. This requires discussion in the separated session about what will be shared. The therapist who constantly remembers that their role is to increase communication between the generations, and does not get caught up in valuing the separate relationship with one or other person in the family, is least likely to be disabled by this problem. If one therapist works with both parents and patient, the danger that too great a disconnection will develop is likely to be averted. In the final analysis, if one or both sides are making progress impossible by insisting on not sharing information then the therapist may need to say so and insist on a renegotiation of the therapeutic contract.

Introducing therapy themes

There is a danger that family therapy for anorexia becomes very repetitive and sterile. The format proposed in the FBT manual is one in which progress with weight restoration takes precedence, and other discussions are deferred until sufficient progress has been made. Sometimes, because of a lack of progress with weight restoration, discussion about other issues can be deferred indefinitely. There is really no objective reason to accept that this should be so. The dilemma facing the therapist is much the same as that faced by family therapists in many other situations where concerns with the management of a symptomatic problem dominate sessions. This being so therapists might well prefer to aim to limit discussion of eating and refeeding, with a view to exploring with families those issues which research indicates to be significant. If the therapist presents these as a "programme" to be worked through families may feel less self-conscious in thinking about them. At the same time, by providing notice of the intention to discuss these issues, family members are given the chance to think about how they might address them. This may make it more likely that families will be able to raise emotionally loaded issues in sessions. Therapists may therefore find it helpful to have a general frame of reference for the discussion, as well as one that is based on observation of the individual family.

It often feels difficult to raise such issues with the families. They are emotionally loaded because they are issues that parents themselves may have difficulty managing, and because of the guilt, even shame, which may be triggered in some parents by the discussion. If that feeling inhibits the therapist from raising issues then that is an indication of the need to revisit the discussion of the therapy situation, and address the secure base issues again, perhaps in a more intensive way, for example by drawing on the suggestions Hughes (2007) makes about the problem of shame and how it should be managed. At this point the therapist could also take the opportunity to set an agenda for future sessions. This should be presented along the lines of saying "With this type of problem we find it helpful to talk about …" and list issues of the sort that research has shown to be relevant. This would be the point to put the issue of comforting, and the family's experience across three generations, on the agenda. Other issues to mention here as topics for discussion would be family attitudes to eating and weight, the way that parents and adolescents take decisions together, conflict and conflict resolution, framing these as things that adolescents often have strong feelings about. In addition, the therapist might want to help the family to focus on anxieties that the children may have about their parents individually and about their parent's relationship.

Family attitudes to emotional expression

Attachment therapy approaches are especially rich in this area. As Dallos (2006) says "Throughout our lives we need to turn to others to help us manage difficult feelings, problems, conflicts, distress, humiliations and anxieties ... An attachment perspective focuses on how family members have come to feel that they cannot comfort each other. ... One helpful approach can be to trace patterns of comforting trans-generationally to discuss what the parents' experience of it has been ..." Dallos (2006, p. 126). He also proposes that the therapist should enquire into times when parents have been able to offer comfort. These issues can be discussed in conjoint family sessions. Sometimes the family genogram might be used in these discussions to help the family think about this issue as it has been played out in each relationship in the current family, and in the parents' families of origin. Dallos describes use of the family genogram in exploring issues about emotional expression and relationships in a family with a daughter with anorexia. The genogram is used to explore trans-generational patterns. Used in this context the questions arising from the use of the genogram would be about such issues as patterns of comforting in families, how parents had experienced this in their families of origin, what they hoped to bring to their current family, and how they might want their current family to be different. Future oriented questions would be about how the younger generation might be in their own future relationships and with their own children. Dallos provides a very helpful set of suggestions about how to apply this approach under the heading "Formats for exploration", as well as a case study illustrating its use with a young woman with anorexia and her parents.

Family attitudes to eating and weight

A therapist can introduce this issue by saying that we all live in a culture in which everybody experiences concerns about weight, shape, physical fitness, and appearance, in some ways. Although this puts particular pressure on girls and young women it is really an issue for both sexes and people of all ages. There are many possible ways that the family therapist can take that discussion forward. For example, the parents could ask the children about how they, each of the children, experience cultural and peer group pressures, and how they deal with this. Parents could also be asked to make their own observations about how they think each child is dealing with this. The children in the family could be asked to question their parents about how they deal with these issues now, and how they experienced them when they were growing up. In some cases the family's response to this sort of enquiry will be greatly at variance with the therapist's observations. In a small number of cases one parent, perhaps very occasionally both parents, are currently suffering from a major eating disorder such as anorexia or bulimia. In a larger number of cases one, or occasionally, both, parents will be suffering from a subclinical eating disorder. The family often denies these parental difficulties, at least in the early stages of the work. The exception to this is that the patient herself may reveal the truth by saying, in effect, "Why should I eat? You don't", or "Why shouldn't I exercise? You do". In such a situation the therapist needs to intervene in a way that supports both sides, so that the parent can feel that the therapist is concerned for their feelings, but at the same time to ensure that the patient is not silenced by parental denial.

There are many possible signs that these difficulties exist. For example parents, or one parent, may have great difficulty accepting the quantities of food necessary for refeeding. Occasionally this may extend to parental interference with the refeeding programme in an in-patient unit. Sometimes one parent never eats with the family, something that Waugh and Bulik (1999) identified as common for mothers who themselves suffered from severe eating disorders. Parents with less severe eating difficulties themselves may be unduly preoccupied with "healthy eating" in a way that communicates itself to the younger generation. Exercise, too, is an important issue, with some parents having what would clearly be a pathological drive to exercise, and others over-valuing exercise to the point that they have difficulty changing their behaviour even when they see that they are modelling behaviour that is inappropriate for their daughter. Parental obesity, as a long-term effect of bulimia or binge eating, or just emotional eating, also occurs in a small number of cases. Since obesity is often a cause of extreme unhappiness, an obese parent may find difficulty in managing refeeding with a daughter, because the daughter's self-control in relation to food appears such an enviable quality to them. They could also experience their daughter's food refusal as an implicit criticism of them. Insofar as parents reveal that they do have their own serious eating difficulties the therapist would naturally approach those with the same degree of sympathy and concern that they display in relation to the patient. Given the sensitivities that people are likely to feel about these issues, the family therapist will need to be fully engaged in supporting family members individually and in their communications with one another.

In families where parents or other family members have their own eating difficulties an ultimate therapy goal must be that the patient, in discussion with her parents, can describe and reject her parents' dysfunctional attitudes and behaviours, in herself, whether or not her parents are able to do that for themselves. She is more likely to be able to do that if her parents can communicate respect for her achievement in doing so. That is the ultimate goal, but the immediate goal must be that parents' or siblings' difficulties should not be secret, since secrets freeze the process of therapy. Hence the therapist's goal should be to help family members name the difficulty, viewing it in the same sympathetic way that one views the problem of the patient herself.

Of course family attitudes to eating, weight, fitness and so on, are often caught up in more general family processes. For example, men who criticise women's weight often display misogynistic attitudes. In such a situation a daughter who develops anorexia can be seen to be both avoiding her father's negative judgement of her, and defeating his control of her. She could also be seen as expressing her resentment to her mother for failing to protect her from her father's behaviour. Here the ultimate goal is that the patient could speak for herself about the impact on her of comments aimed at other women, at her mother and sisters, or at her herself, and, ideally, that the father should be able to apologise for what he has said. The immediate goal must be that the issue is treated as one of the realities of the family's life, one that creates difficulties for all the women in the family. The dynamic may be much the same as that in which a mother is physically abused by her husband, but assumes that this does not affect the children, or that the children do not know about it. In such circumstances there is a negative impact on the younger generation's relationship with both parents and both sets of relationship difficulties need to be addressed.

Family attitudes to control

The treatment manual for FBT approaches the issue of parental control through the medium of a discussion about the negotiation of adolescent autonomy That is to say it approaches the question as one of concrete decision making. No doubt this has some value, but there is a danger that the therapist argues the case for the patient's autonomy, relieving her of the need to do so. Instead, the therapy goal should be to create a context in which she is able to argue the case for herself. The research evidence on adolescent development indicates that it is not just the issue of negotiating separate activities that is crucial in adolescence. Instead, what matters most is the younger generation's ability to verbalise differences from their parents, and the parents' ability to support and value this. Given the evidence we have seen about the relationship between parental psychological control, perfectionism and anorexia, this is likely to be a particularly important area for change, if the patient is to achieve a full recovery.

This is another area that might be addressed in thinking about three generations. It can be seen as an issue relating to parents' corrective and replicative scripts, that is to say, ways that parents are trying to be unlike their own parents in raising their children, or ways that they are, perhaps unwittingly, being the same. Here the therapist's enquiries would be directed to the question of how parents had dealt with their own parents when they were adolescents, and the extent to which they had felt able to hold to and express their own ideas. This then would lead to discussion of how parents wanted their children to be able to do this, and to any areas in which the children might feel that in fact this was difficult for them. Future oriented questions would consider how they might address these issues together, for example when the younger generation are adults.

Such a conversation would be a context for thinking what it is that stops the younger generation, that is, the parents in their own family of origin, and the children in the current family, from saying what they think. Here such difficulties as fear of eliciting anger or disapproval, or feeling a need to protect others' feelings, can be explored. Changes in communication about these topics, such as the ability of a child to tell a parent that they are afraid of their anger, or of their disapproval, sometimes have substantial impact on the relationship.

Family attitudes to conflict and conflict resolution

Discussion of family issues about control leads naturally into a discussion of conflict and conflict resolution. Here there are two issues. First, how is conflict expressed and resolved in the relationship between the patient, and her siblings, on the one hand, and her parents on the other. The other is the question of what the children have learned from their parents' way of expressing and resolving conflict. Here it may be helpful for the therapist to offer some psycho-educational input along the lines of saying that children are helped to learn the importance of doing this by seeing their parents do it, and learn something about how to do it in the same way. This opens up various possibilities for further exploration. Some children will have been subjected to an alarming degree of conflict between their parents at some stage. This then becomes an opportunity for them to express something of their anxieties on this score, for example anxieties about a parent leaving or coming to harm, which they may not have been able to express in the past. This often comes as a surprise to parents. They may regard any conflicts as relatively minor and not appreciate the significance this can have in the minds of children. In other cases the younger generation may be puzzled by an absence of any expressions of parental conflict. This then might present an opportunity for them to consider how they will feel in a future relationship with a partner when disagreements have to be managed.

Children's concerns about parents

A common issue is that the patient, and sometimes siblings also, feel concern for one or both, parents. Sometimes parents are surprised to learn about the extent of their children's concerns about this. They may need to be helped to address this issue, bearing in mind that the children need reassurance, as far as possible, that parents will be constructive in relation to one another, and can take responsibility for their own welfare. In other words there may be a need both to promote some communication in this area, so that parents will know if the younger generation are unduly burdened by concerns about them, but also a need for boundary making if the patient, for example, is being given too much information to process at a particular moment in time.

Therapeutic impasse

Family therapy has a long standing approach to the problems of stuckness, impasse, and treatment failure. There is not space to discuss this here, but a useful summary is to be found in Burnham (1986).

The approach that has been outlined here has a number of additional implications relevant to the problem of impasse. First, attachment theory contains the idea that some people protect themselves by keeping feelings and intimate relationship at a distance for fear of being overwhelmed by emotions that they have not been able to process. In general such people seek to put on a competent front. In that case initial attempts to discuss therapy as a secure base may be responded to in a superficial way that does not get to grips with the reality of family members' vulnerabilities. Therapists need to note this and be ready to return to the issue. They need to revive discussion of the secure base issues when they see signs that family members are in an area that is uncomfortable for them. The proposals that Dallos (2006) makes about the family's need to say when things are going too fast for them need to kept in mind. One difficulty is that people who have not had the experience of working through difficult emotions commonly feel ashamed if they are overwhelmed by emotion, so that events that may seem to be "breakthroughs" to the therapist may be dreaded as "breakdowns" by the family. A similar issue arises in relation to the issue of blame. If, as appears to be the case, many parents are highly conscientious, but are invested in the rigid performance of roles, then a challenge to their role is likely to elicit guilt or, even more problematically, shame. Yet, in order to become a separate person the patient needs to be able to challenge her parents' behaviour. For example, a girl who had recovered her weight under parental supervision but remained very depressed managed after many therapy sessions to tell her very conscientious father that she was frightened of him when he was angry. In this instance the father was able to listen to what his daughter had to say. In this instance the patient's mental state improved dramatically after this event in therapy and the family sessions ended at that point. Had the therapist taken the opportunity to talk about the parent's experiences of anger, and their anxieties about it, more might have been achieved at this point. A therapist working with a trans-generational understanding of the origins of anorexia might well have done so.

A related issue is the issue of blame. Hughes (2007) is very insistent on the responsibility of the therapist to monitor his or her relationship with the family and to take the initiative in addressing the issue if he or she feels they have made anyone feel blamed. The concern is that a person who feels blamed will respond with a sense of shame that causes them to withdraw, physically or psychologically from the therapy situation. This is another issue about impasse since it is possible that, if progress is not being made, one or more family members may have emotionally withdrawn from the therapy situation because they feel blamed, or because the therapist has elicited a feeling of shame in them. Here the impasse might be addressed by a review of what people have hoped and feared about the therapy situation since the beginning. The therapist might also need to name events or comments that have been made that seem to have made a difference. In addition of course, the therapist needs to be willing to apologise for eliciting painful feelings if this is what has occurred.

Sometimes impasse arises for less complex reasons. The therapist may be over-invested in an alliance with one family member, or in some view of the family. In that case it is probably an issue for supervision. The model presented in this book suggests a range of issues that the therapist may need to address and considering the whole range in supervision may help the therapist to notice things that have been missed or need further exploration.

The end of treatment

The end of treatment is a time to reflect on the process of the therapy and to think about what has changed and what still needs to change. The therapist should be realistic, not unduly pessimistic, but not unduly optimistic either, since undue optimism, although comforting in the short-term, discourages realistic appraisal. In addition, the patient should be encouraged to talk with her family about the psychological process she went through when anorexia develops. At this stage one would expect the patient to be able to give a realistic account of her own psychological process, what it was that made her so unhappy that she turned to self-starvation as a solution. Her family could reasonably expect that she would have a plan in place to deal with the situation if that should start to happen again. Essentially the question is how she will deal with distress in the future, and what her parents' roles will be in helping her to do that.

The therapist will say goodbye, but leave a line of communication open. Ideally there would be some follow-ups arranged in the course of the following year or two.

A model of change

It was proposed at the beginning of the book that the onset of anorexia coincides with a time when the patient needed to use parental support but did not do so. It represents a moment she turned away from the attachment relationship and hit upon a false solution to her distress about herself. The initial therapeutic task, in which the parents take charge of her eating, challenges this pattern. In undertaking the task, the parents make themselves available, and availability is one requirement for secure attachment. The other is attunement. If parents undertake the task in a resentful, rejecting, critical way, then the outcome is a shift towards a mental state temporarily improved by the improvement of nutrition. Such a shift is accompanied by reactivated distress about the self, which will drive continuing eating disorder preoccupations and/or other symptomatic difficulties, such as depression and anxiety. However, if the task is undertaken by parents who are not only available but also attuned, then the parents can be reinstated as a source of support, and the patient will be able to use their support to negotiate her distress. If that occurs then she should be able to tackle her difficulties in the family. In particular, she should be able to use the family therapy to express to her parents what the difficulties are for her, in her relationship with them. It seems likely that it will be the patient who finds her voice in that way which will show the greatest psychological improvement in relation to self-esteem and underlying psychopathology. To put it another way, parents are helped to challenge their daughter's use of anorexia as a distancing manoeuvre, and to make themselves both available and attuned. The patient is supported in expressing her difficulties in the relationship with her parents. Her experience of engaging in direct, honest communication with them improves her self-esteem. The relationship is strengthened, with the result that the patient becomes more confident in herself, and more able to use her parents for emotional support in the future. The parents experience confirmation of their worth and competence as parents. The new situation should be self-sustaining. This is somewhat like the structural theory of change, but gives more emphasis to the emotional communication in the parental relationship, rather than the directive aspects of parenting. Moreover, whereas the structural theory of change addresses only the issues of family interaction, a model based on attachment theory has implications for individual change. Family members' relationship to "internal working models" of relationships should be changed by the therapy process. For the patient the expectation would be that the perception of her parents would shift from an experience of parents as overwhelming demanding or needy to seeing them as moderately vulnerable individuals with their own strengths and weaknesses, arising from their own family backgrounds. For parents it would be expected to be a similar shift in the direction of a more realistic appraisal of themselves and each other; a more realistic balancing of appreciation with guilt and blame.

Supervision

Supervision, whether in the form of live supervision in the room or via a one-way screen, or retrospective supervision using recordings or the therapist's notes and recollections, is an intrinsic part of any family therapy approach. The more difficult the family the more crucial is the role of the supervisor. Therapists can easily be drawn into alignments with some family members against others, or into a negative perception of the family. The supervisor's role is to help the therapist stand back from that intense involvement and consider matters afresh. Supervision should be considered as an essential part of therapy. The availability of a supervisor whose frame of reference is congruent with that of the therapist is as important as the availability of the therapist.

In working with patients with anorexia therapists might use the framework presented here to consider with their supervisor their own family experiences and attitudes as they relate to the work. A useful exercise for a therapist will be to consider their own experience in their family of origin, and their family of procreation, in relation to their own attachment style, and what this makes them comfortable with and uncomfortable with in the consulting room. Likewise, therapists might usefully consider their experience of the development of autonomy during adolescence and young adult life, and their attitudes to their own actual or potential children. Therapists' experiences bearing on general attitudes about weight, fitness, and acceptable self-presentation, and how this relates to perceptions of men and women, might also be reviewed here since these attitudes need to be considered in discussions with families. In the therapy situation the therapist's unconscious expectations and prejudices may well communicate themselves to the family.

Implications for research

This chapter supports the proposal made by Dallos (2006) that attachment approaches can be used in work with anorexia. It outlines ways to use them in a context in which the usual treatment strategy is the one that has been shown to be effective in much research, putting parents in charge of their daughter's eating at the outset. In addition it proposes that therapists should address the issues that research indicates are relevant to the development of anorexia. The proposal is that they should do so in a structured way.

There are a number of implications for research. The big question is whether such an approach would produce better quality outcomes than those achieved by therapists who are guided by the Maudsley Model or those who follow the FBT treatment manual. A related question is whether it can improve the outcomes for patients who are hard to treat. These are large questions requiring a considerable research effort. Nevertheless, they might be addressed in collaborative research involving groups of therapists in CAMHS. Another question is whether this approach would facilitate communication and assertion by the patient, and whether, as has been proposed, this in turn would lead to greater levels of psychological recovery. This question could be addressed at the level of the case study, or in larger scale research. Less ambitious research questions that are more likely to be manageable for a small group of therapists working together could focus on the acceptability of the components of such an approach, such as the use of the attachment framework, and the programmatic approach to family issues relevant to anorexia.

CHAPTER TWELVE

Treatment in context

Family therapists work in the context of teams and organisations. Ideally, these would assess the quality of treatment outcomes using an audit method, in order to ensure that outcomes are as good as they can be. Teams seldom have sufficient information or benchmarks against which to compare their own effectiveness. This, in turn, makes it difficult for clinicians to know whether their treatment approaches, their teamwork and their interaction with other teams, such as in-patient teams, are as effective as they could be.

The effectiveness of treatment in the UK

Family therapy has long been recognised as the most effective treatment for young people with anorexia. Almost all this information comes from centres of excellence that have resources for teaching and research. Research evidence about outcomes from "routine treatment" is seldom available. Today we would expect the CAMHS services to see family therapy for anorexia delivered on an out-patient basis, as the first-line treatment for anorexia. If the family cannot be recruited to this, or if the patient's weight loss is critical, then admission to an adolescent psychiatric unit or specialist adolescent eating disorder unit is often the only other choice available to meet that situation. Such admissions are now generally regarded as a regrettable necessity in some cases in order to protect the patient from the effects of starvation, but one that has serious, unhelpful consequences. Moreover, general CAMHS services often admit patients to units belonging to other organisations, whose policies they cannot influence. This situation contributes to a lack of coherence at the different levels of the service received by the patient and family. Sometimes individual treatments such as CBT are also offered to these patients. There are arguments for and against doing this. The question is how to provide a coherent service within teams and across levels of service, in a way that produces the best possible outcomes, freeing the patient from anorexia and other symptoms and problems commonly associated with it.

A little information is available about the efficacy of treatment services for young people with anorexia offered by mainstream CAMHS services in the UK.

The effectiveness of out-patient treatment in the UK

Gowers et al (2007) published outcomes from treatment of young people with anorexia in three treatments, one of which was CAMHS treatment as usual provided by thirty-five community CAMHS teams. By definition this treatment could not be specified, but was described as usually a multidisciplinary, family-based approach, with variable dietetic, individual supportive therapy and paediatric (medical) liaison. Treatment duration was six months. At one-year follow-up treatment outcome using the Morgan-Russell criteria was 18% good, 56% intermediate, and 24% poor, with 2% (one individual) lost to follow-up. After two years outcomes were 36% good, 36% intermediate and 26% poor. It follows that overall, over 70% of patients were weight restored at one year in that they were at least no longer in the anorexic weight range. However, these results fall short of those reported in published trials of family therapy, Maudsley Model Family Therapy, and FBT, mainly in respect of the lower proportion of good outcomes achieved at both one and two year follow-ups.

Gowers et al (2007) also reported the outcomes for a CBT treatment provided by a specialist eating disorders team. Again duration of treatment was limited to six months. This was a treatment mainly involving the patient on an individual basis, although there was some involvement of parents. The trend was that weight recovery was slower for this group, but they had largely caught up after two years. These differences between the treatments did not achieve statistical significance. At the two-year follow-up 75% were weight recovered but only 24% had a good outcome. It follows that after treatment as usual and CBT treatment, many patients were still struggling with eating disorder symptoms.

* * *

Out-patient treatment may often break down, and the patient is admitted to a psychiatric unit. As would be expected this happened in some of the cases allocated to out-patient treatments in the Gowers et al (2007) study.

Effects of admissions following unsuccessful out-patient treatment

In the Gowers et al (2007) study, fifty-five patients were randomly allocated to each of the two out-patient treatments. Despite this, 28% of the patients allocated to these treatments were admitted during the course of the study. This is a relatively small proportion compared to that usually reported by CAMHS which is typically around 40%. Outcomes for these patients were unsatisfactory, with only one (3%) of the thirty-one patients achieving a good outcome after one year, and still only three (10%) after two years. In another study, Gowers et al (2000) followed up seventy-five patients with anorexia treated by a specialist adolescent eating disorder service two to seven years after the end of treatment. Twenty-one patients had been admitted. Of these only three (14%) had a good outcome at the time of the follow-up, compared to thirty-one (61%) of those treated only as out-patients. Psychiatric admission was the strongest predictor of a poor outcome at follow-up, and the severity of anorexia at the first presentation was the second strongest. Gowers et al argued that there may be unhelpful aspects of in-patient admissions and that these may reduce the patients' chances of recovery. He argued that some patients with anorexia experienced such admissions as providing a safe refuge and welcomed the care that was given. However, in those cases it was very difficult for the patient to readjust to a situation in which they had to take responsibility on discharge. He also argued that patients often experienced the treatment as imposed, and that this undermined their self-esteem.

The effectiveness of admissions as a primary treatment

In the study by Gowers et al (2007) fifty-seven patients were allocated to an in-patient treatment in any one of four adolescent units, without any prior attempt at out-patient treatment. This treatment was intended to last for a minimum of six weeks. However, twenty-nine of these patients were not admitted, usually because the offer of admission prompted a degree of weight recovery in the period between the assessment and the admission. Patients who avoided admission in this way did better than those who were admitted, being three times as likely to have a good outcome at one year, and still twice as likely at two years. Patients who accepted admission did relatively badly, only three (11%) had a good outcome at one year, and six, (22%) at two years. Audit information confirms such disappointing results. For example, Allen et al (2014) in a report of an audit of admissions of adolescent patients with anorexia to out of area admissions (mostly private specialist adolescent eating disorder units) found that 70–80% relapsed to an unhealthy weight following discharge.

Outreach services

One approach to improving outcomes and reducing admissions is the development of outreach services. These services offer an intensive input in the home situation for variable periods of time. Some are specialised and work only with young patients with eating disorders. Others do this work as part of a more extensive service to young people with other mental disturbances. Some evidence suggests that they reduce the need for admissions, reduce the duration of admissions, and improve the quality of outcomes. Outreach services have been based in in-patient units, in specialist community-based eating disorder teams, in specialist community-based adolescent teams, and in CAMHS teams.

Jaffa and Percival (2004) report the impact of an outreach service based in an in-patient unit. It was available for patients referred for or waiting for admission. The service could remain involved during and after an admission. It was also able to support the work of the children's ward of a general hospital when young patients with anorexia were admitted there. They argued that the involvement of the outreach service reduced admissions, as some patients were engaged and made progress. They noted that in a study of twenty-five cases referred for admission and seen by one outreach worker, thirteen made such progress that admission became unnecessary. Three case studies were presented in which it was demonstrated that even some severely underweight young people, and patients who were hard to engage in treatment, made good progress given this service.

Allen et al (2014) presented an outreach service based in a community-based specialist eating disorder service. The outreach service was for young people with anorexia. The team provided FBT for this patient group. The outreach service was seen as an addition to this, specifically an input that was seen as adding to the first phase of FBT, supporting parents in refeeding their teenager. The input by the outreach service was limited to six weeks duration. They found that, compared to years when the service had not been available, admissions were reduced, and the number of "bed-days" used by young patients with anorexia was reduced by 65%. Family-Based Treatment was ongoing and continued after the outreach service had completed its work with the family.

Goel and Darwish (2008) provide a very brief report of the service for young people with anorexia provided by a Community Intensive Therapy Team (CITT). The CITT worked with a wide range of young people at risk of admission because of various psychiatric disorders. They reported that thirty patients with anorexia had been treated. Only two cases had needed a hospital admission, and both were supported by the CITT during admissions to the children's ward of a general hospital. There were no psychiatric admissions. Most patients achieved rapid weight recovery but the team remained involved and supported the patient and family in the process of "normalisation" of their lives. The average duration of the team involvement was seventeen months, ranging from five months to three years six months. The treatment philosophy was based on the idea of normalisation, not on a family therapy model. CAMHS Teams also treated some of these patients, so they may also have had family therapy.

Specialist services and coherent treatment

Given the limited success that CAMHS teams seem to achieve in promoting recovery and preventing unhelpful admissions, many clinicians argue the need for specialist services for patients with anorexia.

Advantages of specialist services

It has been argued that specialist services improve outcomes and reduce admissions. The advantages of specialist services are obvious. Clinicians can concentrate on a relatively homogeneous group of families and develop a high level of skills in engagement and treatment. Such a group of clinicians may develop high prestige and contribute to training and research. Their prestige alone may aid engagement and treatment effectiveness. In addition, such a service may be better able to develop a coherent approach across levels of service, between in-patient and out-patient services, and even within their own approach to therapy. House et al (2012) found that studies demonstrated that the admission rate for teenagers treated by CAMHS teams was 35% or more for teenage patients and 50% for younger patients. She found that 42% of a group of anorexic and sub-clinical patients with anorexia who started treatment with general non-specialist CAMHS services were referred on to other teams during the course of a year. This usually means they were referred for admission. The rate of in-patient admissions was two and a half times higher for patients treated in general CAMHS than for those treated in specialist treatment services.

A specialist service may also provide better liaison and education to other parts of the health system, such as to General Practitioners (GPs). Another important finding of the study by House et al (2012) was that twice as many adolescents with anorexia or bulimia were referred by GPs in the areas that received these services. House et al argued that this reflected better communication with and education of GPs. This facilitated the identification and referral of more cases. This, of course, may lead to earlier intervention and to better outcomes.

Disadvantages of specialist services

An obvious disadvantage of specialist services is that since anorexia is relatively rare the number of such services would naturally be limited. Such services may have to be at a considerable distance from some families' homes. Hence, specialist services are more likely to be a viable option for metropolitan areas than for rural areas. Another disadvantage of this kind of service model is that a small number of clinicians may have a monopoly of skills and thinking about the patient group. This has the potential to de-skill clinicians in generic services. They would have little reason to maintain their skills, and not much argument for updating their training in this area of work. Then, if the specialist service became overloaded or temporarily unable to function effectively because key individuals are unavailable, generic services may have difficulty in meeting the patient's needs. Possibly an even bigger disadvantage is that specialist services may not serve all patients, or serve them through the course of their career as a patient. Some hard to engage families may refuse to travel to a distant specialist service. Moreover, specialist services may often see themselves providing an acute therapy service within a limited period of time. Such services often struggle to continue to work with long-term problems because they can be experienced as taking up too much time. Significant proportions of patients either still have anorexia, or significant ongoing eating disorders and other neurotic problems for more than a year. Some severe and complex cases need long-term input. In this case, there is the possibility that, notwithstanding the involvement of specialist services, the most treatment resistant cases will return to the clinicians in CAMHS. These will be the clinicians who will be seen as having the lowest level of skills with this group of patients.

Coherence across levels of service and the impact of admission

Specialist services may be better able to offer a coherent service. This may be more difficult for non-specialist CAMHS. If the individual patient with anorexia has often been seen as caught up in unhelpful, unresolved processes between her parents, so too the patient and her family can often be seen as caught up in such processes between in-patient and out-patient services. Possibly existing specialist services achieve greater coherence in this respect, although evidence on this point is lacking.

A common difficulty in integrating services arises in this way. A therapist has attempted to work with the family using some version of the family therapy model that has included putting parents in charge of their daughter's eating. The therapist has not yet succeeded in helping the parents with this, and because of continuing weight loss the therapist has requested admission of the patient to the local adolescent unit or, in some cases, a private eating disorders unit. At this point three relationships are at a crucial stage. These are the relationship between the therapist and the patient's parents, the relationship between the parents and their daughter, and the relationship between the daughter and the therapist. Considering each of these relationships in turn, the therapist probably has a critical view of the parents, and the parents probably have a critical view of the therapist. Usually these views have not been expressed. Instead parents and therapist may be united in a critical view that the daughter is too difficult, or too "ill" to be managed at home. The daughter has seen her parents fail to achieve the task set by the therapist. She can protect herself from feeling that her parents have failed her only by seeing herself as impossible. Her choice is between investing either in idealisation of the family, or in a criticism of her parents that further reduces her security in the attachment relationship with them. The implicit or explicit criticism between the daughter and her parents is now about to be solidified by her removal from home in a context in which neither side will honestly express their views, in order to "protect" the other. In this transition the patient's diagnostic label is reinforced, pushing her in the direction of the identification with the position of being "an anorexic", a shift that in itself tends to favour chronicity. The dynamic between the patient and the therapist is much the same as that between her and her parents. The therapist has failed in their quasi-parental role of mobilising the parents to provide safety by setting limits. The same issues arise. To protect her self-esteem the patient must devalue the therapist. To protect her hope in the therapist she must devalue herself. The process damages each relationship, yet these are the relationships that will be required to deliver change when the patient comes home.

Further difficulty arises from the professional culture of the service, especially in relation to the in-patient unit. From the perspective of many clinicians outside specialist services these are often seen as the real experts on treating anorexia. The staff of the adolescent unit is likely to be invested in this view. They have a programme of refeeding, individual and group therapy, and other activities. The focus of all this is overwhelmingly on the individual patient. Each profession has its own stake in this situation. For example the clinical psychologist is often committed to individual approaches to treatment. He or she is likely to wish to undertake CBT with the patient. This is perfectly possible so long as three shifts of nurses are available to stand over the patient and insist that she eat three meals and three snacks a day. In these circumstances, patients with anorexia can be rewarding to work with as individuals. They are likeable, vulnerable and often keen to please.

Usually the psychologist can offer this treatment only while the patient is an in-patient, so the psychologist's wishes are likely to align with the parents' anxieties, and sometimes the anxieties of the family therapist too, in pushing for a long admission. In the same way the Consultant Psychiatrist in the in-patient unit is almost always involved only during the admission, and for this reason also has a professional interest in longer admissions. Since the psychiatrist, psychologist and other staff rarely see the patient after discharge their impressions are formed by the apparent progress made during the admission. Since weight gain leads to an improved mental state they have a strong sense that in-patient treatment, and therapeutic techniques used during admissions such as CBT and so on, are highly effective with these patients. Moreover, it is rarely the case that adolescent units seek follow-up information about the medium-term outcomes of admissions. If they did so they would gain a very different impression of the effectiveness of these admissions.

Given the anxiety that anorexia arouses, the admission is the moment for the parents, and quite possibly the therapist too, to sink into the arms of the in-patient team, expressing delight that at last "something is going to be done". Really what is happening is that the patient is being ejected from her family and the most effective treatment strategy for her is being abandoned, often permanently, but no one comments on this. In addition, the unit as a whole will welcome the patient, offering her a temporary place in the "family" of the unit, which will make her feel cared for, and grateful, reinforcing her experience that care is gained so long as she is "ill". The transition is perfectly designed to reinforce the break in the attachment relationship between the girl and her parents, and the attachment break between the family and the family therapist. The patient's inability to trust the relationship with her parents is fully validated by these events. In the same way the in-patient unit intervention routinely undermines the therapeutic system in the CAMHS team. It is only with great difficulty that this can recover. Often it never does.

Problems in community CAMHS teams

If community CAMHS teams produce poorer results than specialist centres this may reflect a range of difficulties for those teams. Clinicians in CAMHS teams generally work under high pressure. Resources are not sufficient to provide optimal input to all the cases referred to teams. In the past this was often managed by running waiting lists. Current commissioning arrangements rightly discourage that, but fail to address the issue of matching resources to work loads. For this reason it is commonly the case that team managers and clinicians struggle with the issue of managing case throughput. The situation contains many potential difficulties for relationships between managers and clinicians, and between clinicians themselves. Often a knock on effect is that clinicians limit the input available to clients, but do so without discussing with the client the nature of the resource issues that drive clinical decisions. In some instances there is a danger that the clinician does not feel able to inform the client about what they think is needed. This is an important professional issue for all clinicians in CAMHS. The issue has implications for the management of young people with anorexia. There may be pressure to assume that family therapy should produce rapid results, and that longer therapies are not justified when these are not achieved in the short-term. Yet that is not what the outcome literature demonstrates.

A more significant problem may be that community CAMHS teams are organised around the idea of a multi-disciplinary service that provides a wide range of inputs. While it is difficult to disagree with that in principle it may not be the most helpful approach when a highly focused input is needed. There is often only one family therapist in a community CAMHS team. The family therapy approach has always seen team working and live supervision as important, but that is hard to achieve when there is only one family therapist. Moreover, whereas a specialist service like that at the Maudsley is likely to have a genuine consensus in the Maudsley Model of treatment this is much less likely to exist in community CAMHS. This in turn is likely to reduce the ability of the team to find its way through the difficulties that present themselves in the course of providing family therapy for these patients. In particular, the family therapist bringing such difficulties to the team for discussion is likely to be faced with a set of competing voices from professionals who want to help but offer inputs that cut across the family therapy model. One possible way to improve the support for the family therapist facing this difficulty is to provide specialist supervision, another is to organise family therapists in neighbouring teams into supportive clinical networks.

Alternative models: clinical networks

An alternative approach to the specialist service is a clinical network in which clinicians within CAMHS teams devote a specified part of their time to delivering treatment for patients with anorexia and their families. In such a model, clinicians in neighbouring CAMHS teams can support one another by co-working, providing specialist supervision, sharing skills and working methods, joining in running groups, such as multi-family groups, and commissioning training to support their work. Sometimes models of this sort are designed to offer interventions for eating disorders in general, rather than simply as a service for anorexia. Such a model can include ambitious proposals to provide a range of treatments including many of those that are offered to adults with anorexia, such as Cognitive Behaviour Therapy, Interpersonal Therapy, Cognitive Analytic Therapy and Psychodynamic Therapy. Such proposals are commendably inclusive, yet evidence that such treatments are effective for anorexia in adults is sparse, and scarcely exists for adolescents. The inclusion of these models may reflect the inclusion of patients with other eating disorders, such as bulimia, who often have different needs. The negative payoff from this could be that the specialism of the team is somewhat diluted, too many different skills are needed, and the potential advantage of the network over the general CAMHS team is lost. Once again the clinician may be faced with competing voices offering inputs that cut across family therapy models. So far there does not seem to be any research evidence that compares the effectiveness of the clinical network approach with that of a pure specialist service on the one hand, and a generic service on the other. To take account of this sort of arrangement House et al (2012) drew a distinction between general CAMHS and Specialist CAMHS. However, although Specialist CAMHS services were identified, numbers were not sufficient to test the possibility that Specialist CAMHS improved service continuity or that they reduced admissions, Eisler (2014).

Potential advantages and disadvantages of clinical networks

The existence of a clinical network bringing together clinicians from different teams seems likely to be helpful in fostering skills, reducing the isolation of therapists and promoting an active agenda within the agency, an agenda that can address the need for specialist supervision and training, and the organisation of services, as well as audit and research. A network could exist to facilitate the delivery of one model of treatment to a narrowly defined group of patients. For example, a network could be set up to provide family therapy for young people with anorexia. Alternatively, a network could be set up with a broader remit to provide for all the needs of a broadly defined group, all patients with eating disorders for example. However, the broader the remit of the network the more it may intrude on the structure and work of the CAMHS teams themselves. The broader the remit, the greater the number of clinicians who would be involved. Moreover, the broader the remit the less internal coherence the network is likely to have, and the less effective it may be in supporting the delivery of any one component of its service. For the family therapist delivering a family intervention for anorexia a network with a broad remit may present the same difficulty that is presented by the CAMHS team. Competing voices offer help, but in ways that undermine the treatment model.

Applying an attachment-based family therapy approach to anorexia: implications for the organisation of services

Out-patient treatment in CAMHS

Clinicians at the major centres that developed approaches to family therapy for anorexia did not work in isolation. At these centres, therapists often worked as trainees receiving live supervision from a more experienced colleague or sometimes with the participation of a team. Even when the therapist has worked alone, he or she did so in the context of a team which contained other clinicians with a similar orientation to their own. The family therapist in CAMHS is in a very different situation since he or she is usually the only person trained in family therapy in the team. Moreover, even within the relatively narrow field of family therapy for anorexia there are competing models. An effective service is likely to be one that works around some sort of consensus so that the clinicians support rather than competing with one another. A family therapist who chose to work along the lines proposed in this book would need to seek like-minded colleagues. A clinic that provided family therapy for anorexia along attachment lines would need the support of the CAMHS clinicians in doing so, as well as that of the team manager.

Family therapy has always emphasised the advantages of co-working cases, using a live supervision model. This argument is as applicable to the attachment approach as to any other. Unfortunately, there does not seem to be any objective evidence that demonstrates that co-working is more effective in achieving better outcomes or in reducing the overall duration of cases, or, in anorexic cases, in reducing admissions. This is a potential area for research. In the absence of such objective evidence it is not surprising if service managers see co-working as having the potential to halve the capacity of the service in the pursuit of uncertain benefits. One could argue that anorexia is sufficiently serious to justify the use of two therapists, and audit or research outcomes to test this. Alternatively it would be possible to argue for less intensive inputs that maintained some aspects of co-working. For example in each case a second clinician could have the role of supervisor and reviewer. Their role would be to discuss progress with the therapist at regular intervals, and/or to conduct live reviews with the therapist and family at set intervals.

Policies

The attachment approach has implications for policy. A policy that should be in place irrespective of the treatment model is that cases of anorexia are urgent and they are not kept waiting for assessment or treatment. The implication of the attachment model is that placing the patient on a waiting list is a statement that the "carers", in the form of the clinicians, are not available, or are unwilling to acknowledge the urgency of the family's needs. By contrast a rapid and timely response to referrals is consistent with an approach that aims to set up the clinical situation as a secure base for the family.

Another policy implication is that therapist's connections with the family should be maintained through thick and thin. In particular connections should be maintained through the course of admissions. This has implications for time management, because the therapist will need to be available in the in-patient unit at least once a week initially. This level of direct input to the unit might be reduced if, subsequently, the patient is on leave, for example at weekends, and the family can attend the out-patient clinic before her return, for example on a Monday morning. But in that case the therapist will still need to find time to communicate about progress with the in-patient unit.

Lastly, the implication of the attachment model is that there should be no rush to close cases. The therapist and family should be able to keep in touch for quite some time after treatment. This requires a challenge to management policies that promote case closure as a signifier of case turnover, as well as policies that insist that CAMHS cases are closed when the patient reaches age eighteen.

Interface with outreach services

The important issue here is to reduce the gap between the therapy and the outreach service. The approach described by Allen et al (2014) serves as a useful model. In this the therapist refers cases to the outreach team and meets the team to discuss the care plan. A member of the outreach team then attends a therapy appointment to meet the family and discuss the involvement of their team. The involvement of the team is not intended to take over from parents in the management of meals, but to empower them to do this using modelling and support. The goal is that parents will make changes to meal plans in discussion with the team, but the team does not take this function away from the parents. The outreach workers have a frame of reference about management of meals that they share with parents. This addresses questions such as what is talked about during meals, and the sort of things that are said when the patient is struggling to eat, and about problem solving in that situation. The intervention is time limited, and the frequency of visits is reduced after the first three weeks, and faded out over the next three weeks. Clearly this kind of intervention is likely to be experienced as supportive by parents, and so should contribute to the sense of the therapy situation as a secure base. In reducing the need for admissions it is also likely to help ensure that the out-patient therapy remains a secure base for the family, and the family a secure base for the patient.

An interesting problem arises in that the outreach worker may well find that relationships at home are far more difficult than has been presented to the family therapist. This presents the question of how to prevent a split in the therapy system while at the same time protecting the relationship of the outreach worker to the family. It might be useful to incorporate subsequent visits of the outreach worker to the family therapy sessions in the approach. The outreach worker could then discuss with the family how they would relate their observations of the family to the therapist or therapy team before a session of that sort took place.

The model described by Allen (2014) was time limited. However, in some of the most difficult cases a service delivered at home, perhaps more along the lines described by Goel and Darwish (2008) might be appropriate. They were especially concerned to prevent the sort of deterioration in patients that they thought resulted from psychiatric admissions. Families who were very stressed by adolescent disturbances but did not wish their children to go to hospital welcomed their input. A longer term input along these lines, but with an emphasis on concurrent family intervention, might support the engagement of families with parents who are themselves very vulnerable, and not yet able to take on the difficult task of refeeding a daughter with anorexia. This might allow the therapists time to work engaging the parents and addressing their unresolved attachment problems, along the lines suggested by Dallos (2006) and by Hughes (2007).

Children's ward admissions

The reader might wonder why, if admissions are as unhelpful as has been suggested, the early studies often used a short period of refeeding in hospital as a prelude to family therapy and this proved successful at the time. Sargent et al (1985) described the management of these admissions at the Children's Hospital of Philadelphia in the 1970s and 1980s. The in-patient unit was not a psychiatric unit. Admissions were managed by paediatricians in close liaison with the child psychiatrist. The admissions were designed to maximise parental involvement. Crucially, parents were required to be present at frequent reviews of progress and to make the decisions about refeeding, for example about the amount of food offered. The hospital's role was to give feedback to the parents about the effects of these decisions. At the same time, as the case studies in Minuchin et al (1978) illustrate, energetic therapeutic engagement with the family focused on getting the patient home safely. Sargent et al recorded that, as the therapy team became more confident of its approach, these admissions were only necessary in 15% of cases. Because of the close liaison between the therapists and the paediatricians the admission provided an opportunity for intensive engagement with the family. Today, in the United Kingdom, patients with anorexia may well be admitted to a children's ward of a general hospital, and a similar policy could be adopted there. This would require a high level of mutual understanding between the CAMHS service and the paediatrician. Family therapists working in CAMHS in the UK may not have this option. Of course it is always possible to arrange for the admission of a seriously compromised patient to an appropriate children's ward in a general hospital. However, achieving the degree of co-operative work with a pediatrician that the Philadelphia group achieved might be very difficult because of the extreme pressures on such resources. The paediatrician would be likely to see the patient as appropriate for a psychiatric facility such as an NHS Adolescent Unit or private adolescent unit. Systematic use of children's ward admissions as a potential preventive measure for psychiatric admission is an issue that needs to be addressed at the level of service commissioning. It is much more likely to succeed if it is supported by an outreach service.

Psychiatric admissions

Psychiatric admission units are not usually integrated with CAMHS and a referral to one is likely to lead to a long admission, typically lasting about six months, in which most therapeutic efforts are addressed to the individual patient. Family therapy plays little part in these admissions and they are usually unsuccessful in the medium term, as we have seen. After one of these admissions the patient becomes one of those patients who have had "previous treatment" and will be more resistant to the family therapy treatment that could have been an effective treatment in the first place.

Another problem is that rigid rules about the patients' eligibility for treatment based on her age stand in the way of offering effective treatment. Managers will usually insist that patients are handed over to adult services at age eighteen. These services do not use the family therapy treatment model. Such transfers of care, which are entirely contrary to the patient's clinical needs, are a common occurrence in Britain today. A long period in an adolescent unit wastes the patient's time and reduces the chance she will be offered effective treatment. The family therapist therefore faces a dilemma. Irrespective of what he or she thinks about the level of treatment resistance the patient's best chance of recovery depends on the attempt to work with the family in outpatient treatment and this usually involves putting parents in charge of their daughter's eating at the beginning. This can be a severe test for the therapist's ability to join and take a position of leadership with the family at the outset because in the most difficult cases parents will hardly be ready to take this role so soon.

Therapeutic use of adolescent psychiatric unit admissions

It has been argued that psychiatric admissions usually cut across the family treatment model, and that they undermine the therapeutic system composed of family therapist and family. The process of these admissions can be counter-therapeutic. How might this be changed in order to support the therapeutic system? To begin with the adolescent unit would need to make a shift of focus and decide to see the therapeutic system, the family and therapist, as the unit that it will support. This is consistent with the frame of reference proposed by Bruggen et al (1973) whose approach was rooted in both systemic and attachment thinking. Bruggen was writing from the perspective of an adolescent psychiatric unit that was working with a wide range of patients. It was not working with patients with anorexia. In their approach the adolescent unit's role was to engage first the referrer, then the referrer and family, in discussing the need for the admission. The focus of discussion was the reason why treatment could not continue at home. The patient was not seen alone at all. The service making the referral was regarded as remaining responsible for the therapy. The adolescent unit was seen as a safe place that could be used while the family and the agencies working with them achieved resolution of the issues that required admission. Parents were required to make the final decision about admission and discharge. In this way they were not allowed to step aside from their position of leadership in the family. In this context the unit essentially offered a safe place and respite while the therapeutic system recovered therapeutic manoeuvrability. The unit and its staff did not diagnose or "treat" the patient.

In anorexic cases the request for admission usually arises because progress cannot be made in the family therapy. Most often the difficulty has to do with failure to achieve weight recovery, but sometimes it may be because of low mood and self-destructive or agitated behaviour in the weight recovered or recovering patient. Either way the unit needs to address the issue of treatment failure, and its consequences, at the outset. This means that the unit (Bruggen would say the family therapist in the unit) needs to have an initial discussion with the therapist making the referral. This would be about the reason that therapy was not creating a safe situation for the patient at home. The conversation would then be repeated at a meeting between the in-patient staff, the out-patient therapist, and the family. This would be an opportunity to talk together about what it is that needs to change in what each person, including the therapist, is doing, in such a way as to progress towards greater safety.

It follows from this way of thinking that in-patient staff do not become therapists in these cases. Instead, the in-patient unit can provide safety for the patient in the short-term, if this is what is needed. Its primary focus is on helping the therapeutic system to provide a secure base. In this way the unit avoids undermining the therapeutic system. Instead it provides containment for it and offers a consultation to the therapeutic system.

To change the role of the adolescent unit in the way that has been outlined would be a major challenge to managers and clinicians. Clinicians in these units are invested in their therapeutic expertise in the treatment of anorexia, despite the fact that evidence does not support the view that their input promotes recovery. Currently, these admissions provide a safe place for the patient in the short-term, at the expense of undermining the therapeutic system that might lead to recovery in the medium term. Hence short-term advantage to the therapist, the patient and her family are purchased at very high cost.

Second-line treatments in CAMHS

Multi-Family Group Therapy

Multi-family group day treatment (MFGT) for anorexia was described by Dare and Eisler (2000), and Eisler (2005). It is an approach to treatment in which a group of families meet for a series of whole days, often grouped together initially into a whole week, and address issues to do with refeeding the patient, and many other issues bearing on the family and anorexia. The approach, as described by Dare and Eisler (2000) and by Eisler (2005) draws on the Maudsley Model approach, but provides a wide range of experiences for families beyond those that can be provided in single-family therapy. Families eat together, in the presence of the staff, so that in this context the family meal re-enactment has been revived by the Maudsley, in a very different form. The way that parents manage the meals is a focus of discussion in the group, and parents, patients, and their siblings, can exchange thoughts about that. A detailed account of the MFGT approach is beyond the scope of this book. Asen and Scholz (2010) provide many practical suggestions for the use of the multi-family approach with a wide range of problems, including eating disorders. Currently the approach is being evaluated as a first line treatment, but at the present time, little evidence is available about its effectiveness. However, Mehl et al (2013) described the outcome of treatment for fifteen young people in the age range fourteen to twenty-three years, a year after the treatment ended. More than half the group had a more than three-year history of anorexia, and there had been numerous previous attempts at treatment. This being so this was a relatively treatment resistant group. On average, the patients BMI increased after treatment, and their quality of life improved, according to their responses to a questionnaire measure. However, their scores on the Rosenberg Self-Esteem Scale declined. Mehl et al concluded that although there were positive outcomes from the treatment the patients were struggling to come to terms with the weight gain, and that it was this that compromised their self-esteem. One interpretation of this would be that the approach was more successful in helping parents to take charge of refeeding than it was in helping to improve family communication and hence promote the psychological recovery of the patient.

Rhodes et al (2008) described a much less intensive intervention for families in treatment using the Maudsley Model or FBT approach in which the parents of successfully treated patients with anorexia have a single meeting with parents who are at an early stage of treatment. In this the focus of discussion is on the way that the successful parents had tackled the anorexia. They compared outcomes for ten patients treated in the standard Maudsley Model or FBT approach, and ten who had that treatment plus the consultation session with parents from another treated family. There was no difference in outcomes from treatment, although some evidence that the rate of weight recovery in the patient improved at the time of the parent-to-parent consultation.

Honig (2005) described a multi-family group for families with a daughter with anorexia in the context of an adolescent, specialist, in-patient unit. The group was offered as an alternative to individual family therapy. Honig provided evidence that parents responded positively to this, but no objective evidence about the effect on outcome.

So far it seems clear that clinicians' and families' experiences of the multi-family therapy approach to anorexia are positive but there is little concrete evidence as to its efficacy as either a first-line or second-line treatment. However, it may be that the approach is likely to lose much of its effectiveness if the patients are in-patients during the group treatment, since in that case the families experience of managing the eating situation, and their relationships with one another, is greatly diluted. Instead, the families may be preoccupied with discussing their experiences of relating to the in-patient unit.

A single CAMHS team would find it difficult to use this approach as a first or second-line treatment because the number of anorexic cases managed in such a team at any one time would not be sufficient. An advantage of specialist services serving a wide area, or the development of clinical networks across CAMHS would be that both are in a better position to offer this treatment. It could be offered alongside single-family therapy as an additional input that may be especially useful for families who do not make rapid progress in single-family therapy. A clinical network of CAMHS teams, or eating disorder clinics within CAMHS teams, could also co-operate to provide multi-family treatment, as an addition to ongoing family therapy. The approach may be of special value for some parents who find the family therapy treatment situation difficult. In particular it may be supposed that parents who feel criticised by the therapist may feel more able to engage with a situation where they feel supported by other parents who are "in the same boat". However, the clinicians who developed this approach emphasised the need to have a mix of cases. A group consisting only of treatment resistant cases would be very hard to manage.

Individual treatments

As we have seen one kind of discontinuity arises when the family therapist is unable in the initial stages of treatment to help the parents gain influence in the eating situation. In this case the likely outcome is admission to an in-patient unit and a hand over to another team. Another kind of discontinuity often arises when the therapist has been able to help the parents with the initial task, but has not been able to help them to improve communication in the family. In that case the patient remains very distressed and preoccupied in the context of a weight recovery that remains unacceptable to her, and/or, develops other symptoms, such as OCD or depression. There is then a danger that a decision will be made to change the approach to one focused on individual treatment. This may create a great sense of relief for the therapist and the parents, who can walk away from a situation of unresolved tension, and often may be glad to do so. The individual treatment most likely to be offered in that situation is CBT. There is no evidence about the effectiveness of that specifically in the context of this scenario. Moreover, we should expect that the transition from a situation in which an unhappy teenager manages her feelings by starving, to one in which she finds her way back into a real relationship with her parents will be a difficult one. What the evidence does suggest is that family therapy can produce very full recoveries, and that this takes time. Clearly, if time passes without progress the therapist should consider the issues of therapeutic impasse discussed in the last chapter, and these should become a subject for discussion in supervision.

Many clinicians have had the experience that after a change of direction in therapy that takes the parents out of the therapeutic system, the patient will often express difficulties about the family situation, or issues that she has not been willing to discuss with her parents and that she has not expressed before. It may then be very difficult to re-convene the family, since the therapist feels bound by rules of confidentiality, while the patient feels great anxiety about how her parents would react. These anxieties range from fear of parental anxiety and rejection, to fears about parental vulnerability, up to and including fears that a parent might commit suicide. While there may be some therapeutic value in the patient's revelations in the context of individual therapy very often they seem to produce little change. Probably it would often have been better to persevere with family therapy, exploring issues about communication using the kind of programmatic structure that has been outlined. The conjecture is driven by the expectation that during the adolescent stage of development the family therapy situation presents the possibility of reparative interventions of much greater power than can be achieved in individual therapy at this or any later life stage with patients with anorexia. This way of looking at it is consistent with the evidence that family therapy with a person with anorexia at this life stage produces greater and more lasting change than it can produce at a later stage, and greater and more lasting change than is produced by other approaches. The decision to abandon the family therapy approach to these patients will very often be an acceptance that the patient will continue with a chronic problem needing long-term management. As Steinhausen's (2002) meta-analysis of results demonstrated, there is little reason for optimism about the results of that. Moreover, in the context of NHS treatment, that is the only kind of treatment the patient is likely to be offered when and if she makes the transition to adult services, whatever her needs might be.

Audit

Unfortunately, at the time of writing the NHS is being driven into an increasing fragmentary state with many competing organisations seeking contracts to provide services. This is not an encouraging scenario given that openness about results is very desirable from a clinical point of view, but agencies are unlikely to wish to lay themselves open to criticism if their outcomes could be seen as inferior to those produced by competing service providers. One thing that might help would be an agreed basis for an outcome audit. Currently many services do audit their outcomes, but these figures are not generally available, and it would be difficult for any organisation to release figures if these were to be compared with those other agencies had produced on a different basis. There is pressure to demonstrate favourable results. This being so there is a need for an agreed design for routine outcome assessment to use in audit. This would need to define the patient population and detail the observations and measures to be used with that population. There probably is already a fair degree of agreement about some of these issues, but by no means all. For example, while some services audit outcomes for patients with anorexia, others audit outcomes for people with all eating disorders. Such audits are impossible to compare. However, within an audit of all eating disorder patients it would be possible to have a sub-set of information about the patients with anorexia. Another issue is that some services may lose patients from their audits when those are moved on to in-patient units, especially if those are run by another agency. A thorough approach would maintain those patients in the audit in order to assess the effectiveness of the whole treatment package. If this is not done many CAMHS services could lose as many as 40% of patients with anorexia from their audits.

Generally there is likely to be a fair degree of agreement about measures, with most services favouring the use of either the Eating

Disorders Examination, (EDE) Fairburn and Cooper (1993), or the Eating Disorders Examination Questionnaire (EDEQ) Fairburn and Beglin (1994). The questionnaire is derived from the EDE and follows its structure in content and scoring. Binford et al (2005) considered it to be a cheaper and more convenient way of collecting data and found that it produced an acceptable level of agreement with results produced by the interview in a study of adolescents with anorexic and/or bulimia.

A complication is that the patient's motivation in an interview, or when completing a questionnaire, can influence results. Patients who are keen to avoid treatment or avoid returning to it naturally are inclined to under-report symptoms, and occasionally patients who seek treatment may overstate them. There is no perfect method but there is a lot to be said for clinicians making follow-ups with patients at set intervals in order to gain more knowledge of the effects of the work. In that context the EDE could be used to structure clinical observations, while a simple questionnaire such as the EAT-26, Garner et al (1982) would provide useful self-report information.

All the measures mentioned so far are measures of eating disorder symptoms, but the research shows that patients often have significant residual psychopathology. That can be taken as an indication that family therapy has been less successful than it might be. Measures of self-esteem, depression, anxiety and obsessionality can be added, as they were in the Maudsley studies, to obtain an overview of this. That is necessary in order both to obtain an adequate estimate of the effects of the intervention, and to assess the patient's continuing needs.

Conclusion: why family therapists and CAMHS services should invest in the new model

The advantage of the model of treatment presented in this book is that it takes the psychopathology of the patient with anorexia and that of her parents seriously. To put this another way, it concerns itself with the vulnerabilities of all the family members, and how they interact. The model is rooted in developmental research. It provides practical ways of addressing the needs of the family, ways that reflect that research. It is not viable to argue that Maudsley Model of FBT approaches have been shown to be superior to older family therapy approaches. They have not been. While it is clear that Maudsley Model and FBT approaches can be used to achieve weight recovery, and that a degree of symptomatic improvement is achieved, the patient's recovery is often partial, as Lock and Le Grange (2013) admitted.

The attachment approach to treatment needs to be tested. It is likely to be most valuable for the most vulnerable patients and families. It is intended to address the vulnerability of parents in ways that will allow them to be parents despite their own difficulties; ways that will allow their daughter to be an adolescent daughter, finding her adolescent voice in her relationship with them. This, the model predicts, will lead to a more complete and lasting recovery for the patient, and that is what the CAMHS service exists to achieve.

REFERENCES

Ablow, J. C., & Measelle J. R. (2010). In: M. S. Shulz, M. K. Pruett, P. K. Kerig, & R. D. Parke (Eds.) *Strengthening Couple Relationships for Optimal Development* (pp. 41–57). Washington DC: American Psychological Association.

Abramowitz, B. A. (2000). Five-year-old girls' ideas about dieting are predicted by mothers' dieting. *Journal of the American Dietetic Association, 100*: 1157–1163.

Adambegan, M., Wagner, G., Nader, I., Fernandez-Aranda, F., Treasure, J., & Kauwautz, A. (2012). Internalising and externalising behavioural problems in the childhood contribution to the development of anorexia and bulimia nervosa—a study comparing sister pairs. *European Eating Disorders Review, 20*: 116–120.

Ainsworth, M. D. S., Blehar, M. C., Waters, E., & Wall, S. (1978). *Patterns of Attachment: A Psychological Study of the Strange Situation*. Hillsdale, NJ: Erlbaum.

Alden, L. E., Wiggins, J. S., & Pincus, A. L. (1990). Construction of circumplex scales for the Inventory of Interpersonal Problems. *Journal of Personality Assessment, 55*: 521–536.

Allen, J. P. (2008). The attachment system in adolescence. In: J. Cassidy & P. R. Shaver (Eds.), *Handbook of Attachment Theory, Research and Clinical Implications* (pp. 419–435). New York: Guilford.

Allen, J., Clark-Stone, S., Winter, K., & Wintle, M. (2014). *The Child and Adolescent Home Treatment Team*. Unpublished Presentation. Eating Disorder Service, 2gether NHS Foundation Trust.

Allen, J. P., & Hauser, S. T. (1996). Autonomy and relatedness in adolescent-family interactions as predictors of young adults' states of mind regarding attachment. *Development and Psychopathology, 64*: 254–263.

Allen, J. P., Hauser, S. T., Eickholt, C., Bell, K. L., & O'Connor, T. G. (1994). Autonomy and relatedness in family interaction as predictors of negative adolescent affect. *Journal of Research in Adolescence, 4*: 535–552.

Allen, J. P., & Land, D. (1999). Attachment in Adolescence. In: J. Cassidy & P. R. Shaver, (Eds.) *Handbook of attachment: Theory, research, and clinical applications* (pp. 319–335). New York: Guilford.

Allen, J. P., McElhaney, K. B., Kuperminc, G. P., & Jodl, K. M. (2004). Stability and Change in Attachment Security Across Adolescence. *Child Development, 75*: 1792–1805.

Anderluh, M. B., Tchanturia, K., Rabe-Hesketh, S., & Treasure, J. (2003). Childhood obsessive-compulsive personality traits in adult women with eating disorders: defining a broader eating disorder phenotype. *American Journal of Psychiatry, 160*: 242–247.

Anschutz, D. J., Kanters, L. J. A., Van Strien, T., Vermust, A. A., & Engels, R. C. M. E. (2009). Maternal behaviors and restrained eating and body dissatisfaction in young children. *International Journal of Eating Disorders, 42*: 54–61.

Aponte, H., & Hoffman, L. (1973). The open door: A structural approach to a family with an anorectic child. *Family Process, 12*: 1–44.

Asarnow, J. R., Tompson, M., Hamilton, E. B., Goldstein, M. J., & Guthrie, D. (1994). Family-expressed emotion, childhood-onset depression, and childhood-onset schizophrenia spectrum disorders: Is expressed emotion a non-specific correlate of child psychopathology or a specific risk factor for depression? *Journal of Abnormal Child Psychology, 22*: 129–146.

Asen, E., & Scholz, M. (2009). *Multi-Family Therapy: Concepts and Techniques*. Routledge. London and New York.

Bachar, E., Latzer, Y., Canetti, L., Gur, E., Berry, E., & Bonne, O. (2002). Rejection of life in anorexic and bulimic patients. *International Journal of Eating Disorders, 31*: 43–48.

Bachar, E., Kanyas, K., Latzer, Y., Canetti, L. Bonne, O., & Lerer, B. (2008). Depressive tendencies and lower levels of self-sacrifice in mothers, and selflessness in their anorexic daughters. *European Eating Disorders Review, 16*: 184–190.

Bachner-Melman, R., Zohar, A. H., Ebstein, R. P., & Bachar, E. (2007). The relationship between selflessness levels and the severity of anorexia nervosa symptomatology. *European Eating Disorders Review, 15*: 213–241.

Back, E. A. (2011). Effects of parental relations and upbringing in troubled adolescent eating behaviors. *Eating Disorders: The Journal of Treatment & Prevention, 19*: 403–424.

Baker, C. W., Whisman, M. A., & Brownell, K. D. (2000). Studying intergenerational transmission of eating attitudes and behaviors: Methodological and conceptual questions. *Health Psychology, 19*: 376–381.

Barbarin, O. A. (1992). *Manual: Family Relations Scale*. Michigan: University Centre for the Child and Family.

Barber, B. K., & Buehler, C. (1996). Family cohesion and enmeshment: different constructs, different effects. *Journal of Marriage and the Family, 58*: 433–441.

Barber, B. K., & Harmon, E. L. (2002). Violating the Self: Parental Psychological Control of Children and Adolescents. In: B. K. Barber (Ed.), *Intrusive Parenting—How Psychological Control Affects Children and Adolescents* (pp. 15–22). Washington DC. American Psychological Association.

Barber, B. K., Stolz, H. E., & Olsen, J. A. (2005). Parental support, psychological control, and behavioural control: Assessing relevance across time, method and culture. *Monographs for the Society for Research in Child Development, 70*: 7. Serial number 276.

Barcai, A. (1971). Family therapy in the treatment of anorexia nervosa. *American Journal of Psychiatry, 128*: 286–290.

Barone, L., & Guiducci, V. (2009). Mental representations of attachment states in eating disorders: a pilot study using the Adult Attachment Interview. *Attachment and Human Development, 11*: 405–417.

Baumrind, D. (1966). Effects of authoritative parental control on child behaviour. *Child Development, 37*: 887–907.

Beavers, W. R., & Hampson, R. B. (1990). *Successful families: Assessment and intervention*. New York. W. W. Norton.

Becker-Stoll, F., Fremmer-Bombik, E., Wartner, U., Zimmerman, P., & Grossman, K. E. (2008). Is attachment at ages 1, 6 and 16 related to autonomy and relatedness behaviour of adolescents in interaction towards their mothers? *International Journal of Behavioural Development, 32*: 372–380.

Beglin, S. J., & Fairburn, C. G. (1992). Women who choose not to participate in surveys on eating disorders. *International Journal of Eating Disorders, 12*: 113–116.

Benedikt, R., Wertheim, E. H., & Love, A. (1998). Eating attitudes and weight-loss attempts in female adolescents and their mothers. *Journal of Youth and Adolescence, 27*: 43–57.

Berger, L. E., Jodl, K. M., Allen, J. P., McElhaney, K. B., & Kuperminc, G. P. (2005). When adolescents disagree with others about their symptoms: Differences in attachment organization as an explanation of discrepancies between adolescent-, parent-, and peer-reports of behaviour problems. *Development and Psychopathology, 17*: 489–507.

Binford, R. B., Le Grange, D., & Jellar, C. C. (2005). Eating Disorders Examination versus Eating Disorders Examination Questionnaire in adolescents with full and partial-syndrome bulimia nervosa and anorexia nervosa. *International Journal of Eating Disorders, 37*: 44–49.

Bishop, D., Epstein, K., & Keitner, G. (1987). *The McMaster Structured Interview of Family Functioning*. Providence, RI: Brown/Butler Family Research Programme.

Blair, C. (1996). The Edinburgh Family Scale: A new measure of family functioning. *International Journal of Methods in Psychiatric Research, 6*: 15–22.

Blair, C., Freeman, C., & Cull, A. (1995). The families of anorexia nervosa and cystic fibrosis patients. *Psychological Medicine, 25*: 985–993.

Blatt, S. J. (2004). *Experiences of depression: Theoretical, clinical, and research perspectives*. Washington DC. American Psychological Association.

Bohanek, J. G., Marin, K. A., Fivush, R., & Duke, M. P. (2006). Family narrative interaction and children's sense of self. *Family Process, 45*: 39–54.

Boraska, V., Davis, O. S. P., Cherkas, L. F., Helder, S. G., Harris, J., Krug, I., Lao, T. P., Treasure, J., Ntalla, I., Karhunen, L., Keski-Rahkonen, A., Christakopoulou, D., Raevuori, A., Shin., S. -Y., Dedoussis, G. V., Kaprio, J., Soranzo, N., Spector, T. D., Collier, D. A., & Zeggini, E. (2012). Genome-wide association analysis of eating disorder-related symptoms, behaviors, and personality traits. *American Journal of Medical Genetics, B. 159*: 803–811.

Botta, R. A., & Dumlao, R. (2002). How do conflict and communication patterns between daughters and fathers contribute to or offset eating disorders? *Health Communication, 14*: 199–219.

Bowlby, J. (1982). *Attachment and Loss: Vol. 1*. Attachment. New York: Basic Books.

Brookings, J. B., & Wilson, J. F. (1994). Personality and family-environment predictors of self-reported eating attitudes and behaviors. *Journal of Personality Assessment, 63*: 313–326.

Brown, R., & Ogden, J. (2004). Children's eating attitudes and behaviour: a study of the modelling and control theories of parental influence. *Health Education Research, 19*: 261–271.

Bruch, H. (1974). *Eating Disorders: Obesity, Anorexia Nervosa and the Person Within*. London: Routledge and Kegan Paul.

Bruch, H. (1981). Developmental considerations of anorexia nervosa, and obesity. *Canadian Journal of Psychiatry, 26*: 212–216.

Bruggen, P., Byng-Hall, J., & Pitt-Aikens, T. (1973). The reason for admission as a focus of work for an adolescent unit. *British Journal of Psychiatry, 122*: 319–329.

Brumariu, L. E., & Kerns, K. A. (2010a). Parent–child attachment and internalizing symptoms in childhood and adolescence: A review of empirical findings and future directions. *Development and Psychopathology, 22*: 177–203.

Brumariu, L. E., & Kerns, K. A. (2010b). Mother–child attachment patterns and different types of anxiety symptoms: Is there a specificity of relations? *Child Psychiatry and Human Development, 41*: 663–674.

Buchholz, A., Henderson, K., Hounsell, A., Wagner, A., Norris, M., & Spettigue, W. (2007). Self-silencing in a clinical sample of female adolescents with eating disorders. *Journal of the Canadian Academy of Child and Adolescent Psychiatry, 16*: 158–163.

Buehler, C., Benson, M. J., & Gerard, J. M. (2006). Interparental hostility and early adolescent problem behaviour: The mediating role of specific aspects of parenting. *Journal of Research on Adolescence, 16*: 265–292.

Bulik, C. M., Sullivan, P. F., Wade, T. D., & Kendler, K. S. (2000). Twin studies of eating disorders: A review. *International Journal of Eating Disorders, 27*: 1–20.

Burnham, J. B. (1986). *Family Therapy: first steps towards a systemic approach.* London: Tavistock.

Button, E. J., Sonuga-Barke, E. J. S., Davies, J., & Thompson, M. (1996). A prospective study of self-esteem in the prediction of eating problems in adolescent schoolgirls: Questionnaire findings. *British Journal of Clinical Psychology, 35*: 193–203.

Byely, L., Archibald, A. B., Graber, J., & Brooks-Gunn, J. (2000). A prospective study of familial and social influences on girls' body image and dieting. *International Journal of Eating Disorders, 25*: 155–164.

Calam, R., & Waller, G. (1998). Are eating psychosocial characteristics in early teenage years useful predictors of eating characteristics in early adulthood? A 7-year longitudinal study. *International Journal of Eating Disorders, 24*: 351–362.

Calati, R., De Ronch, D., Bellini, M., & Serretti, A. (2011). The 5-HTTLPR polymorphism and eating disorders: A meta-analysis. *International Journal of Eating Disorders, 44*: 191–199.

Carper, J. L., Fisher, J. O., & Birch, L. L. (2000). Young girls' emerging dietary restraint and disinhibition are related to parental control in child feeding. *Appetite, 32*: 121–129.

Casper, R. C. (1983). Some provisional ideas concerning the psychological structure in anorexia nervosa and bulimia. In: P. L. Darby (Ed.), *Anorexia Nervosa: Recent Developments in Research* (pp. 387–392). New York: Alan R. Liss.

Casper, R. C., Offer, D., & Ostrov, E. (1981). The self-image of adolescents with anorexia nervosa. *Journal of Pediatrics, 98*: 656–661.

Casper, R. C., & Troiani, M. (2001). Family functioning in anorexia nervosa differs by subtype. *International Journal of Eating Disorders, 30*: 338–342.

Castro-Fornieles, J., Gual, P., Lahortiga, F., Casuala, V., Fuhrmann, C., Imirizaldu, M., Saura, B., Martinez, E., & Toro, J. (2007). Self-oriented perfectionism in eating disorders. *International Journal of Eating Disorders, 40*: 562–568.

Cella, S., Iannaccone, M., & Cotrufo, P. (2014). How perceived parental bonding affects self-concept and drive for thinness: A community-based study. *Eating Behaviors, 15*: 110–115.

Claes, L., Soenens, B., Vansteenkiste, M., & Vandereycken, W. (2012). The scars of the inner critic: Perfectionism and nonsuicidal self-injury in eating disorders. *European Eating Disorders Review, 20*: 196–202.

Cleveland, E., & Reese, E. (2005). Maternal structure and autonomy support in conversations about the past: Contributions to children's autobiographical memory. *Developmental Psychology, 41*: 376–388.

Cleveland, E., Reese, E., & Grolnick, W. (2007). Children's engagement and competence in personal recollection: Effects of parents' reminiscing goals. *Journal of Experimental Child Psychology, 96*: 131–149.

Cockell, S. J., Hewitt, P. L., Seal, B., Sherry, S., Goldner, E. M., Flett, G. L., & Remick, R. A. (2002). Trait and self-presentational dimensions of perfectionism among women with Anorexia Nervosa. *Cognitive Therapy and Research, 26*: 745–758.

Cole-Detke, H., & Kobak, R. (1996). Attachment processes in eating disorder and depression. *Journal of Consulting and Clinical Psychology, 64*: 282–290.

Colonnesi, C., Draijer, E. M., Stams, G. J. J. M., Van der Bruggen, C. O., Bogels, S. M., & Noom, M. J. (2011). The relation between insecure attachment and child anxiety: A meta-analytic review. *Journal of Clinical Child and Adolescent Psychology, 40*: 630–645.

Cook-Darzens, S., Doyen, C., Falissard., B., & Mouren, M. (2005). Self-perceived family functioning in 40 French families of anorexic adolescents: implications for therapy. *European Eating Disorders Review, 13*: 223–236.

Cooper, M., & Burrows, A. (2001). Underlying assumptions and core beliefs related to eating disorders in the mothers of overweight girls. *Behavioural and Cognitive Psychotherapy, 29*: 143–149.

Cooper, P. J., Whelan, E., Woolgar, M., Morrell, J., & Murray, L. (2004). Association between childhood feeding problems and maternal eating disorder: role of the family environment. *British Journal of Psychiatry, 184*: 210–215.

Cooper, Z., & Fairburn, C. (1987). The Eating Disorder Examination: A semi-structured Interview for the assessment of the specific psychopathology of eating disorders. *International Journal of Eating Disorder, 6*: 485–494.

Corning, A. F., Gondoli, D. M., Bucchianeri, M. M., & Blodgett Salafia, E. H. (2010). Preventing the development of body issues in adolescent girls through intervention with their mothers. *Body Image, 7*: 289–295.

Couturier, J., Isserlin, L., & Lock, J. (2010). Family-Based Treatment for adolescents with Anorexia Nervosa: a dissemination study. *Eating Disorders, 18*: 199–209.

Craddock, A. E., Church, W., & Sands, A. (2009). Family of origin characteristics as predictors of perfectionism. *Australian Journal of Psychology, 6*: 136–144.

Crittenden, P. (1997). Truth, error, omission, distortion, and deception: an application of attachment theory to the assessment and treatment of psychological disorder. In: S. M. Clany Dollinger & L. F. DiLalla (Eds.) *Assessment and Intervention Issues Across the Lifespan* (pp. 35–76). London: Lawrence Erlbaum.

Cummings, E. M., & Merrilees, C. E. (2010). Identifying the Dynamic Processes Underlying Links Between Marital Conflict and Child Adjustment. In: M. S. Shulz, M. K. Pruett, P. K. Kerig, & R. D. Parke (Eds.) *Strengthening Couple Relationships for Optimal Development* (pp. 27–40). Washington DC: American Psychological Association.

Cummings, E. M., Schemerhorn, A. C., Davies, P. T., Goeke-Morey, M. C., & Cummings, J. S. (2006). Interparental discord and child adjustment: Prospective investigations of emotional security as an explanatory mechanism. *Child Development, 77*: 132–152.

Cummings, E. M., & Wilson, A. (1999). Contexts of Marital Conflict and Children's Emotional Security: Exploring the distinction between Constructive and Destructive Conflict. In: M. J. Cox & J. B. Brooks-Gunn (Eds.) *Conflict and Cohesion in Families* (pp. 105–129). Mahwah, NJ: Lawrence Erlbaum Associates.

Cunha, A. L., Relvas, A. P., & Soares, I. (2009). Anorexia nervosa and family relationships: Perceived family functioning, coping strategies, beliefs, and attachment to parents and peers. *International Journal of Clinical and Health Psychology, 9*: 229–240.

Cutting, T. M., Fisher, J. O., Grimm-Thomas, K., & Birch, L. L. (1999). Like mother, like daughter: Familial patterns of overweight are mediated by mothers' dietary disinhibition. *American Journal of Clinical Nutrition, 69*: 608–613.

Dallos, R. (2004). Attachment Narrative Therapy: integrating ideas from narrative and attachment theory in systemic family therapy with eating disorders. *Journal of Family Therapy, 26*: 40–66.

Dallos, R. (2006). *Attachment Narrative Therapy*. Maidenhead. Open University Press.

Dallos, R., & Densford, S. (2008). A qualitative exploration of relationship and attachment themes in families with an eating disorder. *Clinical Child Psychology and Psychiatry, 1*: 305–322.

Dallos, R., & Vetere, A. (2009). *Systemic Therapy and Attachment Narratives*. London. Routledge.

Dancyger, I., Fornari, V., & Sunday, S. (2006). What may underlie differing perceptions of family functioning between mothers and their adolescent daughters with eating disorders? *International Journal of Adolescent Medicine and Health, 18*: 281–286.

Dare, C., Chania, E., Eisler, I., Hodes, M., & Dodge, E. (2000). The Eating Disorder Inventory as an instrument to explore change in adolescents in family therapy for Anorexia Nervosa. *European Eating Disorders Review, 8*: 369–383.

Dare, C., Eisler, E., Colahan, M., Crowther, C., Senior, R., & Asen, E. (1995a). The listening heart and the chi square: clinical and empirical perceptions in the family therapy of anorexia nervosa. *Journal of Family Therapy, 17*: 31–57.

Dare, C., & Eisler, I. (1995b). Family Therapy. In: G. Szmuckler, C. Dare & J. Treasure (Eds.) *Handbook of Eating Disorders* (pp. 333–350). Chichester: Wiley.

Dare, C., & Eisler, I. (1997). Family therapy for anorexia nervosa. In: D. M. Garner & P. E. Garfinkel (Eds.), *Handbook of Treatment for Eating Disorders. (2nd edn.)* (pp. 307–324). New York: Guilford.

Dare, C., & Eisler, I. (2000). A multi-family group day treatment programme for adolescent eating disorder. *European Eating Disorders Review, 8*: 4–18.

Dare, C., Eisler, I., Russell, G. F. M., & Szmuckler, G. I. (1990). The clinical and theoretical impact of a controlled trial of family therapy in Anorexia Nervosa. *Journal of Marital and Family Therapy, 16*: 39–57.

Dare, C., & Key, A. (1999). Family functioning and adolescent anorexia nervosa. *British Journal of Psychiatry, 175*: 89–90.

Dare, C., Le Grange, D., Eisler, I., & Rutherford, J. (1994). Redefining the psychosomatic family. *International Journal of Eating Disorders, 16*: 211.

Davila, J., La Greca, A., Starr, L. R., & Landoll, R. R. (2010). Anxiety disorders in adolescence. In: J. G. Beck (Ed.), *Interpersonal Processes in the Anxiety Disorders: Implications for Understanding Psychopathology and Treatment* (pp. 97–124). Washington DC: American Psychological Association.

Davis, C., Shuster, B., Blackmore, E., & Fox, J. (2004). Looking good—family focus on appearance and the risk of eating disorders. *International Journal of Eating Disorders, 35*: 136–144.

Davison, K. K., Markey, C. N., & Birch, L. L. (2000). Etiology of body dissatisfaction and weight concerns among 5-year-old girls. *Appetite, 35*: 143–151.

Delogu, A. M., Tortolani, D., & Zavattini, G. C. (2008). The appraisal of attachment in anorexic families. *Infanzia e Adolenza, 7*: 98–109.

Diamond, G. S., & Stern, R. S. (2003). Attachment-based family therapy for depressed adolescents: Repairing attachment failures. In: S. M. Johnson & V. E. Whiffen (Eds.), *Attachment Processes in Couple and Family Therapy*. (pp. 191–212). New York: Guilford.

Dixon, R., Adair, V., & O'Connor, S. (1996). Parental influences on the dieting beliefs and behaviors of adolescent females in New Zealand. *Journal of Adolescent Health, 19*: 303–307.

Dozier, M., Stovall-McClough., K. C., & Albus, K. E. (2008). Attachment and Psychopathology in Adulthood. In: J. Cassidy & P. R. Shaver (Eds.) *Handbook of Attachment Theory, Research and Clinical Applications* (pp. 718–744). New York: Guilford.

Dring, G. (2014). Anorexia runs in families: Is this due to genes or the family environment? *Journal of Family Therapy. Published online at http://onlinelibrary.wiley.com/journal/10.1111/(ISSN)1467–6427/earlyview*. Last accessed 06/11/2014.

Dring, G. J., Singlehurst, P., & Hutton, S. (2004). Can adolescents perceptions of their weight be used in screening for eating disorders? A pilot study of a short screening questionnaire. *European Eating Disorders Review, 12*: 327–330.

Eddy, K. T., Celio Doyle, A., Hoste, R. R., Herzog, D. B., & Le Grange, D. (2008). Eating disorders not otherwise specified in adolescents. *Journal of the American Academy of Child and Adolescent Psychiatry, 47*: 156–164.

Eggert, J., Levendosky, A., & Klump. K. (2007). Relationships among attachment styles, personality characteristics, and disordered eating. *International Journal of Eating Disorders, 40*: 149–155.

Eisler, I. (2004). Personal Communication.

Eisler, I. (2005). The empirical and theoretical base of family therapy and multiple family day therapy for adolescent anorexia nervosa. *Journal of Family Therapy, 27*: 104–131.

Eisler, I. (2014). Personal Communication.

Eisler, I., Dare, C., Hodes, M., Russell, G., Dodge, E., & Le Grange, D. (2000). Family therapy for adolescent Anorexia Nervosa: The results of a controlled study of two family interventions. *Journal of Child Psychology and Psychiatry, 41*: 727–736.

Eisler, I., Dare, C., Russell, G. F. M., Szmuckler, G., Le Grange, D., & Dodge, E. (1997). Family and individual therapy for Anorexia Nervosa: A 5-year follow-up. *Archives of General Psychiatry, 54*: 1025–1030.

Eisler, I., Lock, J., & Le Grange, D. (2010). Family-Based Treatments for adolescents with Anorexia Nervosa: single-family and multi-family approaches. In: C. M. Grillo & J. E. Mitchell (Eds.), *The Treatment of Eating Disorders* (pp. 150–174). New York: Guilford.

Eisler, I., Simic, M., Russell, G. F. M., & Dare, C. (2007). A randomised controlled treatment trial of two forms of family therapy in adolescent anorexia nervosa: a five-year follow-up. *Journal of Child Psychology and Psychiatry, 48*: 552–560.

Elfhag, K., & Linne, Y. (2005). Gender differences in associations of eating pathology between mothers and their adolescent offspring. *Obesity Research, 13*: 1070–1076.

Epstein, N. B., Baldwin, L. M., & Bishop, D. S. (1983). The McMaster Family Assessment Device. *Journal of Marital and Family Therapy, 9*: 171–180.

Erol, A., Yazici, F., & Toprak, G. (2007). Family functioning of patients with an eating disorder compared with that of patients with obsessive compulsive disorder. *Comprehensive Psychiatry, 48*: 47–50.

Espina, A., Ochoa de Alda, I., & Ortego, A. (2003). Dyadic adjustment in parents of daughters with an eating disorder. *European Eating Disorders Review, 11*: 349–362.

Evans, J., & Le Grange, D. L. (1995). Body size and parenting in eating disorders: A comparative study of the attitudes of mothers towards their children. *International Journal of Eating Disorders, 18*: 39–48.

Fahy, T. & Treasure, J. (1989). Children of mothers with bulimia nervosa. *British Medical Journal, 299*: 1031.

Fairburn, C. G., & Beglin, S. J. (1994). Assessment of eating disorders: Interview or self-report questionnaire? *International Journal of Eating Disorders, 16*: 363–370.

Fairburn, C. G., & Cooper, Z. (1993). The Eating Disorders Examination (12th edn.). In: C. G. Fairburn & G. T. Wilson (Eds.), *Binge eating: nature, assessment and treatment* (pp. 317–332). New York: The Guilford Press.

Fairburn, C. G., & Beglin, S. J. (1994). Assessment of Eating Disorders: Interview or self-report questionnaire. *International Journal of Eating Disorders, 16*: 363–370.

Fearon, R. M. P., Van IJzendoorn, M. H., Fonagy, P., Bakermans-Kranenburg, M. J., Schuengel, C., & Bokhorst, C. L. (2006). In search of shared and nonshared environmental factors in security of attachment: a behavior-genetic study of the association between sensitivity and attachment security. *Developmental Psychology, 42*: 1026–1040.

Fennig, S., Hadas, A., Itzaky, L., Roe, D., Apter, A., & Shahar, G. (2008). Self-criticism is a key predictor of eating disorder dimensions among adolescent females. *International Journal of Eating Disorders, 41*: 762–765.

Fernandez-Aranda, F., Pinheiro, A. P., Tozzi, F., Thornton, L. M., Plotnicov, H., Kaye, W. H., Fichter, M. M., Halmi, K. A., Kaplan, A. S., Woodside, D. B., Klump, K. L., Strober, M., Crow, S., Mitchell, J., Rotondo, A., Keel, P.,

Berrettini, W. H., Rickels, K. E., Crawford, S. F., Brandt, H., Johnson, C., & Bulik, C. M. (2007). Symptom Profile of Major Depressive Disorder in Women with Eating Disorders. *Australia and New Zealand Journal of Psychiatry, 41*: 24–31.

Field, A. E., Camargo, C. A., Taylor, C. B., Berkey, C. S., Roberts, S. B., & Colditz, G. A. (2001). Peer, parent, and media influences on the development of weight concerns and frequent dieting among preadolescent and adolescent girls and boys. *Pediatrics, 107*: 54–60.

Fivush, R. (2002). Voice and silence: A feminist model of autobiographical memory. In: J. Lucariello, J. A., Hudson, R. Fivush & P. J. Bauer (Eds.), *The mediated mind: essays in honor of Katherine Nelson* (pp. 79–99). Mahwah, NJ: Erlbaum.

Fivush, R., Haden, C., & Reese, E. (2006). Elaborating on elaborations: Maternal reminiscing style and children's socioemotional outcome. *Child Development, 77*: 1568–1588.

Fletcher, K. L., Shim, S. S., & Wang, C. (2012). Perfectionistic concerns mediate the relationship between psychologically controlling parenting and achievement goal orientation. *Personality and Individual Differences, 52*: 876–881.

Flett, G. L., Hewitt, P. L., Oliver, J. M., & Macdonald, S. (2002). Perfectionism in children and their parents: a developmental analysis. In: G. L. Flett, & P. L. Hewitt, (Eds.), *Perfectionism. Theory, Research and Treatment* (pp. 89–132). Washington DC: American Psychological Association.

Fonagy, P., Gergely, G., Jurist, E., & Target, M. (2004). *Affect Regulation, Mentalization, and the Development of the Self*. London: Karnac.

Fonagy, P., Leigh, T., Steele, M., Kennedy, R., Mattoon, G., Target, M., & Gerber, A. (1996). The relation of attachment status, psychiatric classification, and response to psychotherapy. *Journal of Consulting and Clinical Psychology, 64*: 22–31.

Fornari, V., Wlodarczyk-Bisarga, K., Matthews, M., Sandberg, D., Mandel, F. S., & Katz, J. L. (1999). Perception of family functioning and depressive symptomatology in individuals with anorexia or bulimia. *Comprehensive Psychiatry, 40*: 434–441.

Fulkerson, J. A., McGuire, M. T., Neumark-Sztainer, D., Story, M., French, S. A., & Perry, C. L. (2002). Weight related behaviors of adolescent boys and girls who are encouraged to diet by their mothers. *International Journal of Obesity, 26*: 1579–1587.

Furnham, A., & Adam-Saib, S. (2001). Abnormal eating attitudes and behaviours and perceived parental control: a study of white British and British-Asian school girls. *Social Psychiatry and Epidemiology, 36*: 462–470.

Garfinkel, P. E., Garner, D., Rose, J., Darby, P., Brandes, J. S., O'Hanlon, J., & Walsh, N. (1983). A comparison of characteristics in the families of patients with anorexia and normal controls. *Psychological Medicine, 13*: 821–828.

Garner, D. M., Olmstead, M. P., Bohr, Y., & Garfinkel, P. E. (1982). The eating attitudes test: psychometric features and clinical correlates. *Psychological Medicine, 14*: 871–878.

Garner, D. M., Olmstead, M. P., & Polivy, J. (1983). Development and validation of a multidimensional eating disorder inventory for anorexia and bulimia. *International Journal of Eating Disorders, 2*: 15–34.

Geller, J., Cockell, S. J., Hewitt, P. L., Goldner, E. M., & Flett, G. L. (2000). Inhibited expression of negative emotions and interpersonal orientation in anorexia nervosa. *International Journal of Eating Disorders, 28*: 8–19.

George, C., Kaplan, N., & Main, M. (1984). Adult Attachment Interview protocol. Unpublished manuscript, University of California at Berkeley.

George, C., Kaplan, N., & Main, M. (1984). Adult Attachment Interview protocol. (2nd edition) Unpublished manuscript, University of California at Berkeley.

George, C., Kaplan, N., & Main, M. (1984). Adult Attachment Interview protocol (3rd edition). Unpublished manuscript, University of California at Berkeley.

Gillett, K. S., Harper, J. M., Larson, J. H., Berrett, M. E., & Hardman, R. K. (2009). Implicit Family Process Rules in Eating-Disordered and Non-Eating-Disordered Families. *Journal of Marital and Family Therapy, 35*: 159–175.

Gilligan, C. (1982). *In a different voice: Women's conceptions of self and morality*. Cambridge, MA: Harvard University Press.

Goel, A., & Darwish, A. (2008). An alternative to conventional care for young people with anorexia nervosa. *Psychiatric Bulletin, 32*: 437.

Goldner, E. M., Cockell, S. J., & Srikameswaran, S. (2002). Perfectionism and Eating Disorders. In: G. L. Flett & P. L. Hewitt (Eds.), *Perfectionism: Theory, Research and Treatment* (pp. 319–340). Washington DC: American Psychological Association.

Gowers, S., Clark, A., Roberts, C., Griffiths, A., Edwards, V., Bryan, C., Smethurst, N., Byford, S., & Barrett, B. (2007). Clinical effectiveness of treatments for anorexia nervosa in adolescents. *British Journal of Psychiatry, 191*: 427–435.

Gowers, S., & North, C. (1999). Difficulties in family functioning and adolescent anorexia nervosa. *British Journal of Psychiatry, 174*: 63–66.

Gowers, S., Weetman, J., Shore, A., Hossain, F., & Elvins, R. (2000). Impact of hospitalisation on the outcome of adolescent anorexia nervosa. *British Journal of Psychiatry, 176*: 138–141.

Grotevant, H. D., & Cooper, C. R. (1986). Individuation in Family relationships: A perspective on individual differences in the development of identity and role-taking skills in adolescence. *Human Development, 29*: 82–100.

Grych, J. H., & Fincham, F. D. (1993). Children's appraisals of marital conflict: Initial investigations of the cognitive-contextual framework. *Child Development, 64*: 1648–1661.

Guttman, H. A., & Laporte, L. (2002). Family members' retrospective perceptions of intrafamilial relationships. *Contemporary Family Therapy: An International Journal, 24*: 505–521.

Habermas, T., & de Silveira, C. (2008). The development of global coherence in life narratives across adolescence: Temporal, causal and thematic aspects. *Developmental Psychology, 44*: 707–721.

Haden, C. A., Haine, R. A., & Fivush, R. (1997). Developing narrative structure in parent–child reminiscing across the preschool years. *Developmental Psychology, 33*: 295–307.

Haines, J., Neumark-Sztainer, D., Hannan, P., & Robinson-O'Brien, R. (2008). Child versus Parent Report of Parental Influences on Children's Weight-related Attitudes and behaviors. *Journal of Paediatric Psychology, 33*: 783–788.

Hall, A., Leibrich, J., Walkey, F. H., & Welch, G. (1986). Investigation of "weight pathology" of 58 mothers of anorexia nervosa patients and 204 mothers of schoolgirls. *Psychological Medicine, 16*: 71–76.

Halmi, K. A. (2005b). Obsessive-Compulsive Personality Disorder and Eating Disorders. *Eating Disorders, 13*: 85–92.

Halmi, K. A., Sunday, S. R., Strober, M., Kaplan, A., Woodside, D. B., Fichter, M., Treasure, J., Berrettini, W. H., & Kaye, W. H. (2000). Perfectionism in anorexia nervosa: variation by clinical subtype, obsessionality, and pathological eating behavior. *American Journal of Psychiatry, 157*: 1799–1805.

Halmi, K. A., Tozzi, F., Thornton, L. M., Crow, S., Fichter, M., Kaplan, A. S., Keel, P., Klump, K., Lilenfeld, L. R., Mitchel, J. E., Plotnicov, K. H., Pollice, C., Rotondo, A., Strober, M., Woodside, D. B., Berrettini, W. H., Kaye, W. H., & Bulik, C. M. (2005a). The Relation between Perfectionism, Obsessional-Compulsive Personality Disorder, and Obsessional-Compulsive Disorder in Individuals with Eating Disorders. *International Journal of Eating Disorders, 38*: 371–374.

Harding, T. P., & Lachenmeyer, J. R. (1986). Family interaction patterns and locus of control as predictors of the presence and severity of anorexia nervosa. *Journal of Clinical Psychology, 42*: 440–448.

Harper, J. M., Stoll, R. W., & Larson, J. H. (2007). *Development and psychometric properties of the Family Implicit Rules Profile*. Unpublished manuscript, Brigham Young University. Provo: UT.

Hartmann, A., Zeeck, A., & Barrett, M. S. (2010). Interpersonal problems in eating disorders. *International Journal of Eating Disorders, 43*: 619–627.

Haworth-Hoeppner, S. (2000). The Critical Shapes of Body Image: The Role of the Culture and Family in the Production of Eating Disorders. *Journal of Marriage and the Family, 62*: 212–227.

Hesse, E. (2008). The Adult Attachment Interview. In: J. Cassidy & P. R. Shaver (Eds.), *Handbook of Attachment. 2nd edn.* (pp. 552–598). New York: Guilford.

Hewitt, P. L., Flett, C. L., & Ediger, E. (1995). Perfectionism traits and perfectionistic self-presentation in eating disorder attitudes, characteristics, and symptoms. *International Journal of Eating Disorders, 18*: 317–326.

Hill, A. J., & Franklin, J. A. (1998). Mothers, daughters and dieting: Investigating the transmission of weight control. *British Journal of Clinical Psychology, 37*: 3–13.

Hill, A. J., & Pallin, V. (1998). Dieting awareness and low self-worth: related issues in 8-year-old girls. *International Journal of Eating Disorders, 24*: 405–413.

Hill, A. J., Weaver, C., & Blundell (1990). Dieting concerns of 10-year-old girls and their mothers. *British Journal of Clinical Psychology, 29*: 346–348.

Hock, E., Eberly, M., Bartle-Haring, S., Ellwanger, P., & Widaman, F. (2001). Separation Anxiety in Parents of Adolescents: Theoretical Significance and Scale Development. *Child Development, 72*: 284–298.

Hodes, M., Dare, C., Dodge, E., & Eisler, I. (1999). The Assessment of Expressed Emotion in a Standardised Family Interview. *Journal of Child Psychology and Psychiatry, 40*: 617–625.

Hodes, M., Timimi, S., & Robinson, P. (1997). Children of Mothers with Eating Disorders: A Preliminary Study. *European Eating Disorders Review, 5*: 11–24.

Hodges, E. L., & Cochrane, C. E. (1998). Family characteristics of binge-eating disorder patients. *International Journal of Eating Disorders, 23*: 145–151.

Holland, A. J., Hall, A., Murray, R., Russell, G. F. M., & Crisp, A. H. (1984). Anorexia nervosa: a study of 34 twin pairs. *British Journal of Psychiatry, 145*: 414–419.

Holland, A. J., Sicotte, N., & Treasure, J. (1988). Anorexia nervosa: evidence for a genetic basis. *Journal of Psychosomatic Research, 32*: 561–571.

Honig, P. (2005). A Multi-family Group Programme as Part of an Inpatient Service for Adolescents with a Diagnosis of Anorexia Nervosa. *Clinical Child Psychology and Psychiatry, 10*: 465–475.

Horesh, N., Apter, A., Lepkifker, E., Ratzoni, G., Weizmann, R., & Tyano, S. (1995). Life events and severe anorexia nervosa in adolescence. *Acta Psychiatrica Scandinavica, 91*: 5–9.

Horowitz, L. M., Rosenberg, S. E., Baer, B. A., Ureno, G., & Villasenor, V. S. (1988). Inventory of Interpersonal Problems: Psychometric properties and clinical applications. *Journal of Consulting and Clinical Psychology, 56*: 885–892.

House, J., Schmidt, U., Craig, M., Landau, S., Simic, M., Nichols, D., Hugo, P., Berelowitz, M., & Eisler, I. (2012). Comparison of Specialist and Nonspecialist Care Pathways for Adolescents with Anorexia Nervosa and Related Eating Disorders. *International Journal of Eating Disorders, 45*: 949–956.

Hughes, D. A. (2007). *Attachment-Focussed Family Therapy*. New York: W. W. Norton.

Hughes, P., Turton, P., Hopper, E., McGauley, G. A., & Fonagy, P. (2001). Disorganised attachment behaviour among infants born subsequent to stillbirth. *Journal of Child Psychology and Psychiatry, 42*: 791–801.

Humphrey, L. L. (1986b). Family relations in bulimic-anorexic and non-distressed families. *International Journal of Eating Disorders, 5*: 223–232.

Humphrey, L. L. (1989). Observed family interactions among sub-types of eating disorders using structural analysis of social behavior. *Journal of Consulting and Clinical Psychology, 57*: 206–214.

Humphrey, L. L., Apple, R. F., & Kirschenbaum, D. S. (1986a). Differentiating Bulimic-Anorexic From Normal Families Using Interpersonal and Behavioral Observation Systems. *Journal of Consulting and Clinical Psychology, 54*: 190–195.

Jack, D. C., & Dill, D. (1992). The Silencing the Self Scale: Schemas associated with depression in women. *Psychology of Women Quarterly, 16*: 97–106.

Jacobi, C., Agras, W. S., & Hammer, L. (2001). Predicting children's reported eating disturbances at 8 years of age. *Journal of the American Academy of Child and Adolescent Psychiatry, 40*: 364–372.

Jaffa, T., & Percival, J. (2004). The impact of outreach on admissions to an adolescent anorexia nervosa inpatient unit. *European Eating Disorders Review, 12*: 317–320.

Jordan, J., Joyce, P. R., Carter, F. A., Horn, J., McIntosh, V. V. W., Luty, S. E., McKenzie, J. M., Frampton, C. M. A., Mulder, R. T., & Bulik, C. M. (2008). Specific and Nonspecific Comorbidity in Anorexia Nervosa. *International Journal of Eating Disorders, 41*: 47–56.

Juster, H. R., Heimberg, R. G., Frost, R. O., Holt, C. S., Mattia, J. I., & Faccenda, K. (1996). Social Phobia and Perfectionism. *Personal and Individual Differences, 21*: 403–410.

Kalucy, R. S., Crisp, A. H., & Harding, B. (1977). A study of 56 families with anorexia nervosa. *British Journal of Medical Psychology, 50*: 381–395.

Kamins, M. L., & Dweck, C. S. (1999). Person versus process praise and criticism: Implications for contingent self-worth and coping. *Developmental Psychology, 35*: 835–847.

Karwautz, A., Nobis, G., Haidvogl, M., Wagner, G., Hafferl-Gattermeyer, A., Wober-Bingol, C., & Friedrich, M. H. (2003). Perceptions of family relationships in adolescents with anorexia and their unaffected sisters. *European Child and Adolescent Psychiatry, 12*: 128–135.

Katz, L. F., & Hunter, E. C. (2007). Maternal Meta-emotion Philosophy and Adolescent Depressive Symptomatology. *Social Development, 16*: 343–360.

Katz, L. F., Wilson, B., & Gottman, J. M. (1999). Meta-Emotion Philosophy and Family Adjustment: Making an Emotional Connection. In: M. J. Cox & J. B. Brooks-Gunn, *Conflict and Cohesion in Families* (pp. 131–165). Mahwah, NJ. Lawrence Erlbaum Associates.

Kaye, W. H., Bulik, C. M., Thornton, L., Barbarich, N., & Masters, K. (2004). Comorbidity of Anxiety Disorders With Anorexia and Bulimia. *American Journal of Psychiatry, 161*: 2215–2221.

Kaye, W. H., Klump, K. L., Frank, G. K. W., & Strober, M. (2000). Anorexia nervosa and bulimia. *Annual Review of Medicine, 51*: 299–313.

Keery, H., Eisenberg, M. E., Boutelle, K., Neumark-Sztainer, D., & Story, M. (2006). Relationships between maternal and adolescent weight-related behaviours and concerns: The role of perception. *Journal of Psychosomatic Research, 61*: 105–111.

Kerig, P. (1995). Triangles in the Family Circle: Effects of Family Structure on Marriage, Parenting, and Child Adjustment. *Journal of Family Psychology, 9*: 28–43.

Kerig, P. A., & Swanson, J. A. (2010). Ties That Bind: Triangulation, Boundary Dissolution, and the Effects of Interparental Conflict on Child Development. In: M. S. Shulz, M. K. Pruett, P. K. Kerig, & R. D. Parke (Eds.) *Strengthening Couple Relationships for Optimal Development* (pp. 59–76). Washington DC: American Psychological Association.

Kerig, P. K., & Brown, C. A. (1996). *The Parent–Child Boundary Scale. Department of Psychology*. Simon Fraser University.

Kinston, W., & Loader, P. (1984). Eliciting whole-family interaction with a standardized clinical interview. *Journal of Family Therapy, 6*: 347–363.

Klump, K. L., Miller, K. B., Keel, P. K., McGue, M., & Iacono, W. G. (2001). Genetic and environmental influences in a population based twin study. *Psychological Medicine, 31*: 737–740.

Krcmar, M., Giles, S., & Helme, D. (2008). Understanding the Process: How Mediated and Peer Norms Affect Young Women's Body Esteem. *Communication Quarterly, 56*: 111–130.

Krug, I., Treasure, J., Anderluh, M., Bellodi, L., Cellini, E., Collier, D., di Bernardo, M., Granero, R., Karwautz, A., Nacmias, B., Penelo, E., Ricca, V., Sorbi, S., Tchanturia, K., Wagner, G., & Fernandez-Aranda, F. (2009). Associations of individual and family eating patterns during childhood and early adolescence: a multicentre European study of associated eating disorder factors. *British Journal of Nutrition, 101*: 909–918.

Kobak, R. R., Cole, H. E., Ferenz-Gilles, R., & Fleming, W. S. (1993). Attachment and Emotion Regulation during Mother–Teen Problem Solving: A Control Theory Analysis. *Child Development, 64*: 231–245.

Kog, E., & Vandereycken, W. (1989). Family Interaction in Eating Disorder Patients and Normal Controls. *International Journal of Eating Disorders, 8*: 11–23.

Kog, E., Vandereycken, W., & Vertommen, H. (1985). The psychosomatic family model: A critical analysis of family interaction concepts. *Journal of Family Therapy, 7*: 31–44.

Kog, E., Vertommen, H., & Vandereycken, W. (1987). Minuchin's Psychosomatic Family Model Revised: A Concept-Validation Study Using a Multitrait-Multimethod Approach. *Family Process, 26*: 235–253.

Kortegaard, L. S., Hoerder, K., Joergensen, J., Gillberg, C., & Kyvik, K. O. (2001). A preliminary population-based twin study of self-reported eating disorder. *Psychological Medicine, 31*: 361–365.

Lacey, J. H., & Smith, G. (1987). Bulimia nervosa. The impact of pregnancy on mother and baby. *British Journal of Psychiatry, 150*: 777–781.

Laghai, A., & Joseph, S. (2000). Attitudes towards emotional expression: Factor structure, convergent validity and associations with personality. *British Journal of Medical Psychology, 73*: 381–384.

Laliberte, M., Boland, F. J., & Leichner, P. (1999). Family climates: Family factors specific to disturbed eating and bulimia nervosa. *Journal of Clinical Psychology, 55*: 1021–1040.

Lam, C. B., & McHale, S. M. (2012). Developmental Patterns and Family Predictors of Adolescent Weight Concerns: A Replication and Extension. *International Journal of Eating Disorders, 45*: 524–530.

Lattimore, P. J., Wagner, H. L., & Gowers, S. (2000a). Autonomic arousal and conflict avoidance in anorexia nervosa: A pilot study. *European Eating Disorders Review, 8*: 31–39.

Lattimore, P. J., Wagner, H. L., & Gowers, S. (2000b). Conflict avoidance in anorexia nervosa: An observational study of mothers and daughters. *European Eating Disorders Review, 8*: 355–368.

Latzer, Y., & Gaber, L. B. (1998). Pathological conflict avoidance in anorexia nervosa: Family perspectives. *Contemporary Family Therapy: An International Journal, 20*: 539–551.

Latzer, Y., Hochdorf, Z., Bachar, E., & Canetti, L. (2002). Attachment style and family functioning as discrimination factors in eating disorders. *Contemporary Family Therapy, 24*: 581–599.

Lee, Y., & Lin, P. -Y. (2010). Association between serotonin transporter gene polymorphism and eating disorders: A meta-analytic study. *International Journal of Eating Disorders, 43*: 498–504.

Le Grange, D., Binford, R. & Loeb, K. L. (2005). Manualised Family-Based Treatment for Anorexia Nervosa: A Case Series. *Journal of the American Academy of Child & Adolescent Psychiatry, 44*: 41–46.

Le Grange, D., Eisler, I., Dare, C., & Hodes, M. (1992b). Family criticism and self-starvation: a study of expressed emotion. *Journal of Family Therapy, 14*: 177–192.

Le Grange, D., Eisler, I., Dare, C., & Russell, G. F. M. (1992a). Evaluation of Family Treatments in Adolescent Anorexia Nervosa: A Pilot Study. *International Journal of Eating Disorders, 12*: 347–357.

Le Grange, D., Hoste, R. R., Lock, J., & Bryson, S. W. (2011). Parental expressed emotion of adolescents with anorexia nervosa: Outcome in Family-Based Treatment. *International Journal of Eating Disorders, 44*: 731–734.

Le Grange, D., Lock, J., Loeb, K. L., & Nicholls, D. (2010). Academy for Eating Disorders Position Paper: The Role of the Family in Eating Disorders. *International Journal of Eating Disorders, 43*: 1–5.

Leon, G. R., Fulkerson, J. A., Perry, C. L., & Dube, A. (1994). Family influences, school behaviors, and risk for the later development of an eating disorder. *Journal of Youth and Adolescence, 23*: 499–515.

Leung, F., Schwartzman, A., & Steiger, H. (1996). Testing a dual-process family model in understanding the development of eating pathology: A structural equation modeling analysis. *International Journal of Eating Disorders, 20:* 367–375.

Levine, M., Smolak, L., Moodey, A. F., Shuman, M. D., & Hessen, L. D. (1994). Normative Developmental Challenges and Dieting and Eating Disturbances in Middle School Girls. *International Journal of Eating Disorders, 15*: 11–20.

Lieberman, S. (1995). Anorexia nervosa: The tyranny of appearances. *Journal of Family Therapy, 17*: 133–138.

Lilenfeld, L. R., Kaye, W. H., Greeno, C. G., Merikangas, K. R., Plotnocov, K., Police, C., Rao, R., Strober, M., Bulik, C. M., & Nagy, L. (1998). A controlled family study of anorexia nervosa and bulimia nervosa. *Archives of General Psychiatry, 55*: 603–610.

Linville, D., Stice, E., Gau, J., & O'Neil, M. (2011). Predictive effects of mother and peer influences on increases in adolescents eating disorder risk factors and symptoms: A 3-year longitudinal study. *International Journal of Eating Disorders, 44*: 745–751.

Lock, J., Agras, W. S., Bryson, S., & Kraemer, H. C. (2005). A Comparison of Short and Long-Term Family Therapy for Adolescent Anorexia Nervosa. *Journal of the American Academy of Child and Adolescent Psychiatry, 44*: 632–639.

Lock, J., Couturier, J., & Agras, S. (2006a). Comparison of Long-Term Outcomes in Adolescents With Anorexia Nervosa Treated With Family Therapy. *Journal of the American Academy of Child and Adolescent Psychiatry, 45*: 666–672.

Lock, J., & Le Grange, D. (2013). *Treatment Manual for Anorexia Nervosa: A Family-Based Approach. 2nd edn*. New York: Guilford.

Lock, J., Le Grange, D., Forsberg, S., & Hewell, K. (2006b). Is Family Therapy Useful for Treating Children with Anorexia Nervosa? Results of a Case Series. *Journal of the American Academy of Child and Adolescent Psychiatry, 45*: 1323–1328.

Lock, J., Le Grange, D., Agras, W. S., & Dare, C. (2001). *Treatment Manual for Anorexia Nervosa: A Family-Based Approach*. New York: Guilford.

Lock, J., Le Grange, D., Agras, W. S., Moye, A., & Bryson, S. W. (2010). Randomised clinical trial comparing Family-Based Treatment with adolescent-focused individual therapy for adolescents with anorexia nervosa. *Archives of General Psychiatry, 67*: 1025–1032.

Loeb, K. L., Walsh, T., Lock, J., Le Grange, D., Jones, J., Marcus, S., Weaver, J., & Dobrow, I. (2007). Open Trial of Family-Based Treatment for Full and Partial Anorexia Nervosa in Adolescence: Evidence of Successful Dissemination. *Journal of the American Academy of Child and Adolescent Psychiatry, 46*: 792–800.

Lowes, J., & Tiggemann, M. (2003). Body dissatisfaction, dieting awareness and the impact of parental influence in young children. *British Journal of Health Psychology, 8*: 135–147.

Lyon, M., & Chatoor, I. (1997). Testing the hypothesis of the multidimensional model of anorexia nervosa in adolescents. *Adolescence, 32(125)*: 101–112.

Main, M., & Solomon, J. (1986). Discovery of a new insecure disorganised/disoriented attachment pattern. In: T. B. Brazelton & M. Yogman (Eds.), *Affective Development in Infancy* (pp. 95–124). Norwood, NJ.: Ablex.

Manassis, K., Bradley, S., Goldberg, S., Hood, J., & Swinson, R. P. (1994). Attachment in mothers with anxiety disorders and their children. *Journal of the American Academy of Child and Adolescent Psychiatry, 33*: 1106–1113.

Martin, F. E. (1985). The treatment and outcome of anorexia nervosa in adolescents: A prospective study of five year follow-up. *Journal of Psychiatric Research, 19*: 509–514.

McCabe, M. P., & Ricciardelli, L. A. (2005). A prospective study of pressures from parents, peers, and the media on extreme weight change behaviors among adolescent boys and girls. *Behaviour Research and Therapy, 43*: 653–658.

McDermott, B. M., Batik, M., Roberts, L., & Gibbon, P. (2002). Parent and child report of family functioning in a clinical child and adolescent eating disorder sample. *Australian and New Zealand Journal of Psychiatry, 36*: 509–514.

McEwen, C., & Flouri, E. (2009). Fathers' parenting, adverse life events, and adolescents' emotional and eating disorder symptoms: the role of emotion regulation. *European Child and Adolescent Psychiatry, 18*: 206–216.

Mehl, A., Tomanova, J., Kubena, A., & Papezova, H. (2013). Adapting multifamily therapy to families who care for a loved one with an eating disorder in the Czech Republic combined with a follow-up pilot study of efficacy. *Journal of Family Therapy, 35(S1):* 82–101.

Meyer, C., Leung, N., Barry, L., & De Feo, D. (2010). Emotion and eating Psychopathology: Links with Attitudes Toward Emotional Expression Among Young Women. *International Journal of Eating Disorders, 43*: 187–189.

Meyer, C., McPartlan, L., Sines, J., & Waller, G. (2009). Accuracy of Self-Reported Weight and Height: Relationship with Eating Psychopathology among Young Women. *International Journal of Eating Disorders, 42*: 379–381.

Micucci, J. A. (2009). *The Adolescent in Family Therapy: Harnessing the Power of Relationships. (2nd edn.)*. New York: Guilford.

Mikulincer, M. (1995). Attachment Style and Mental Representation of the Self. *Journal of Personality and Social Psychology, 69*: 1203–1215.

Miller-Day, M., & Marks, J. D. (2006). Perceptions of Communication Orientation, Perfectionism, and Disordered Eating Behaviours of Sons and Daughters. *Health Communication, 19*: 153–163.

Millon, T. (1998). DSM narcissistic personality disorder: Historical reflections and future directions. In: E. Ronningstam (Ed.), *Disorders of narcissism: Diagnostic, Clinical and Empirical Implications* (pp. 75–101). Washington DC: American Psychiatric Association.

Milos, G., Spindler, A., Schnyder, U., & Fairburn, C. (2005). Instability of eating disorder diagnoses: prospective study. *British Journal of Psychiatry, 187*: 573–578.

Minuchin, S. (1970). The use of an ecological framework in the treatment of a child. In: E. J. Anthony & C. Koupernik (Eds.), *The child in the family* (pp. 41–57). New York: John Wiley.

Minuchin, S. (1974). *Families and Family Therapy*. London: Routledge.

Minuchin, S., Baker, L., Rosman, B. L., Liebman, R., Milman, L., & Todd, T. C. (1975). A Conceptual Model of Psychosomatic Illness in Children. *Archives of General Psychiatry, 32*: 1031–1038.

Minuchin, S., & Fishman, H. C. (1981). *Family Therapy Techniques*. Cambridge, MA: Harvard University Press.

Minuchin, S., Rosman, B. L., & Baker, L. (1978). *Psychosomatic Families: Anorexia Nervosa in Context*. Cambridge, MA: Harvard University Press.

Moos, R. H., & Moos, B. S. (1980). *Family Environment Scale*. Palo Alto, CA. Consulting Psychologists Press.

Moreno, A., & Thelen, M. H. (1993). Parental factors related to bulimia nervosa. *Addictive Behaviors, 18*: 681–689.

Moretti, M., & Holland, R. (2003). The Journey of Adolescence. Transitions in Self in the Context of Attachment Relationships. In: S. M. Johnson & V. E. Whiffen (Eds.), *Attachment Processes in Couple and Family Therapy* (pp. 234–257). New York: Guilford.

Morgan, H. G., & Russell, G. F. M. (1975). Value of family background and clinical features as prediction of long-term outcome in anorexia nervosa: A follow-up of 41 patients. *Psychological Medicine, 5*: 355–372.

Mueller, C. M., & Dweck, C. S. (1998). Praise for intelligence can undermine children's motivation and performance. *Journal of Personality and Social Psychology, 75*: 33–52.

Mukai, T., Crago, M., & Shisslak, C. M. (1994). Eating attitudes and weight preoccupation among female high school students in Japan. *Journal of Child Psychology and Psychiatry, 35*: 677–688.

Nakabyashi, K., Komaki, G., Tajima, A., Ando, T., Ishikawa, M., Nomoto, J., Hata, K., Oka, A., Inoko, H., & Sasazuki, T. (2009). Identification of novel candidate loci for anorexia nervosa at 1g41 and 11q22 in Japanese by a genome wide association analysis with microsatellite markers. *Journal of Human Genetics, 54*: 531–537.

Newcombe, R., & Reese, E. (2004). Evaluations and orientations in mother–child narratives as a function of attachment security: A longitudinal investigation. *International Journal of Behavioral Development, 28*: 230–245.

Nilsson, K., Sundbom, E., & Hagglof, B. (2008). A longitudinal study of perfectionism in adolescent onset anorexia nervosa-restricting type. *European Eating Disorders Review, 16*: 386–394.

North, C., Gowers, S., & Byram, V. (1995). Family functioning in adolescent anorexia nervosa. *British Journal of Psychiatry, 167*: 673–678.

North, C., Gowers, S., & Byram, V. (1997). Family functioning and life events in the outcome of adolescent anorexia nervosa. *British Journal of Psychiatry, 171*: 545–549.

Ogden, J., & Elder, C. (1998). The role of family status and ethnic group on body image and eating behavior. *International Journal of Eating Disorders, 23*: 309–315.

Ogden, J., & Steward, J. (2000). The role of the mother–daughter relationship in explaining weight concern. *International Journal of Eating Disorders, 28*: 78–83.

Olson, D., McCubbin, H., Barnes, H., Larsen, A., Muxen, M., & Wilson, M. (1985). *Family inventories—Inventories used in a national survey of families across the life cycle*. St Paul: University of Minnesota.

Olson, D. H., Bell, R., & Portner, J. (1978). *Family Adaptability and Cohesion Evaluation Scale*. St Paul. MN: Family Social Science Press.

Olson, D. H., Sprenkle, D. H., & Russell, C. S. (1979). Circumplex model of marital and family systems: 1. Cohesion and adaptability dimensions, family types, and clinical applications. *Family Process, 18*: 3–28.

O'Shaughnessy, R., & Dallos, R. (2009). Attachment Research and Eating Disorders.: A Review of the Literature. *Clinical Child Psychology and Psychiatry, 14*: 559–575.

Palazzoli, M. S. (1974). *Self starvation: from the intrapsychic to the transpersonal approach to anorexia nervosa*. Oxford: Chaucer.

Palazzoli, M. S., Boscolo, L., Cecchin, G., & Prata, G. (1978). *Paradox and Counterparadox*. New York: Jason Aronson.

Parker, G., Tupling, H., & Brown, L. (1979). A parental bonding instrument. *British Journal of Medical Psychology, 52*: 1–10.

Pasupathi, M., & McClean, K. C. (2010). Where have you been, and where are you going? Narrative identity in adolescence. In: K. C. McLean & M. Pasupathi, (Eds.), *Narrative Development in Adolescence: Creating the Storied Self* (pp. xix–xxxiii). New York: Springer.

Paterson, G., Power, K., Yellowlees, A., Park, K., & Taylor, L. (2007). The relationship between two dimensional self-esteem and problem solving style in anorexic patients. *European Eating Disorders Review, 15*: 70–77.

Paulson-Karlsson, G., Engstrom, I., & Nevonen, L. (2009). A Pilot Study of a Family-Based Treatment for Adolescent Anorexia Nervosa: 18- and 36-Month Follow-ups. *Eating Disorders, 17*: 72–88.

Perry, J. A., Silvera, D. H., Neilands, T. B., Rosenvinge, J. H., & Hanssen, T. (2008). A study of the relationship between parental bonding, self-concept and eating disturbances in Norwegian and American college populations. *Eating Behaviors, 9*: 13–24.

Pike, K. M., Hilbert, A., Wilfley, D. E., & Fairburn, C. G. (2008). Toward an understanding of risk factors for anorexia nervosa: a case-control study. *Psychological Medicine, 38*: 1443–1454.

Pike, K. M., & Rodin, J. (1991). Mothers, daughters, and disordered eating. *Journal of Abnormal Psychology, 100*: 198–204.

Pinheiro, A. P., Bulik, C. M., Thornton, L. M., Sullivan, P. F., Root, T. L., Bloss, C. S., Berrettini, W. H., Schork, N. J., Kaye, W. H., Bergen, A. W., Magistretti, P., Brandt, H., Crawford, S., Crow, S., Fichter, M. M., Goldman, D., Halmi, K. A., Johnson, C., Kaplan, A. S., Keel, P. K., Klump, K. L., La Via, M., Mitchell, J. E., Strober, M., Rotondo, A., Treasure, J., & Woodside,

D. B. (2010). Association study of 182 candidate genes in anorexia nervosa. *American Journal of Medical Genetics Part B, 153B*: 1070–1080.

Powers, S. I., & Welsh, D. P. (1999). In: M. J. Cox & J. B. Brooks-Gunn (Eds.), *Conflict and Cohesion in Families* (pp. 243–281). Mahwah, NJ: Lawrence Erlbaum Associates.

Puhl, R. M., & Schwartz, M. B. (2003). If you are good you can have a cookie: How memories childhood food rules link to adult eating behaviors. *Eating Behaviors, 4*: 283–293.

Raevuori, A., Kaprio, J., Hoek, H. W., Sihvola, E., Rissanen., A., & Keski-Rahonen, A. (2008). Anorexia and Bulimia Nervosa in Same-Sex and Opposite-Sex Twins: Lack of Association With Twin Type in a Nationwide Study of Finnish Twins. *American Journal of Psychiatry, 165*: 1604–1610.

Raney, T. J., Thornton, L. M., Berrettini, W., Brandt, H., Crawford, S., Fichter, M. M., Halmi, K. A., Johnson, C., Kaplan, A. S., LaVia, M., Mitchell, J., Rotondo, A., Strober, M., Woodside, D. B., Kaye, W. H., & Bulik, C. M. (2008). Influence of overanxious disorder of childhood on the expression of anorexia nervosa. International Journal of Eating Disorders, *41*: 326–332.

Rastam, M., & Gillberg, C. (1991). The Family Background of Anorexia Nervosa: A Population-based Study. *Journal of the American Academy of Child and Adolescent Psychiatry, 30*: 283–289.

Rastam, M., Gillberg, C., & Gillberg, I. C. (1996). A Six-Year Follow-up Study of Anorexia Nervosa with Teenage Onset. *Journal of Youth and Adolescence, 25*: 439–453.

Reese, E. (2008). Maternal coherence in the Adult Attachment Interview is linked to maternal reminiscing and to children's self-concept. *Attachment and Human Development, 10*: 451–464.

Reese, E., Yan, C., Jack, F., & Hayne, C. (2010). Emerging identities: narrative and self from early childhood to early adolescence. In: K. C. McLean & M. Pasupathi, (Eds.), *Narrative Development in Adolescence: Creating the Storied Self* (pp. 23–44). New York: Springer.

Rhodes, P., Baillee, A., Brown, J., & Madden, S. (2008). Can parent-to-parent consultation improve the effectiveness of the Maudsley Model of Family-Based Treatment for anorexia nervosa? A randomized control trial. *Journal of Family Therapy, 30*: 96–108.

Rieves, L., & Cash, T. F. (1996). Social developmental factors and women's body-image attitudes. *Journal of Social Behavior and Personality, 11*: 63–78.

Ringer, F., & Crittenden, P. M. (2007). Eating Disorders and Attachment: The Effects of Hidden Family Processes on Eating Disorders. *European Eating Disorders Review, 15*: 119–130.

Robin, A. L. (1994). Family Therapy versus Individual Therapy for Adolescent Females with Anorexia Nervosa. *Developmental and Behavioral Pediatrics, 15*: 111–116.

Robin, A. L., Siegel, P. T., & Moye, A. (1995). Family Versus Individual Therapy for Anorexia: Impact on Family Conflict. *International Journal of Eating Disorders, 17*: 313–322.

Robin, A. L., Siegel, P. T., Moye, A. W., Gilroy, M., Dennis, A. B., & Sikand, A. (1999). A controlled comparison of family versus individual therapy for adolescents with anorexia nervosa. *Journal of the American Academy of Child and Adolescent Psychiatry, 38*: 1482–1489.

Romans, S. E., Gendall, K. A., Martin, J. L., & Mullen, P. E. (2001). Child sexual abuse and later disordered eating: A New Zealand Epidemiological Study. *International Journal of Eating Disorders, 29*: 380–392.

Root, T. L., Szatkiewicz, J. P., Jonassaint, C. R., Thornton, L. M., Pinheiro, A. P., Strober, M., Bloss, C., Berrettini, W., Schork, N. J., Kaye, W. H., Bergen, A. W., Magistretti, P., Brandt, H., Crawford, S., Crow, S., Fichter, M. M., Goldman, D., Halmi, K. A., Johnson, C., & Kaplan, A. S. (2011). Association of Candidate Genes with Phenotypic Traits Relevant to Anorexia Nervosa. *European Eating Disorders Review, 19*: 487–493.

Rosman, B. L., Minuchin, S., & Liebman, R. (1975). Family lunch session: an introduction to family therapy in anorexia nervosa. *American Journal of Orthopsychiatry, 45*: 846–853.

Ross, C. (2006). Overestimates of the Genetic Contribution to Eating Disorders. *Ethical Human Psychology and Psychiatry, 8*: 123–133.

Rowa, K., Kerig, P. K., & Geller, J. (2001). The family and anorexia nervosa: examining parent–child boundary problems. *European Eating Disorders Review, 9*: 97–114.

Russell, G. F. M., Szmuckler, G. I., Dare, C., & Eisler, I. (1987). An evaluation of family therapy in anorexia nervosa and bulimia nervosa. *Archives of General Psychiatry, 44*: 1047–1056.

Sands, E. R., & Wardle, J. (2003). Internalization of ideal body shapes in 9–12-year-old girls. *International Journal of Eating Disorders, 33*: 193–204.

Sargent, J., Liebman, R., & Silver, M. (1985). Family Therapy for Anorexia Nervosa. In: D. M. Garner & P. E. Garfinkel, (Eds.), Handbook of Psychotherapy for Anorexia Nervosa and Bulimia (pp. 257–279). New York: Guilford.

Schaefer, E. (1965). Children's reports of parental behaviour: an inventory. *Child Development, 36*: 413–424.

Schmidt, U., & Treasure, J. (2006). Anorexia nervosa: Valued and visible. A cognitive-interpersonal maintenance model and its implications for research and practice. *British Journal of Clinical Psychology, 45*: 343–366.

Serpell, L., Neiderman, M., Haworth, E., Emmanuel, F., & Lask, B. (2003). The use of the Pros and Cons of Anorexia Nervosa (P-CAN). Scale with children and adolescents. *Journal of Psychosomatic Research, 54*: 567–571.

Serpell, L., Treasure, J., Teasdale, J., & Sullivan, V. (1999). Anorexia nervosa: Friend or foe? *International Journal of Eating Disorders, 25*: 177–186.

Sharpe, T. M., Killen, J. D., Bryson, S. W., Shisslak, C. M., Estes, L. S., Gray, N., Crago, M., & Taylor, C. B. (1998). Attachment styles and weight concerns in preadolescent and adolescent girls. *International Journal of Eating Disorders, 23*: 39–44.

Shisslak, C. M., McKeon, R. T., & Crago, M. (1990). Family dysfunction in normal weight bulimic and bulimic anorexic families. *Journal of Clinical Psychology, 46*: 185–189.

Shoebridge, P., & Gowers, S. G. (2000). Parental high concern and adolescent-onset anorexia nervosa. *British Journal of Psychiatry, 176*: 132–137.

Sim, L. A, Homme, J. H., Lteif, A. N., Vande Voort, J. L, Schak, K. M., & Ellingson, J. (2009). Family functioning and maternal distress in adolescent girls with anorexia nervosa. *International Journal of Eating Disorders, 42*: 531–539.

Sippola, L., & Bukowski, W. M. (1996). *Relational authenticity in adolescence: associations between "voice", friendship and adolescent adjustment*. Unpublished Manuscript. Concordia University.

Skinner, H. A., Steinhauer, P. D., & Santa-Barbara, J. (1983). The Family Assessment Measure. *Canadian Journal of Community Mental Health, 2*: 91–103.

Smith, C., Feldman, S., Nasserbakht, A., & Steiner, H. (1993). Psychological Characteristics and DSM-111-R Diagnoses at 6-Year Follow-up of Adolescent Anorexia Nervosa. *Journal of the American Academy of Child and Adolescent Psychiatry, 32*: 1237–1245.

Smith, G. T., Hohlstein, L. E., & Atlas, J. G. (1992). Accuracy of self-reported weight: Covariation with binger or restrainer status and eating disorder symptomatology. *Addictive Behaviors, 17*: 1–8.

Smolak, L., Levine, M. P., & Schermer, F. (1999). Parental input and weight concerns among elementary school children. *International Journal of Eating Disorders, 25*: 263–271.

Smolak, L., & Munstertieger, B. F. (2002). The relationship of gender and voice to depression and eating disorders. *Psychology of Women Quarterly, 26*: 234–241.

Snoek, H. M., van Strien, T., Janssens, J. M. A. M., & Engels, R. C. M. E. (2009). Longitudinal relationship between fathers', mothers', and adolescents' restrained eating. *Appetite, 52*: 461–468.

Soenens, B., Elliot, A. J., Goosens, L., Vansteenkiste, M., Luyten, P., & Duriez, B. (2005b). The intergenerational transmission of perfectionism: Parents psychological control as an intervening variable. *Journal of Family Psychology, 19*: 358–366.

Soenens, B., Luyckx, K., Vansteenkiste, M., Luyten, P., Duriez, B., & Goosens, L. (2008a). Maladaptive perfectionism as an intervening variable between psychological control and adolescent depressive symptoms: A three-wave longitudinal study. *Journal of Family Psychology, 22*: 465–474.

Soenens, B., Vansteenkiste, M., Duriez, B., & Goosens, L. (2006). In Search of the Source of Psychologically Controlling Parenting: The Role of Parental Separation Anxiety and Parental Maladaptive Perfectionism. *Journal of Research on Adolescence, 16*: 539–559.

Soenens, B., Vansteenkiste, M., Luyten, P., Duriez, B., & Goosens, L. (2005a). Maladaptive perfectionistic self-representations: The mediational link between psychological control and adjustment. *Personality and Individual Differences, 38*: 487–498.

Soenens, B., Vansteenkiste, M., & Luyten, P. (2010). Toward a domain-specific approach to the study of parental psychological control: Distinguishing between dependency-oriented and achievement-oriented psychological control. *Journal of Personality, 78*: 217–256.

Soenens B., Vansteenkiste, M., Vandereycken, W., Luyten, P., Sierens, E., & Goosens, L. (2008b). Perceived parental psychological control and eating-disordered symptoms: Maladaptive perfectionism as a possible intervening variable. *Journal of Nervous and Mental Disease, 196*: 144–152.

Sokol, M. S., Carroll, A. K., Heebink, D., Hoffman-Rieken, K. M., Goudge, C. S., & Ebers, D. D. (2009). Anorexia Nervosa in identical triplets. *CNS Spectrums, 14*: 156–162.

Spielberger, C. D., Johnson, E. H., Russell, S. F., Crane, R. J., Jacobs, G. A., & Worder, T. J. (1985). The experience and expression of anger: Construct validation of an anger expression scale. In: M. A. Chesney & R. H. Rosenman (Eds.), *Anger and hostility in cardiovascular and behavioural disorders* (pp. 5–30). New York: McGraw Hill.

Squire-Dehouk, B. (1993). *Evaluation of conjoint family therapy versus family counselling in adolescent anorexia nervosa patients: A two year follow-up study*. Unpublished dissertation for MSc. in Clinical Psychology, Institute of Psychiatry, University of London/Surrey University.

Srinivasagam, N. M., Kaye, W. H., Plotnikov, K. H., Greenco, C., Weltzin, T. E., & Rao, R. (1995). Persistent perfectionism, symmetry. and exactness after long-term recovery from anorexia nervosa. *American Journal of Psychiatry, 152*: 1630–1634.

Steiger, H., Liquornik, K., Chapman, J., & Hussain, N. (1991). Personality and family disturbances in eating-disordered patients: comparison of "restrictors" and "bingers" to normal controls. *International Journal of Eating Disorders, 10*: 501–512.

Steiger, H., Stotland, S., Ghadirian, A. M., & Whitehead, V. (1995). Controlled study of eating concerns and psychopathological traits in relatives of eating-disordered probands: do familial traits exist? *International Journal of Eating Disorders, 18*: 107–118.

Steiger, H., Stotland, S., Trottier, J., & Ghanirian, A. M. (1996). Familial eating concerns and psychopathological traits: Causal implications of transgenerational effects. *International Journal of Eating Disorders, 19*: 147–157.

Stein, A., & Fairburn, C. G. (1989). Children of mothers with bulimia nervosa. *British Medical Journal, 299*: 777–778.

Stein, A., Stein, J., Walters, E. A., & Fairburn, C. G. (1995). Eating habits and attitudes among mothers of children with feeding disorders. *British Medical Journal, 310*: 228.

Stein, A., Woolley, H., Cooper, S. D., & Fairburn, C. G. (1994). An observational study of mothers with eating disorders and their infants. *Journal of Child Psychology andPsychiatry, 35*: 733–748.

Stein, A., Woolley, H., Cooper, S. D., Winterbottom, J., Fairburn, C. G., & Cortina-Borja, M. (2006). Eating habits and attitudes among 10-year-old children of mothers with eating disorders. *British Journal of Psychiatry, 189*: 324–329.

Steinberg, L. (1990). Autonomy, conflict, and harmony in the family relationship. In: S. S. Feldman & G. R. Elliott (Eds.), *At the threshold: The developing adolescent* (pp. 255–276). Cambridge, Mass: Harvard University Press.

Steinhausen, H. (2002). The Outcome of Anorexia in the 20th Century. *American Journal of Psychiatry, 159*: 1284–1293.

Stern, S. L., Dixon, K. N., Jones, D., Lake, M., Nemzer, E., & Sansome, R. (1989). Family Environment in Anorexia and Bulimia. *International Journal of Eating Disorders, 8*: 25–31.

Stice, E., Mazotti, L., Krebs, M., & Martin, S. (1998). Predictors of adolescent dieting behaviors: a longitudinal study. *Psychology of Addictive Behaviors, 12*: 195–205.

Stice, E., Agras, W. S., & Hammer, L. D. (1999). Risk Factors for the Emergence of Childhood Eating Disturbances: A Five-Year Prospective Study. *International Journal of Eating Disorders, 25*: 375–387.

Stierlin, H., & Weber, G. (1989). *Unlocking the Family Door: A Systemic Approach to the Understanding and Treatment of Anorexia Nervosa.* Philadelphia, PA: Brunner/Mazel.

Stoavall-McClough, K. C., & Cloitre, M. (2006). Unresolved attachment, PTSD, and dissociation in women with childhood abuse histories. *Journal of Consulting and Clinical Psychology, 74*: 219–228.

Stonehill, E., & Crisp, A. H. (1977). Psychoneurotic characteristics of patients with Anorexia Nervosa before and after treatment and at follow-up 4–7 years later. *Journal of Psychosomatic Research, 21*: 187–193.

Strauss, J., & Ryan, R. M. (1987). Autonomy disturbances in sub-types of anorexia. *Journal of Abnormal Psychology, 96*: 254–258.

Striegel-Moore, R. H., & Kearney Cooke, A. (1994). Exploring parents' attitudes and behaviors about their children's physical appearance. *International Journal of Eating Disorders, 15*: 377–385.

Strober, M. (1980). Personality and symptomological features in the young, nonchronic Anorexia Nervosa patients. *Journal of Psychosomatic Research, 24*: 353–359.

Strober, M. (1981). The significance of bulimia in juvenile Anorexia Nervosa: An exploration of possible etiologic factors. *International Journal of Eating Disorders, 1*: 28–43.

Strober, M. (1991). Disorders of the self in anorexia nervosa: An organismic-developmental paradigm. In: C. L. Johnson (Ed.), *Psychodynamic treatment of anorexia and bulimia* (pp. 354–373). New York: Guilford.

Strober, M., Freeman, R., Lampert, C., Diamond, J., & Kaye, W. (2000). Controlled family study of anorexia nervosa and bulimia nervosa: Evidence of shared liability and transmission of partial syndromes. *American Journal of Psychiatry, 157*: 393–401.

Szabo, C. P., Goldin, J., & Le Grange, D. (1999). Application of the family relations scale to a sample of anorexics, bulimics and non-psychiatric controls: a preliminary study. *European Eating Disorders Review, 7*: 37–46.

Szmuckler, G. I., Eisler, I., Russell, G. F. M., & Dare, C. (1985). Anorexia Nervosa, parental "expressed emotion" and dropping out of treatment. *British Journal of Psychiatry, 147*: 265–271.

Tafarodi, R. W., & Swann, W. B. (2001). Two-dimensional self-esteem: Theory and measurement. *Personality and Individual Differences, 31*: 635–673.

Tata, P., Fox, J., & Cooper, J. (2001). An investigation into the influence of gender and parenting styles on excessive exercise and disordered eating. *European Eating Disorders Review, 9*: 194–206.

Tetley, A., Moghaddam, N. G., Dawson, D. L., & Rennoldson, M. (2014). Parental bonding and eating disorders: A systematic review. *Eating Behaviors, 15*: 49–59.

Thelen, M. H., & Cormier, J. F. (1996). Desire to be thinner and weight control among children and their parents. *Behavior Therapy, 26*: 85–99.

Thienemann, M., & Steiner, H. (1993). Family Environment of Eating Disordered and Depressed Adolescents. *International Journal of Eating Disorders, 14*: 43–48.

Timimi, S., & Robinson, P. (1996). Disturbances in children of parents with eating disorders. *European Eating Disorders Review, 4*: 183–188.

Troisi, A., Massaroni, P., & Cuzzolaro, M. (2005). Early separation anxiety and adult attachment style in women with eating disorders. *British Journal of Clinical Psychology, 44*: 89–97.

Troop, N. A., & Treasure, J. L. (1997). Setting the scene for eating disorders, II. Childhood helplessness and mastery. *Psychological Medicine, 27*: 531–538.

Truglia, E., Mannucci, E., Lassi, S., Rotella, C., Faravelli, C., & Ricca, V. (2006). Aggressiveness, anger and eating disorders: A review. *Psychopathology, 39*: 55–68.

Turner, H. M., Rose, K. S., & Cooper, M. J. (2005). Parental bonding and eating disorder symptoms in adolescents: The mediating role of core beliefs. *Eating Behaviours, 6*: 113–118.

van den Berg, P., Keery, H., Eisenberg, M., & Neumark-Sztainer (2010). Maternal and Adolescent Report of Mothers' Weight-Related Concerns and Behaviors: Longitudinal Associations with Adolescent Body Dissatisfaction and Weight Control Practices. *Journal of Paediatric Psychology, 35*: 1093–1102.

van Wezel-Meijler, G., & Wit, J. M. (1989). The offspring of mothers with anorexia nervosa: a high risk group for undernutrition and stunting? *The European Journal of Pediatrics, 149*: 130–135.

Vaughan, C. E., & Leff, J. (1976). The measurement of expressed emotion in the families of psychiatric patients. *British Journal of Social and Clinical Psychology, 15:* 157–165.

Vidovic, V., Juresa, V., Begovac, I., Mahnik, M., & Tokilj, G. (2005). Perceived Family Cohesion, Adaptability and Communication in Eating Disorders. *European Eating Disorders Review, 13*: 19–28.

Vincent, M. A., & McCabe, M. P. (2000). Gender Differences Among Adolescents in Family, and Peer Influences on Body Dissatisfaction, Weight Loss, and Binge Eating Behaviors. *Journal of Youth and Adolescence, 29*: 205–221.

Vostanis, P., Nicholls, J., & Harrington, R. (1994). Maternal expressed emotion in conduct and emotional disorders of childhood. *Journal of Child Psychology and Psychiatry, 35*: 365–376.

Wade, T. D., Bulik, C. M., Neale, M., & Kendler, K. S. (2000). Anorexia nervosa and major depression: Shared genetic and environmental risk factors. *American Journal of Psychiatry, 157*: 469–471.

Wade, T. D., Gillespie, N., & Martin, N. G. (2007). A comparison of early family life events amongst monozygotic twin women with lifetime anorexia nervosa, bulimia nervosa, or major depression. *International Journal of Eating Disorders, 40*: 679–686.

Wade, T. D., Gordon, S., Medland, S., Bulik, C. M., Heath, A. C., Montgomery, G. W., & Martin, N. G. (2013). Genetic Variants Associated with Disordered Eating. *International Journal of Eating Disorders, 46*: 594–608.

Waller, G., & Hartley, P. (1994). Perceived Parental Style and Eating Psychopathology. *European Eating Disorders Review, 2*: 76–92.

Waller, G., Slade, P., & Calam, R. (1990a). Who Knows Best? Family Interaction and Eating Disorders. *British Journal of Psychiatry, 156*: 546–550.

Waller, G., Slade, P., & Calam, R. (1990b). Family Adaptability and Cohesion: Relation to Eating Attitudes and Disorders. *International Journal of Eating Disorders, 9*: 225–228.

Wallin, U., & Hansson, K. (1999). Anorexia nervosa in teenagers: Patterns of family function. *Nordic Journal of Psychiatry, 53*: 29–35.

Wallin, U., Kronvall, P., & Majewski, M. (2000). Body Awareness Therapy in Teenage Anorexia Nervosa: Outcome after 2 Years. *European Eating Disorders Review, 8*: 19–30.

Walters, E. E., & Kendler, K. S. (1995). Anorexia nervosa and anorexia-like syndromes in a population-based female twin sample. *American Journal of Psychiatry, 152*: 64–71.

Wang, K., Zhang, H., Bloss, C. S., Duvvuri, V., Kaye, W., Schork, N. J., Berrettini, W., & Hakonarson, H. (2011). A genome-wide association study on common SNPs and rare CNVs in anorexia nervosa. *Molecular Psychiatry, 16*: 949–959.

Ward, A., Ramsey, R., Turnbull, S., Benedettini, M., & Treasure, J. (2000). Attachment Patterns in Eating Disorders: Past in the Present. *International Journal of Eating Disorders, 28*: 370–376.

Ward, A., Ramsey, R., Turnbull, S., Steele, M., Steele, H., & Treasure, J. (2001). Attachment in anorexia nervosa: A transgenerational perspective. *British Journal of Medical Psychology, 74*: 497–505.

Waters, B. G. H., Beumont, P. J. V., Touyz, S., & Kennedy, M. (1990). Behavioural differences between twin and non-twin sibling pairs discordant for anorexia nervosa. *International Journal of Eating Disorders, 9*: 265–273.

Waugh, E., & Bulik, C. M. (1999). Offspring of Women with Eating Disorders. *International Journal of Eating Disorders, 25*: 123–133.

Webster, J., & Palmer, R. L. (2000). The childhood and family background of women with clinical eating disorders: A comparison with women with major depression and women without psychiatric disorder. *Psychological*

Medicine: A Journal of Research in Psychiatry and the Allied Sciences, 30: 53–60.

Weeks, T. L., & Pasupathi, M. (2010). Autonomy, Identity, and Narrative Construction with Parents and Friends. In: K. C. McLean & M. Pasupathi (Eds.), *Narrative Development in Adolescence: Creating the Storied Self* (pp. 65–92). New York. Springer.

Whelan, E., & Cooper, P. J. (2000). The association between childhood eating problems and maternal eating disorder. *Psychological Medicine, 30*: 69–77.

White, M. (1983). Anorexia nervosa: A transgenerational system perspective. *Family Process, 22*: 255–273.

Whitney, J., & Eisler, I. (2005). Theoretical and empirical models around caring for someone with an eating disorder: The reorganization of family life and inter-personal maintenance factors. *Journal of Mental Health, 14*: 575–585.

Williams, G. -J., Power, K. G., Miller, H. R., Freeman, C. P., Yellowlees, A., Dowds, T., Walker, M., & Parry-Jones, W. L. (1994). Development and validation of the Stirling eating disorder scales. *International Journal of Eating Disorders, 16*: 35–43.

Wonderlich, S. A., & Swift, W. (1990). Perceptions of Parental Relationships in the Eating Disorders: The Relevance of Depressed Mood. *Journal of Abnormal Psychology, 99*: 353–360.

Woodside, D. B., Bulik, C. M., Halmi, K. A., Fichter, M. M., Kaplan, A., Berrettini, W. H., Strober, M., Treasure, J., Lilenfeld, L., Klump, K., & Kaye, W. H. (2002). Personality, perfectionism, and attitudes towards eating in parents of individuals with eating disorders. *International Journal of Eating Disorders, 31*: 290–299.

Woodside, D. B., & Shektar-Wolfson, L. F. (1990). Parenting by patients with anorexia nervosa and bulimia nervosa. *International Journal of Eating Disorders, 9*: 303–309.

Yackobovitch-Gavan, M., Golan, M., Valevski, A., Kreiter, S., Bachar, E., Lieblich, A., Mitrani, E., Weizman, A., & Stein, D. (2009). An Integrative Quantitative Model of Factors Influencing the Course of Anorexia Nervosa Over Time. *International Journal of Eating Disorders, 42*: 306–317.

Yamazaki, Y., & Omori, M. (2011). Gender Differences in Thin-Ideal Internalization and Drive for Thinness among Adolescents: Mothers' Roles in Children's Thin-Ideal Internalisation. *Proceedings, 13*: 79–89.

Zaitsoff, S. L., Geller, J., & Srikameswaran, S. (2002). Silencing the self and suppressed anger: Relationship to eating disorder symptoms in adolescent females. *European Eating Disorders Review, 10*: 51–60.

Zeijmans van Emmichoven, I. A., van Ijzendoorn, M. H., De Ruiter, C., & Brosschot, J. F. (2003). Selective processing of threatening information: Effects of attachment representation and anxiety disorder on attention and memory. *Development and Psychopathology, 15*: 219–237.

Zubery, E., Binsted, N., Zifman, N., & Jecsmien, P. (2005). Adolescents Resisting Treatment: Exploring the Resistance in Eating Disorder Patients to Treatment Within the Family System. *Israeli Journal of Psychiatry and Related Science, 42*: 146–153.

INDEX